The Definitiv

Also by Simon Gray

Fiction
COLMAIN, SIMPLE PEOPLE, LITTLE PORTIA, A COMEBACK
FOR STARK

Non-fiction
AN UNNATURAL PURSUIT, HOW'S THAT
FOR TELLING 'EM, FAT LADY?

Stage plays
WISE CHILD, DUTCH UNCLE, THE IDIOT, SPOILED, BUTLEY,
OTHERWISE ENGAGED, DOG DAYS, MOLLY, THE REAR
COLUMN, CLOSE OF PLAY, STAGE STRUCK, QUARTERMAINE'S
TERMS, CHAPTER 17, THE COMMON PURSUIT, MELON,
HIDDEN LAUGHTER, THE HOLY TERROR

Television plays
THE CARAMEL CRISIS, DEATH OF A TEDDY BEAR, AWAY WITH
THE LADIES, SLEEPING DOG, SPOILED, PIG IN A POKE, MAN IN
A SIDE-CAR, PLAINTIFFS AND DEFENDANTS, TWO SUNDAYS

Television films
AFTER PILKINGTON, QUARTERMAINE'S TERMS, OLD FLAMES,
THEY NEVER SLEPT, THE COMMON PURSUIT

Films
BUTLEY, A MONTH IN THE COUNTRY

THE DEFINITIVE
SIMON GRAY II

faber and faber
LONDON · BOSTON

This collection first published in 1992
by Faber and Faber Limited
3 Queen Square London WC1N 3AU

Photoset by Parker Typesetting Service, Leicester
Printed in England by Cox & Wyman Ltd, Reading, Berks.

All rights reserved

This collection © Simon Gray
Otherwise Engaged, Plaintiffs and Defendants and *Two Sundays* © Simon Gray,
1975
Dog Days © Simon Gray, 1976, 1992
Molly and *Man in a Side-Car* © Simon Gray, 1978
Pig in a Poke © Simon Gray, 1980

Otherwise Engaged was first published in 1975 in a volume (including *Plaintiffs and Defendants* and *Two Sundays*) entitled *Otherwise Engaged and Other Plays* by Eyre Methuen Ltd.
Dog Days was first published in 1976 by Eyre Methuen Ltd; revised version (1986) first published in this collection.
Molly and *Man in a Side-Car* were first published in 1978 in a volume entitled *The Rear Column and Other Plays* by Eyre Methuen Ltd.
Pig in a Poke was first published in 1980 in a volume entitled *Close of Play and Pig in a Poke* by Eyre Methuen Ltd.

All professional and amateur rights in these plays are strictly reserved and applications for permission to perform them must be made in advance to Judy Daish Associates Limited, 83 Eastbourne Mews, London W2 6LQ. Telephone 071-262 1101

This book is sold subject to the condition that it shall not, by way of trade or otherwise, be lent, resold, hired out or otherwise circulated without the publisher's prior consent in any form of binding or cover other than that in which it is published and without a similar condition including this condition being imposed on the subsequent purchaser

A CIP record for this book is available from the British Library

ISBN 0-571-16240-1

1 3 5 7 9 10 8 6 4 2

CONTENTS

Otherwise Engaged   1

Dog Days   55

Molly   113

Pig in a Poke   169

Man in a Side-Car   211

Plaintiffs and Defendants   269

Two Sundays   307

CONTENTS

Otherwise Engaged

For Harold
Two summers 1971 and 1975

Otherwise Engaged was first presented by Michael Codron on 30 July 1975, at the Queen's Theatre. The cast was as follows:

SIMON	Alan Bates
DAVE	Ian Charleson
STEPHEN	Nigel Hawthorne
JEFF	Julian Glover
DAVINA	Jacqueline Pearce
WOOD	Benjamin Whitrow
BETH	Mary Miller
Director	Harold Pinter

ACT ONE

The living-room of the Hench's house in London. It is both elegant and comfortable, but not large. Two sofas, two armchairs, a coffee table, a telephone with an answering machine, an extremely expensive and elaborate hi-fi set, and around the walls shelves to accommodate a great range of books (which are evidently cherished) and an extensive collection of records, in which Wagner and other opera sets can be distinguished.

Stage left is a door that leads onto a small hall, at one end of which is the front door, and at the other a door which, in its turn, when opened, reveals a passage that goes onto stairs going down to the basement. More stairs lead up from the hall to another section of the house. The house has, in fact, recently been divided into two, so that there is a top flat.

Stage right has a door that leads to the kitchen, and as becomes evident, there is a door that opens from the kitchen into the garden.

When the curtain goes up, SIMON *is unwrapping a new record. He takes it out with the air of a man who is deeply looking forward to listening to it – there are several records, in fact – the complete* Parsifal. *He goes to the hi-fi, puts the first record on, listens, adjusts the level, then goes to the sofa and settles himself in it. The opening chords of* Parsifal *fill the theatre.*

The door opens, left. DAVE *enters.* SIMON *turns, looks at him, concealing his irritation as* DAVE *wanders into the kitchen, returns, and sits restlessly in the armchair. A pause in the music.*

DAVE: What's that then?

(SIMON *gets up and switches off the record.*)

SIMON: Wagner. Do you like him?

DAVE: (*Standing up*) No, well I mean he was antisemitic, wasn't he. Sort of early fascist, egomanic type.

SIMON: What about his music, do you like that?

DAVE: Well, I mean, I'm not likely to like his music if I don't like his type, am I?

SIMON: (*Concealing his impatience*) Everything all right? In the

5

flat, that is. No complaints or other urgencies?

DAVE: No, no, that's all right. Oh, you mean about the rent?

SIMON: Good God no, I wasn't thinking about the rent.

DAVE: It's all right if it waits a bit then, is it?

SIMON: Good God yes, pay us this week's when you pay us last week's – next week, or whenever.

DAVE: OK. I'm a bit short, you know how it is. Your wife out again then?

SIMON: Yes, she's gone to (*thinks*) Salisbury. She left last night.

DAVE: That girl in the first year came round last night for something to eat. I dropped down to borrow a chop or something, fish fingers would have done.

SIMON: Would they really?

DAVE: But she wasn't here, your wife.

SIMON: No, she wouldn't have been, as she was either in, or on her way to, Salisbury.

DAVE: So I had to take her out for a kebab and some wine. Then I had to get her to come back.

SIMON: Ah, she stayed the night then? Good for you!

DAVE: No, she didn't.

SIMON: Oh. You managed to get rid of her, then, instead, well done!

DAVE: She just left by herself.

SIMON: Before you had a chance to get rid of her, oh dear, why?

DAVE: Said she didn't fancy me.

SIMON: Good God, why ever not?

DAVE: I don't know. I mean I asked her if she'd like a screw and she said no. Then I asked her why not, and she said she didn't fancy me, that was why not.

SIMON: Still, she's left the door open for a platonic relationship.

DAVE: Yeah, well, then she went off to see something on television with some friend. I haven't got a television.

SIMON: Well, I'm afraid I can't help you there, nor have we.

DAVE: Anyway she said she might be going to that Marxist bookshop down the road today.

SIMON: What time?

DAVE: About lunch time, she said.

SIMON: But good God, lunch will soon be on you, hadn't you better get going – it would be tragic to miss her.

DAVE: Yeah, well that's it, you see. I'm a bit short, like I said. I mean we can't do anything –

(*Pause.*)

SIMON: Can I lend you some?

DAVE: What?

SIMON: Can I lend you some money?

DAVE: Yeah, OK.

SIMON: (*Giving him a fiver*) Is that enough?

DAVE: Yeah. Right. (*Takes it.*) That's five.

SIMON: Well, I'll get back to my music while you're making your own.

STEPHEN: (*Enters, through the kitchen door*) Hello. Oh hello.

SIMON: (*Concealing his dismay*) Oh, Stephen. This is Dave, who's taken over the upstairs flat. Dave, my brother Stephen.

STEPHEN: Oh yes, you're at the Poly, aren't you?

DAVE: That's right.

STEPHEN: What are you studying?

DAVE: Sociology.

STEPHEN: That must be jolly interesting. What aspect?

DAVE: What?

STEPHEN: Of sociology.

DAVE: Oh, the usual stuff.

STEPHEN: Psychology, statistics, politics, philosophy, I suppose.

DAVE: We're sitting in at the moment.

STEPHEN: Really? Why?

DAVE: Oh, usual sort of thing. Well – (*Goes towards the door and out.*)

STEPHEN: What is the usual sort of thing?

SIMON: No idea.

STEPHEN: (*After a pause*) Well, I must say!

SIMON: Oh, he's not as thick as he seems.

STEPHEN: Isn't he? He certainly seems quite thick. (*Sits down.*) I'm surprised a student could afford that flat, what do you charge him?

SIMON: Two pounds a week, I think.

7

STEPHEN: But you could get, good heavens, even through the rent tribunal, ten times that.

SIMON: Oh, we're not out to make money from it.

STEPHEN: Well, *he* seems rather an odd choice for your charity, with so many others in real need. Beth's not here, then?

SIMON: No, she's taken some of her foreign students to Canterbury.

STEPHEN: Did she go with that teacher she was telling Teresa about?

SIMON: Chap called Ned?

STEPHEN: Yes.

SIMON: Yes.

STEPHEN: What do you think of him?

SIMON: Oh, rather a wry, sad little fellow. Bit of a failure, I'd say, from what I've seen of him.

STEPHEN: A failure? In what way?

SIMON: Oh, you know, teaching English to foreigners.

STEPHEN: So does Beth.

SIMON: True, but Beth isn't a middle-aged man with ginger hair, a pigeon-toed gait, a depressed-looking wife and four children to boot.

STEPHEN: You know, sometimes I can't help wondering how people describe me. A middle-aged public school teacher with five children to boot. A bit of a failure too, eh? Anyhow, that's how I feel today.

SIMON: Why, what's the matter?

STEPHEN: That damned interview.

SIMON: Interview?

STEPHEN: For the Assistant Headmastership. You'd forgotten then!

SIMON: No, no of *course* I hadn't. When is it exactly?

STEPHEN: (*Looks at him*) Yesterday.

SIMON: Good God! Was it really? Well, what happened?

STEPHEN: I didn't get it.

SIMON: Well, who did?

STEPHEN: A chap called MacGregor. And quite right too, as he's already Assistant Headmaster of a small public school in

Edinburgh, very capable, written a couple of textbooks – in other words he's simply the better man for the job.

SIMON: I don't see what that's got to do with it. I don't know how your Headmaster had the face to tell you.

STEPHEN: Oh, he didn't. Nobody's had the face or the grace. Yet.

SIMON: Then how do you know he's got it.

STEPHEN: It was written all over MacGregor. I've never seen anyone so perky after an interview.

SIMON: Oh good God, is that all? Of course he was perky. He's a Scot isn't he? They're always perky. Except when they're doleful. Usually they're both at once.

STEPHEN: If you'd seen him come bouncing down the library steps.

SIMON: In my experience a bouncing candidate is a rejected candidate. No, no, Steve, my money's on your paddle feet. (*He sits.*)

STEPHEN: Even though my interview lasted a mere half hour although his lasted fifty-seven minutes? Even though I fluffed my mere half hour, and before a hostile board. Do you know, one of the Governors couldn't get over the fact that I'd taken my degree at Reading. He was unable to grasp that Reading was a university even, he referred to it as if it were some cut-price institution where I'd scraped up some – some diploma on the cheap. MacGregor went to Oxford, needless to say.

SIMON: Did he? Which college?

STEPHEN: And then another Governor harped on the number of our children – he kept saying *five* children, eh? Like that. Five children, eh? As if I'd had – I don't know – five – five –

SIMON: Cheques returned.

STEPHEN: What?

SIMON: That's what you made it sound as if he sounded as if he were saying.

STEPHEN: Anyway, there were the two Governors manifestly hostile.

SIMON: Out of how many?

STEPHEN: Two.

SIMON: Ah, but then your Headmaster was on your side.

STEPHEN: Perhaps. (*Pause*.) At least until I succeeded in putting him off.

SIMON: How?

STEPHEN: By doing something I haven't done since I was twelve years old.

SIMON: (*After a pause*) Can you be more specific?

STEPHEN: You will of course laugh, for which I shan't of course blame you, but I'm not sure that I can stand it if you do laugh at the moment. It was something very trivial, but also very embarrassing. (*Pause*.) You see, the Governor who didn't feel Reading was up to snuff had a rather low, husky voice, and towards the end I bent forward, rather sharply, to catch something he said, and this movement caused me to fart.

(*They stare levelly at each other.* SIMON's *face is completely composed*.)

SIMON: You haven't farted since you were twelve?

STEPHEN: In public, I meant.

SIMON: Oh. Loudly?

STEPHEN: It sounded to me like a pistol shot.

SIMON: The question, of course, is what it sounded like to Headmaster.

STEPHEN: Like a fart, I should think.

SIMON: Oh, he probably found it sympathetically human, you've no grounds for believing he'd hold anything so accidental against you, surely?

STEPHEN: I don't know, I simply don't know. (*He gets up.*) But afterwards when he had us around for some of his wife's herbal coffee –

SIMON: Herbal coffee?

STEPHEN: They paid far more attention to MacGregor than they did to me. I had to struggle to keep my end up. Headmaster was distinctly aloof in his manner – and MacGregor, of course, was relaxed and I suppose a fair man would call it charming.

SIMON: What herbs does she use?

STEPHEN: What? What's that got to do with it? How would I know.

SIMON: Sorry, I was just trying to imagine the – the setting, so to speak.

STEPHEN: You know, what really hurts is that I can't complain that it's unfair. MacGregor really is better qualified, quite obviously an admirable bloke. But what I do resent, and can't help resenting, is the edge Oxford gives him – the simple fact that he went there improves his chances – but I suppose that's the way of the world, isn't it? Almost everybody goes along with it, don't they?

SIMON: Oh, I don't know –

STEPHEN: Of course you know. You subscribe to it yourself, don't you?

SIMON: Certainly not. Why should I?

STEPHEN: Because you went to Oxford yourself.

SIMON: Good God, so what?

STEPHEN: Well, how many other members of your editorial board also went there?

SIMON: Only five.

STEPHEN: Out of how many?

SIMON: Eight.

STEPHEN: And where did the other three go, Cambridge?

SIMON: Only two of them.

STEPHEN: And so only *one* of the nine went elsewhere?

SIMON: No, he didn't go anywhere. He's the Chairman's son.

STEPHEN: I think that proves my point.

SIMON: It proves merely that our editorial board is composed of Oxford and Cambridge graduates, and a half-wit. It proves absolutely nothing about your chances of beating MacDonald to the Assistant Headmastership. And it's my view that poor old MacDonald, whether he be Oxford MacDonald or Cambridge MacDonald or Reading MacDonald or plain Edinburgh MacDonald –

STEPHEN: MacGregor.

SIMON: What?

STEPHEN: His name happens to be MacGregor.

SIMON: Absolutely. Has no chance at all. Even if they do believe
you have too few qualifications and too many children, even
if they suspect that your single fart heralds chronic
incontinence, they'll still have to appoint you. And if they've
been extra courteous to MacDonald it's only to compensate
him for coming all the way from Edinburgh for a London
rebuff.

(*Stands up.*)

STEPHEN: Actually it would be better, if you don't mind, not to
try and jolly me along with reasons and reassurances. I shall
have to face the disappointment sooner or later, and I'd
rather do it sooner – wouldn't you?

SIMON: No, I have a distinct preference for later, myself. I really
do think you'll get it you know.

STEPHEN: Yes, well thanks anyway. I'd better get back. What
time's your friend coming?

SIMON: What friend?

STEPHEN: When I phoned and asked whether I could come
round, you said it mightn't be worth my while as you were
expecting a friend.

SIMON: Good God! Yes. Still, he's one of those people who never
turns up when expected. So if I remember to expect him I
should be all right.

STEPHEN: You mean you don't want him to turn up? Who is he
anyway?

SIMON: Jeff Golding.

STEPHEN: Oh *him*! Yes, well I must say that piece he wrote in one
of last week's Sundays, on censorship and children – I've
never read anything so posturingly half-baked.

SIMON: Oh, I doubt if he was posturing, he really is half-baked.

STEPHEN: I shall never forget – never – how he ruined the dinner
party – the one time I met him – his drunkenness and his
appalling behaviour. And I shall particularly never forget his
announcing that people – he meant me, of course – only went
into public school teaching because they were latent
pederasts.

SIMON: Good God, what did you say?

STEPHEN: I told him to take it back.

SIMON: And did he?

STEPHEN: He offered to take back the latent, and congratulated me on my luck. That was his idea of badinage. By God I don't often lose control but I made a point of cornering him in the hall when he was leaving. I got him by the lapels and warned him that I'd a good mind to beat some manners into him. If Teresa hadn't happened to come out of the lavatory just then – she'd rushed in there in tears – I might have done him some damage. I've never told you that bit before, have I?

SIMON: You haven't told me any of it before, it's very amusing. Tell me, who gave this memorable dinner party?

STEPHEN: You did.

SIMON: Did I really? I don't remember it. It must have been a long time ago.

STEPHEN: Yes, but I have a feeling your friend Jeff Golding will remember it all right.

(*The front door slams and* JEFF GOLDING *enters left.*)

JEFF: Simon – ah, there you are. (*There is a pause.*) Weren't you expecting me?

SIMON: I most certainly was. Oh, my brother Stephen – Jeff Golding. I believe you know each other.

STEPHEN: We do indeed.

JEFF: Really? Sorry, 'fraid I don't remember.

STEPHEN: A dinner party Simon gave – some years ago.

JEFF: (*Clearly not remembering at all*) Nice to see you again. Could I have a Scotch please? (*To* SIMON.)

SIMON: Of course. (*Goes to the drinks table.*) Steve?

STEPHEN: No thank you.

JEFF: (*Collapses into a chair*) Christ! Christ! I've just had a session at the Beeb, taping a piece with Bugger Lampwith. I've got the goods on him at last.

STEPHEN: Lampwith. Isn't he a poet?

JEFF: Not even. He's an Australian. A closet Australian. Went to Oxford instead of Earl's Court. Thinks it makes him one of us. Still, I got him out of his closet with his vowels around his tonsils, once or twice. Thrice, actually. (*Laughs at the recollection.*)

STEPHEN: What exactly have you got against him?

JEFF: Isn't that enough?

STEPHEN: Simply that he's an Australian?

JEFF: They're all right as dentists.

STEPHEN: But could you please explain to me why you have it in for Australians.

JEFF: Once you let them into literature they lower the property values.

STEPHEN: Really? How?

JEFF: They're too fertile, scribble, scribble, scribble like little Gibbons. They breed whole articles out of small reviews, don't mind what work they do, go from sports journalists to movie critics to novelists to poets to television pundits, and furthermore they don't mind how little they get paid as long as they fill our space. So you see if there weren't any Australians around sods like me wouldn't end up having to flog our crap to the *Radio Times* and even the *Shiterary Supplement*, let alone spend Saturday morning interviewing buggers like Bugger Lampwith.

STEPHEN: We've got half a dozen Australian boys in our school at the moment. They're not only friendly, frank and outgoing, they're also intelligent and very hard-working.

JEFF: Exactly, the little buggers. Hey! (*To* SIMON) Roger's been going around telling people I can't face him since my review of his turgid little turd of a novel. Have you read it?

SIMON: Which?

JEFF: My review – first things first.

SIMON: Yes, I did.

JEFF: Well?

SIMON: Some good jokes, I thought.

JEFF: Weren't there? And what did you honestly, frankly and actually think of his turd?

SIMON: I haven't read it.

JEFF: Didn't you publish it?

SIMON: Yes.

JEFF: Well, if you ask me, the blokie you got to write the blurb hadn't read it either, bloody sloppy piece of crap, who did it anyway?

SIMON: Actually I did.

JEFF: D'you know what it bloody is – I'll tell you what it bloody is – I wish I'd come out with it straight when I wrote about it – it's a piece of – *literature*, that's what it bloody is!

STEPHEN: You don't like literature?

JEFF: (*A pause*) I don't like literature, no.

STEPHEN: Why not?

JEFF: Because it's a bloody boring racket.

STEPHEN: You think literature is a *racket*?

JEFF: Are you in it too?

STEPHEN: I happen to teach it, it so happens.

JEFF: Does it, Christ! To whom?

STEPHEN: Sixth formers. At Amplesides.

JEFF: What's Amplesides?

STEPHEN: It happens to be a public school.

JEFF: Does it? Major or minor?

STEPHEN: Let's just say that it's a good one, if you don't mind.

JEFF: I don't mind saying it even if it's not. It's a good one. Christ, I can't remember when I last met a public school teacher.

STEPHEN: Probably when you last met me.

JEFF: But I don't remember that, don't forget.

STEPHEN: Would you like me to remind you? I'm the latent pederast.

JEFF: (*After a pause*) Then you're in the right job.

STEPHEN: (*To* SIMON) I think I'd better go. Before I do something I regret. (*Turns and goes out through kitchen.*)

SIMON: Oh right. (*Making an attempt to follow* STEPHEN) Love to Teresa and the kids. (*Calling it out.*)
(*Sound of door slamming.* JEFF *helps himself to another Scotch.*)

JEFF: Seems a real sweetie, what's he like in real life?

SIMON: Not as stupid as he seems.

JEFF: That still leaves him a lot of room to be stupid in.

SIMON: He *is* my brother.

JEFF: I'm very sorry.

SIMON: Actually, the last time he met you, he offered to fight you.

JEFF: Then he's matured since then. Where's Beth?

SIMON: Gone to Canterbury.

JEFF: With her woggies?

SIMON: Yes.

JEFF: Never seem to see her these days. You two still all right, I take it?

SIMON: Yes, thanks.

JEFF: Christ, you're lucky, don't know how you do it. She's so bloody attractive of course, as well as nice and intelligent. I suppose that helps.

SIMON: Yes, it does really.

JEFF: And she's got that funny little moral streak in her – she doesn't altogether approve of me, I get the feeling. Even after all these years. Christ, women! Listen there's something I want to talk to you about, and I'll just lay down the guide-lines of your response. What I want from you is an attentive face and a cocked ear, the good old-fashioned friendly sympathy and concern for which you're celebrated, O bloody K?

SIMON: Well, I'll do my best.

JEFF: Remember Gwendoline?

SIMON: Gwendoline, no. Have I met her?

JEFF: Hundreds of times.

SIMON: Really, where?

JEFF: With me.

SIMON: Oh. Which one was she – to tell you the truth, Jeff, there've been so many that the only one I still have the slightest recollection of is your ex-wife.

JEFF: Are you sure?

SIMON: Absolutely.

JEFF: Well, that was Gwendoline.

SIMON: Oh, I thought her name was Gwynyth.

JEFF: Why?

SIMON: What?

JEFF: Why should you think her name was Gwynyth?

SIMON: Wasn't she Welsh?

JEFF: No, she bloody was not Welsh.

SIMON: Well, I haven't seen her for years, don't forget, not since the afternoon you threw your drink in her face and walked out on her.

JEFF: And that's all you remember?

SIMON: Well, it *did* happen in my flat, a lunch party you asked me to give so that you could meet the then Arts Editor of the *Sunday Times*, and you did leave her sobbing on my bed, into my pillow, with the stink of Scotch everywhere –

JEFF: Don't you remember anything else about my Gwendoline days, for Christ's sake? What I used to tell you about her?

SIMON: (*Thinks*) Yes. You used to tell me that she was the stupidest woman I'd ever met.

JEFF: *You'd* ever met.

SIMON: Yes.

JEFF: And was she?

SIMON: Yes.

JEFF: Well, you've met some stupider since, haven't you?

SIMON: Probably, but fortunately I can't remember them either.

JEFF: So you rather despised my poor old Gwendoline, did you?

SIMON: Absolutely. So did you.

JEFF: Then why do you think I married her?

SIMON: Because of the sex.

JEFF: Did I tell you that too?

SIMON: No, you told her that, once or twice, in front of me.

JEFF: Christ, what a bloody swine of a fool I was. (*Pours himself another drink.*) Well, now I'm suffering for it, aren't I? Listen, a few months ago I bumped into her in Oxford Street. I hadn't given her a thought in all that time, and suddenly there we were, face to face, looking at each other. For a full minute just looking. And do you know something, she cried. And I felt as if we were – Christ, you know – still married. But in the very first days of it, when we couldn't keep our hands off each other. In a matter of minutes.

SIMON: Minutes?

JEFF: Minutes. Bloody minutes. All over each other.

SIMON: In *Oxford* Street.

JEFF: I'll tell you – I put my hand out, very slowly, and stroked her cheek. The tears were running down, her mouth was trembling – and she took my hand and pressed it against her cheek. Then I took her to Nick's flat – he's still in hospital by the way.

SIMON: Really? I didn't know he'd gone in.

JEFF: They're trying aversion therapy this time, but it won't do any good. He's so bloody addictive that he'll come out hooked on the cure and still stay hooked on the gin, poor sod. Saline chasers. Anyway, I took her to Nick's, and had her, and had her, and had her. Christ! And when she left what do you think I did?

SIMON: Slept, I should think.

JEFF: I cried, that's what I did. Didn't want her to leave me, you see. I'm in love with her. I think I love her. And since then there have been times when I've thought I even liked her. Well?

SIMON: Well Jeff, that's marvellous. Really marvellous.

JEFF: Oh yes, bloody marvellous to discover that you want to marry your ex-wife.

SIMON: But why ever not? It just confirms that you were right the first time. Why not marry her?

JEFF: (*Taking another drink*) Because she's got a new bloody husband, that's why. In fact not so new, five years old. A bloody don in Cambridge called Manfred. Christ knows why he had to go and *marry* her!

SIMON: Perhaps he likes sex too.

JEFF: According to Gwen he likes TV situation comedies, football matches, wrestling, comic books, horror films and sadistic thrillers, but not sex.

SIMON: What does he teach?

JEFF: Moral sciences.

SIMON: Then there's your answer. Philosophers have a long tradition of marrying stupid women, from Socrates on. They think it clever. Does she love him?

JEFF: Of course she does, she loves everyone. But she loves me most. Except for their bloody child. She bloody dotes on the bloody child.

SIMON: Oh. How old is it?

JEFF: Two – three – four – that sort of age.

SIMON: Boy or girl?

JEFF: Can't really tell. The one time I saw it, through my car window, it was trotting into its nursery school with its arm over its face, like a mobster going to the grand jury.

SIMON: Haven't you asked Gwen which it is?

JEFF: Yes, but only to show interest. Anyway, what does it matter, what matters is she won't leave Manfred because of it. She's *my* wife, not his, I had her first, and she admits as much, she'll always be mine, but all I get of her is two goes a week when I drive up to Cambridge – Tuesdays and Thursdays in the afternoon when Manfred's conducting seminars. In the rooms of some smartie-boots theologian.

SIMON: (*Pacing up and down*) Do you mean Manfred conducts his seminars in the rooms of some smartie-boots theologian or you have Gwen in the rooms of some smartie-boots theologian?

JEFF: I have Gwen there. He's a friend of Manfred's you see.

SIMON: So Manfred's asked him to let you use his rooms?

JEFF: Oh no, Manfred doesn't know anything about it. Or about me. No, smartie-boots seems to have some idea that it's part of his job to encourage what he calls sin. Oh Christ, you know the type, a squalid little Anglican queen of a pimp the little sod. Turns my stomach. (*Adds more Scotch.*) Christ, you know, Simon, you want to know something about me?

SIMON: What? (*Sinks into an armchair.*)

JEFF: I'm English, yes, English to my marrow's marrow. After years of buggering about as a cosmopolitan literateur, going to PEN conferences in Warsaw, hob-nobbing with Frog poets and Eyetye essayists, German novelists and Greek composers, I suddenly realise I hate the lot of them. Furthermore I detest women, love men, loathe queers.

D'you know when I'm really at bloody peace with myself?
When I'm caught in a traffic jam on an English road, under
an English heaven – somewhere between London and
Cambridge, on my way to Gwen, on my way back from her,
rain sliding down the window, engine humming, dreaming –
dreaming of what's past or is to come. Wrapped in the
anticipation or the memory, no, the anticipation *of* the
memory. (*Pause.*) Oh Christ – it's my actual bloody opinion
that this sad little, bloody little country of ours is finished at
last. Bloody finished at last. Yes, it truly is bloody well
actually finished at last. I mean that. Had the VAT man
around the other day. That's what we get now instead of the
muffin man. I remember the muffin men, I'm old enough to
remember the muffin men. Their bells and smells and
lighting of the lamps – do you remember? Sometimes I even
remember hansom cabs and crinoline, the music halls and
Hobbes and Sutcliffe . . . (*Smiles.*) Or the memory of the
anticipation, I suppose. Stu Lampwith. Christ, the bugger!
(*Pause.*) Well Christ – I suppose I'd better go and write my
piece. (*He gets to his feet.*) Did I tell you what that cold-
hearted bitch said last night, in bed? Christ!

SIMON: Who?

JEFF: What?

SIMON: What cold-hearted bitch?

JEFF: Davina. (*Takes another Scotch.*)

SIMON: Davina?

JEFF: You don't know about Davina?

SIMON: (*Wearily*) No.

JEFF: You haven't met her?

SIMON: No, no – I don't think –

JEFF: But Christ, I've got to tell you about bitch Davina. (*Sits
down.*)

SIMON: Why?

JEFF: Because she is actually and completely the most utterly and
totally – (*Lifts his hand.*)
(*There is a ring at the doorbell.*)
What?

SIMON: Just a minute, Jeff. (*Goes to the door, opens it.*)

DAVINA: Hello, is Jeff here, by any chance?

(JEFF *groans in recognition and sits down on the sofa.*)

SIMON: Yes, yes he is. Come in.

(DAVINA *enters.* JEFF *ignores her.*)

DAVINA: I'm Davina Saunders. (*To* SIMON.)

SIMON: I'm Simon Hench.

DAVINA: I know.

(*There is a pause.*)

SIMON: Would you like a drink?

DAVINA: Small gin and bitters, please.

(SIMON *goes across to the drinks table.*)

JEFF: How did you know I was here?

DAVINA: You said you would be.

JEFF: Why did I tell you?

DAVINA: Because I asked you.

JEFF: But why did I tell you? Because you see, I wanted a quiet conversation with my friend, Simon, you see.

DAVINA: You're all right then, are you?

JEFF: What?

(*A pause.* SIMON *brings* DAVINA *her drink.*)

DAVINA: How did the interview go?

JEFF: All right.

DAVINA: What's he like?

JEFF: Who?

DAVINA: Bugger Lampwith.

JEFF: OK.

DAVINA: What's OK about him?

JEFF: He's all right.

DAVINA: Good.

JEFF: What do you mean, good?

DAVINA: That he's all right. (*Sits down.*)

JEFF: Well, what d'you want me to say, you follow me across bloody London, you turn up when I'm having a private bloody conversation with my old friend Simon, you're scarcely in the room before you ask me whether I'm drunk –

DAVINA: As a matter of sober precision, I did not ask you whether

21

you were drunk. I asked you whether you were all right.

JEFF: Then as a matter of drunken precision, no, I'm not all right, I'm drunk.

DAVINA: That's surprising, as with you being all right and being drunk are usually precisely synonymous.

JEFF: But now you're here, aren't you, and that alters everything, doesn't it?

DAVINA: Does it?

JEFF: I thought you were going to spend the morning at the British Bloody Museum. I thought we'd agreed not to see each other for a day or two, or even a year or two – (*There is a pause.*)

SIMON: What are you doing at the BM, some research?

JEFF: That's what she's doing. On Major Bloody Barttelot. Got the idea from *my* review of that Life of Stanley – naturally.

SIMON: Really, and who is Major Bloody Barttelot?

DAVINA: Major Barttelot went with Stanley to the Congo, was left in a camp to guard the Rear Column, and ended up flogging, shooting, and even, so the story goes, eating the natives.

JEFF: Pleasant work for a woman, eh?

SIMON: Major Barttelot was a *woman*?

DAVINA: He was an English gentleman. Although he did find it pleasant work from what I've discovered, yes.

SIMON: Really? And are you planning a book?

JEFF: Of course she is, cannibalism, sadism, doing down England all at the same time, how can it miss? Why do you think she's on to it?

SIMON: I must say it sounds quite fascinating. Who's your publisher?

DAVINA: I haven't got one yet.

JEFF: Is that what summoned you away from the BM, the chance of drawing up a contract with my old friend, the publisher Simon? (*Refills his glass.*)

DAVINA: Actually, I haven't been to the BM this morning. I've been on the telephone. And what summoned me here was first that I wanted to give you your key back. (*Throws it over to him.*)

JEFF: (*Makes no attempt to catch it*) Thank you.

DAVINA: And secondly to tell you about the telephone call.

JEFF: What? Who was it?

DAVINA: Your ex-wife's husband. Manfred.

JEFF: What did he want?

DAVINA: You.

JEFF: Why?

DAVINA: He wanted you to know the contents of Gwendoline's suicide letter.

JEFF: (*After a pause*) What? Gwendoline – what – Gwen's dead!

SIMON: Good God!

DAVINA: No.

JEFF: But she tried – tried to commit suicide?

DAVINA: Apparently.

JEFF: What do you mean apparently, you mean she failed?

DAVINA: Oh, I'd say she succeeded. At least to the extent that Manfred was hysterical, I had a wastefully boring morning on the telephone, and you look almost sober. What more could she expect from a mere bid, after all?

JEFF: For Christ's sake, what happened, what actually happened?

DAVINA: Well, Manfred's narrative was a trifle rhapsodic.

JEFF: But you said there was a letter.

DAVINA: He only read out the opening sentences – he was too embarrassed by them to go on.

JEFF: Embarrassed by what?

DAVINA: Oh, Gwendoline's epistolary style, I should think. It was rather shaming.

JEFF: Look, where is she?

DAVINA: In that hospital in Cambridge probably. And if you're thinking of going up there, you should reflect that Manfred is looking forward to beating you to a pulp. A *bloody* pulp was his phrase, and unlike yourself he seems to use the word literally, rather than for rhetorical effect or as drunken punctuation. I like people who express themselves limpidly (*to* SIMON) under stress, don't you?

JEFF: (*Throws his drink at her, splashing her blouse, etc.*) Is that limpid enough for you?

DAVINA: No, tritely theatrical, as usual. But if you're absolutely determined to go, and you might as well because what else have you to do? I advise you not to drive. Otherwise you may have to make do with one of the hospitals *en route*.

SIMON: Yes, you really shouldn't drive, Jeff . . .

(JEFF *turns, goes out, left, slamming the door. There is a pause.*) I'll get you something to wipe your shirt –

DAVINA: Don't bother, it's far too wet. But another drink please. (*Hands him her glass.*)

SIMON: Of course.

(*Takes it, goes to the drinks table.* DAVINA *takes off her shirt and throws it over a chair. She is bra-less. She goes to the large wall mirror, and dries herself with a handkerchief from her bag.* SIMON *turns with the drink, looks at* DAVINA, *falters slightly, then brings her her drink.*)

DAVINA: God, what a stupid man, don't you think?

SIMON: Well, a bit excitable at times, perhaps.

DAVINA: No, stupid really, and in an all-round way. You know, when I was at Oxford one used to take his articles quite seriously – not very seriously but quite. But now of course one sees that his facility, though it may pass in the Arts pages as intelligence and originality, was something merely cultivated in late adolescence for the examination halls. He hasn't developed, in fact his Gwendoline syndrome makes it evident that he's regressed. Furthermore his drunken bravado quickly ceases to be amusing, on top of which he's a fourth-rate fuck.

SIMON: Oh well, perhaps he's kind to animals.

DAVINA: (*Sitting on the sofa*) To think I thought he might be of some use to me. But of course he's out of the habit, if he was ever in it, of talking to women who like to think and therefore talk concisely, for whom intelligence does actually involve judgement, and for whom judgement concludes in discrimination. Hence the appeal, I suppose, of a pair of tits from which he can dangle, with closed eyes and infantile gurglings. Especially if he has to get to them furtively, with a sense of not being allowed. Yes, stupid, don't you agree?

SIMON: Did you really go to Oxford?

DAVINA: Came down two years ago, why?

SIMON: From your style you sound more as if you went to Cambridge.

DAVINA: Anyway, he's nicely gone, you will admit, and four bad weeks have been satisfactorily concluded.

SIMON: Aren't you a little worried about him, though?

DAVINA: Why should I be?

SIMON: Well, Manfred did threaten to beat him to a bloody pulp, after all. And it may not be an idle boast. Men whose wives attempt suicide because of other men sometimes become quite animated, even if they are moral scientists.

DAVINA: Oh, I think the wretched Manfred will be more bewildered than belligerent. I composed that fiction between Great Russell Street and here. Of course I didn't know until I met his glassy gaze and received his boorish welcome whether I was actually going to work it through. It was quite thrilling, don't you think?

SIMON: You mean, Gwendoline didn't try to commit suicide?

DAVINA: Surely you don't imagine that *that* complacent old cow would attempt even an attempted suicide?

SIMON: Why did you do it?

DAVINA: Spite of course. Well, he told me he wanted to bring it all to a climax, although he wanted no such thing of course, prolonged and squalid messes that lead least of all to climaxes being his method, so my revenge has been to provide him with one that should be exactly in character – prolonged, squalid and utterly messy even by Cambridge standards, don't you think? *You're* married, aren't you? To Beth, isn't it?

SIMON: That's right.

DAVINA: I've only just realized she isn't here, is she?

SIMON: Well, I suppose that's better than just realizing she was, isn't it?

DAVINA: I'd like to have met her. I've heard a great deal about you both, you mainly, of course. Are you two as imperturbably, not to say implacably *married* as he and everyone else says?

SIMON: I hope so.

DAVINA: And that you've never been unfaithful to Beth, at least as far as Jeff knows.

SIMON: Certainly never that far.

DAVINA: Don't you even fancy other women?

SIMON: (*Sits in the armchair*) My not sleeping with other women has absolutely nothing to do with not fancying them. Although I do make a particular point of not sleeping with women I don't fancy.

DAVINA: That's meant for me, is it?

SIMON: Good God, not at all.

DAVINA: You mean you do fancy me?

SIMON: I didn't mean that either.

DAVINA: But do you fancy me?

SIMON: Yes.

DAVINA: But you don't like me?

SIMON: No.

DAVINA: Ah, then do you fancy me *because* you don't like me? Some complicated set of manly mechanisms of that sort, is it?

SIMON: No, very simple ones that Jeff, for instance, would fully appreciate. I fancy you because of your breasts, you see. I'm revolted by your conversation and appalled by your behaviour. I think you're possibly the most egocentrically unpleasant woman I've ever met, but I have a yearning for your breasts. I'd like to dangle from them too, with my eyes closed and doubtless emitting infantile gurglings. Furthermore they look deceptively hospitable.

DAVINA: If they look deceptively hospitable, they're deceiving you. (*Comes over and sits on the arm of his chair.*) You're very welcome to a nuzzle. (*Pause.*) Go on then. And then we'll see what *you* can do.

(SIMON *sits, hesitating for a moment, then gets up, gets Davina's shirt, hands it to her.*)

Because of Beth?

SIMON: This is her house, as much as mine. It's *our* house, don't you see?

DAVINA: Fidelity means so much to you?

SIMON: Let's say rather more to me than a suck and a fuck with the likes of you. So, come to that, does Jeff.

DAVINA: Yes, well I suppose that's to be expected in a friend of his. He doesn't begin to exist and nor do you.

SIMON: That's excellent. Because I haven't the slightest intention of letting you invent me.

DAVINA: And what about my Barttelot book?

SIMON: There I'm sure we shall understand each other. If it's any good, I shall be delighted to publish it. And if you've any sense, and you've got a hideous sight too much, you'll be delighted to let me. I shall give you the best advance available in London, arrange an excellent deal with an American publisher, and I shall see that it's edited to your advantage as well as ours. If it's any good.

DAVINA: That means more to me than being sucked at and fucked by the likes of you.

(*They smile.* DAVINA *turns and goes out.*)

(SIMON, *with the air of a man celebrating, picks up the keys and glasses, puts them away. Makes to go to the gramophone, stops, goes to the telephone answering machine.*)

SIMON: (*Records*) 348 0720, Simon Hench on an answering machine. I shall be otherwise engaged for the rest of the day. If you have a message for either myself or for Beth could you please wait until after the high-pitched tone, and if that hasn't put you off, speak. Thank you.

(*Puts the button down, then goes over to the gramophone, bends over to put a record on.*)

(DAVE *enters,* SIMON *freezes, turns.*)

DAVE: She didn't show.

SIMON: What?

DAVE: Suzy. My girl. She didn't show. You know what I'd like to do now, I'd like to get really pissed, that's what I'd like to do.

SIMON: I don't blame you, and furthermore, why don't you? You'll still catch the pubs if you hurry —

DAVE: Well, I'm a bit short, you see.

SIMON: But didn't you have a few pounds —

DAVE: Yeah, well I spent those.

SIMON: Oh, what on?

DAVE: Usual sort of stuff.

SIMON: Well then, let me. (*Pause.*) I've got just the thing.
(*Goes to the drinks table, fishes behind, takes out a bottle of Cyprus sherry.*)
Here. Go on, one of Beth's students gave it to her – it's yours. (*Hands it to* DAVE.) A Cyprus sherry. Nice and sweet. Now you settle down in some dark corner, with a receptacle by your side, and forget yourself completely. That's what I'd want to do if I were you. (*Points him towards the door.*)
(DAVE *goes out.* SIMON *turns back to the hi-fi. Voices in the hall.*)

DAVE: (*Opens the door*) Bloke here for you. (*Withdraws.*)

SIMON: What? (*Turns.*)

WOOD: (*Enters*) Mr Hench?

SIMON: Yes.

WOOD: Can you spare me a few minutes? My name is Wood. Bernard Wood.

SIMON: (*As if recognizing the name, then checks it*) Oh?

WOOD: It means something to you, then?

SIMON: No, just an echo. Of Birnam Wood, it must be, coming to Dunsinane. No, I'm very sorry, it doesn't. Should it?

WOOD: You don't recognize me either, I take it?

SIMON: No, I'm afraid not. Should I?

WOOD: We went to school together.

SIMON: Did we really, Wundale?

WOOD: Yes. Wundale. I was all of three years ahead of you, but I recall you. It should be the other way around, shouldn't it? But then *you* were very distinctive.

SIMON: Was I really, in what way?

WOOD: (*After a little pause*) Oh, as the sexy little boy that all the glamorous boys of my year slept with.

SIMON: (*After a pause*) But you didn't?

WOOD: No.

SIMON: Well, I do hope you haven't come to make good, because it's too late, I'm afraid. The phase is over, by some decades.

28

(*Little pause, then with an effort at courtesy*) I'm sure I would
have remembered you, though, if we had slept together.

WOOD: Well, perhaps your brother Stephen, isn't it? would
remember me as we were in the same year, how is he?

SIMON: Oh, very well.

WOOD: Married, with children?

SIMON: Yes.

WOOD: And you're married?

SIMON: Yes.

WOOD: Good. Children?

SIMON: No.

WOOD: Why not?

SIMON: There isn't enough room. What about you?

WOOD: Oh, as you might expect of someone like me. Married
with children.

(*There is a pause.*)

SIMON: Well . . . um – you said there was something –

WOOD: Yes, there is. It's of a rather personal – embarrassing
nature.

(*Pause.*)

SIMON: (*Unenthusiastically*) Would a drink help?

WOOD: Oh, that's very kind. Some sherry would be nice, if you
have it.

SIMON: Yes, I have it.

WOOD: Then some sherry, if I may.

SIMON: Yes, you may. (*Pours* WOOD *a sherry.*)

WOOD: My many thanks. Your very good health. I thought you
might have heard my name the day before yesterday.

SIMON: Oh, in what context?

WOOD: From my girl, Joanna. In your office, at about six in the
evening.

SIMON: Joanna?

WOOD: She came to see you about getting work in publishing.
She's only just left art school, but you were kind enough to
give her an appointment.

SIMON: Oh yes, yes. I do remember a girl – I'm terrible about
names, a nice girl, I thought.

WOOD: Thank you. How did your meeting go? Just between us?

SIMON: Well, I thought she was really quite promising.

WOOD: But you didn't make her any promises.

SIMON: Well, no, I'm afraid I couldn't. What work of hers she showed me struck me as a – a trifle over-expressive for our needs. (*Pause*.) Why, is her version of our, um, talk different, in any way?

WOOD: She hasn't said anything about it at all.

SIMON: I see. And you've come to me to find out about her potential?

WOOD: Not really, no. I've come to ask you if you know where she is.

SIMON: Have you lost her then?

WOOD: She hasn't been home since I dropped her off at your office.

SIMON: Well, I'm very sorry, but I haven't seen her since she left my office.

WOOD: I only have one rule with her, that she come home at night. Failing that, that at least she let me know where or with whom she is spending the night. Failing that, that at least she telephone me first thing in the morning. Could I be more unreasonably reasonable? So before doing the rounds among her pals, from Ladbroke Grove to Earls Court, I thought it might be worth finding out from you if she let anything slip about her plans.

SIMON: Nothing that I can remember.

WOOD: She didn't mention any particular friend or boyfriend?

SIMON: Just the usual references to this drip and that drip in the modern manner. Look, from what one makes out of today's youth, isn't it likely that she'll come home when she feels in the mood or wants a good meal, eh?

WOOD: I suppose so.

SIMON: I can quite understand your worry –

WOOD: Can you? No, I don't think you can.

SIMON: No, perhaps not. But I really don't see how I can help you any further.

WOOD: Did you have it off with her?

SIMON: What? *What?*

WOOD: Did you have it off with her?

SIMON: Look, Wood, whatever your anxiety about your daughter, I really don't think, old chap, that you should insinuate yourself into people's homes and put a question like that to them. I mean, good God, you can't possibly expect me to dignify it with an answer, can you?

WOOD: In other words, you did.

SIMON: (*After a long pause*) In other words, I'm afraid I did. Yes. Sorry, old chap.

(*Curtain.*)

ACT TWO

Curtain up on exactly the same scene, WOOD *and* SIMON *in exactly the same postures. There is a pause.*

WOOD: Tell me, does your wife know you do this sort of thing?

SIMON: Why, are you going to tell her?

WOOD: Oh, I'm not a sneak. Besides, Joanna would never forgive me. She'd have told me herself, you know. She always does. She thinks it's good for me to know what she and her pals get up to. Do you do it often. (*Smiling.*)

SIMON: Reasonably often. Or unreasonably, depending on one's point of view.

WOOD: And always with girls of my Joanna's age?

SIMON: There or thereabouts, yes.

WOOD: Because you don't love your wife?

SIMON: No, because I do. I make a point, you see, of not sleeping with friends, or the wives of friends, or acquaintances even. No one in our circle. Relationships there can be awkward enough –

WOOD: It's a sort of code, is it?

SIMON: No doubt it seems a rather squalid one, to you.

WOOD: So that's why you chose my Joanna, is it?

SIMON: I didn't really choose her, you know. She came into my office, and we looked at her work, and talked –

WOOD: Until everybody else had gone. You decided, in other words, that she was an easy lay. And wouldn't make any fuss, afterwards.

SIMON: I also realized that I couldn't possibly do her any harm.

WOOD: What about the clap? (*Pause.*) I think I have a right to know.

SIMON: I keep some pills at my office.

WOOD: So your post-coital period together was passed gobbling down anti-VD pills.

SIMON: One doesn't exactly gobble them – one swallows them, as one might digestive tablets.

32

WOOD: What about going back to your wife, reeking of sex?

SIMON: What?

WOOD: What do you do about the stench of your adulteries?

SIMON: I confess I find this enquiry into method rather depressing.
I'd willingly settle for a burst of parental outrage –

WOOD: And I'd far rather satisfy my curiosity. Won't you please
tell me?

SIMON: Very well. I stop off at my squash club, play a few points
with the professional, then have a shower.

WOOD: But you don't suffer from any guilt afterwards? No post-
coital distress, no angst or even embarrassment?

SIMON: Not unless this counts as afterwards.

WOOD: So really, only your sexual tastes have changed, your moral
organism has survived intact since the days when you were
that lucky sod, the Wundale Tart?

SIMON: Look, are you here because I slept around at thirteen, with
the attractive boys of your year, or because I sleep around with
attractive girls of your daughter's generation, at thirty-nine.
Good God Wood, I'm beginning to find something frankly
Mediterranean in this obsession with your child's sex-life –
and mine – after all, let's face it, in the grand scheme of things,
nothing much has happened, and in the Anglo-Saxon scheme
of things, your daughter's well over the age of consent. That
may sound brutal, but it's also true.

WOOD: Except in one important point. She's not my daughter.

SIMON: What? What is she then?

WOOD: My (*hesitates*) fiancée.

SIMON: Is it worth my saying sorry over again, or will my earlier
apologies serve. (*Pause*.) But I thought you said her name was
Wood –

WOOD: Yes.

SIMON: And your name is Wood.

WOOD: Yes. I changed my name as she refuses to change hers, and
won't marry me.

SIMON: In that case you're not Wood of Wundale.

WOOD: No, I'm Strapley – Strapley of Wundale. Known as
Wanker Strapley. Now do you remember me?

SIMON: Strapley – Strapley, Wanker Strapley. No.

WOOD: Well, your brother certainly would. He was known as Armpits Hench. We were two of a kind, in that we were both considered drips – what was the Wundale word for drip?

SIMON: I really can't remember.

WOOD: It was 'plop'.

SIMON: Plop.

WOOD: Those of us who were called it are more likely to remember it than those of you who called us it. Plop. Yes, I'm a plop, Hench. Whom one can now define, after so many years ploppily lived, as a chap who goes straight from masturbation to matrimony to monogamy.

SIMON: Oh, now there I think you're underestimating yourself. After all you have a wife, didn't you say, and now Joanna –

WOOD: I haven't got my wife any more. I doubt if I've got Joanna any more. But it's only appropriate that *you* should be the last common factor in our relationship. The first time I set eyes on her she reminded me of you.

SIMON: Where was that?

WOOD: At our local amateur theatricals. Joanna was playing in *The Winslow Boy*. She came on the stage in grey flannel bags, a white shirt and starched collar. She walked with a modest boy's gait, her eyes were wide with innocent knowledge. So did you walk down the Wundale Cloisters, that first year of yours. So I watched you then as I watched her. And there on my one side, were my two poor old sons, who've never reminded me of anyone but myself. And on the other, my poor old wife, the female plop, who from that second on ceased even to remind me that we shared a ploppy past. The years we'd spent together brooding over her mastoids, my haemorrhoids, and the mortgage on our maisonette, watching over our boys' sad little defeats, their failure to get into Wundale, their scrabbling for four O levels and then two A levels, their respective roles as twelfth man and scorer – they haven't even the competitiveness for sibling rivalry, poor old boys – all seemed, it all seemed such a waste, such a waste.

SIMON: But still you did succeed, to some extent at least, in breaking free. And you did succeed, to some extent I take it, with Joanna – so not altogether a case for predestination, when you think of it.

WOOD: Free meals, lots of gifts, little loans by the usual ploppy techniques of obligation and dependence – not that she felt dependent or obliged. She took what I offered and then asked for more. A generous nature. Did she get anything from you?

SIMON: She didn't ask for anything.

WOOD: Just as you never asked for anything from those boys – Higgens, Hornby, Darcy.

SIMON: It's true that Darcy was very kind with his tuck, but I hope I never took it as payment, nor did he offer it as such.

WOOD: (*Pause*) What was it like with Joanna?

SIMON: Well, it was, um, I'm sure you know – she's a very uninhibited um –

WOOD: It was, then, satisfactory?

SIMON: Well, as these things go.

WOOD: They don't for me. I'm incapacitated by devotion.

SIMON: But you live together?

WOOD: She allows me to share the flat I've leased for her. We have different rooms – I sometimes sit on the side of her bed when she's in it. More often when she's not.

SIMON: You're obviously in the grip of a passion almost Dante-esque in the purity of its hopelessness. You know, I really feel quite envious – for you every moment has its significance, however tortured, I just have to get by on my small pleasures and easy accommodations, my daily contentments –

WOOD: So she actually talks of me as a drip, does she?

SIMON: The ignorance of youth. Drips have neither your capacity for ironic self-castigation, nor more importantly your gift for the futile grand gesture.

WOOD: If she comes back, do you know what she'll do? She'll tell me about the boys she's slept with, the adults she's conned, the pot she's smoked. She'll tell me what a good time she had with you on your office floor –

SIMON: Sofa, actually.

WOOD: If she comes back. And I'll sit listening and yearning and just occasionally I'll soothe myself with the thought that one day she'll be dead, or even better old and unwanted and desperate – what I resent most about you, little Hench, is the way you seem to have gone on exactly as you promised you would at Wundale. If life catches up with everybody at the end, why hasn't it with you?

SIMON: But I haven't got to the end yet, thank God. I'm sure it will eventually.

WOOD: Sweet little Hench from Wundale, who picks off my Jo in an hour at his office, munches down a few pills, and then returns, without a worry in his head, the whole experience simply showered off, to his wife, who is doubtless quite attractive enough – is she?

SIMON: I find her quite attractive enough for me. Though taste in these matters –

WOOD: I'd like to kill you, Hench. Yes – kill you!

STEPHEN: (*Enters through the kitchen*) Si— (*Sees* WOOD.) Oh sorry, I didn't realize . . . Good God, it is, isn't it? Old Strapley, from Wundale?

WOOD: The name's Wood.

STEPHEN: Oh, sorry. You look rather like a chap who used to be at school with us, or rather me, in my year, Strapley.

WOOD: Really? What sort of chap was he?

STEPHEN: Oh actually, a bit of what we used to call a plop, wasn't he, Simon? So you're quite lucky not to be Strapley who almost certainly had a pretty rotten future before him. (*Laughs.*)

WOOD: Thank you for the sherry. (*Turns quickly, goes out.*)

SIMON: Not at all.

STEPHEN: I hope I haven't driven him off.

SIMON: Mmmm. Oh no, it's not you that's driven him off.

STEPHEN: What did he want?

SIMON: He was looking for somebody I once resembled. A case of mistaken identity, that's all.

STEPHEN: Well, if he had been Strapley, he'd hardly have changed at all, except that he's a quarter of a century older.

36

Poor old Wanker Strapley. (*Sits down*.)

(*There is a pause.*)

Well Si, you were quite right, of course.

SIMON: Mmmm?

STEPHEN: I got it.

SIMON: Got what?

STEPHEN: The Assistant Headmastership.

SIMON: Oh. Oh good! (*Pause*.) Goody.

STEPHEN: You can imagine how stunned I was. I was so depressed when I got home, not only because I thought I'd lost the appointment, but because of that friend of yours –

SIMON: What friend?

STEPHEN: Golding. Jeff Golding. That he didn't even remember me, let alone what I'd threatened to do to him – and I could hear the children quarrelling in the garden, the baby crying in her cot, and when I sat down in the sitting-room there was a piece in *The Times* on the phasing out of public schools and private health, lumped together, and it all seemed – well! Then Teresa called out. I couldn't face her, you know how lowering her optimism can be – but I managed to drag myself into the kitchen – she had her back to me, at the oven, cooking up some nut cutlets for the childrens' lunch – and she said: 'Greetings, Assistant Headmaster of Amplesides.' Yes, Headmaster's wife had phoned while I was here, isn't that ironic? I could hardly believe it. So. I crammed down a nut cutlet –

SIMON: What was it like?

STEPHEN: What?

SIMON: The nut cutlet.

STEPHEN: Oh, it was from one of Headmaster's wife's recipes. They're semi-vegetarian, you know.

SIMON: What did it *taste* like?

STEPHEN: Rather disgusting. But she's going to give us some more recipes if we like this one. Perhaps they'll be better.

SIMON: But you didn't like this one.

STEPHEN: (*Pause*) Aren't you pleased or even interested in my news?

SIMON: Of course I am.

STEPHEN: In spite of thinking MacDonald the better man? Well, you needn't worry about him, he's been offered a job too. As head of sixth form English.

SIMON: But you're head of sixth form English.

STEPHEN: Not any more. Headmaster reckons that with my new responsibilities I should step down from some of my teaching. I shall be head of fifth form English.

SIMON: Ah, fewer hours then.

STEPHEN: Actually more hours, but at fifth form level.

SIMON: Ah, less cerebration. That's even better. So – (*loses thread, picks it up*) so justice has been done to two excellent candidates.

STEPHEN: I shall still be senior to MacDonald, you know.

SIMON: Isn't his name MacGregor?

STEPHEN: Yes. (*Little pause.*) Thanks, Si. (*Ironically.*)

SIMON: What for?

STEPHEN: Sharing my triumph with me.

SIMON: Why don't you – have a drink.

STEPHEN: No, thank you. Headmaster's asked Teresa to ask me to look in after lunch for a celebration glass.

SIMON: Oh. Of what?

STEPHEN: Pansy wine, I expect, as that's their favourite tipple.

SIMON: (*After a pause*) Do they make it themselves?

STEPHEN: Headmaster's wife's aunt's husband does.

SIMON: Does he? (*Little pause.*) What's it like?

STEPHEN: You know what it's like.

SIMON: No, I don't. What's it like?

STEPHEN: Why do you want to know what it's like?

SIMON: Because I can't imagine what it's like, I suppose.

STEPHEN: Oh yes you can. Oh yes you can.

(*Turns, goes out through the kitchen.* DAVE *enters left. He's slightly drunk. There is a pause.*)

DAVE: (*Swaying slightly*) She's come. She's upstairs. She came all by herself.

SIMON: Who?

DAVE: That girl. Suzy. She dropped in for a cup of Nescafé.

SIMON: That's very good news, Dave. But should you, now you've got her, leave her to have it all by herself. She sounds a highly-strung creature –

DAVE: Yeah, well the only thing is, I'm out of Nescafé.

SIMON: Oh.

DAVE: Well, have you got any, man?

SIMON: No, I'm sorry, we don't drink it.

DAVE: Anything else?

SIMON: Nothing at all like Nescafé, I'm afraid.

DAVE: What, no coffee at all?

SIMON: Oh yes, we've got coffee. But we use beans, a grinder, and a rather complicated filter process. Metal holders, paper cones –

DAVE: That'll do. Is it in the kitchen? (*He moves towards kitchen.*)

SIMON: Actually, it's rather a precious set.

DAVE: What? (*Returning.*)

SIMON: It's one of those few things I feel rather specially about.

DAVE: You mean you've got something against lending it to me?

SIMON: Not at all. The beans are in a sealed bag in an airtight tin –

DAVE: Oh yes you have. I can tell by your – your tone.

SIMON: My tone? Oh come now, Dave, that's only one possible gloss of my tone. No, you take the grinder, take the filters, the jug, the paper cones and the metal holders, and the coffee beans which come from a small shop in Holborn that keeps uncertain hours and can therefore be easily replaced with a great deal of difficulty, and don't addle your head with questions about my tone, good God! (*Pause.*) Go ahead. Please. (*Wearily.*)

DAVE: No thanks. No thank you! Because you do mind all right, you bloody mind all right.

SIMON: No, I don't.

DAVE: No, you don't, no, you don't bloody mind, do you – why should you, you've got it all already, haven't you? Machines for making coffee, a table covered with booze, crates of wine in your cellar, all the nosh you want, all the books you want, all the discs, the best hi-fi on the bloody market, taxis to work every morning, taxis home in the evening, a whole bloody

house just for you and your sexy little wife – oh, you don't
bloody mind anything you don't, what's there for you to
mind, you shit you!

SIMON: Now that's not quite fair, Dave. It's not really a whole
house, you know, since we converted the top floor at
considerable expense and turned it over to you at an
inconsiderable rent which you don't pay anyway. But then I
don't mind that either.

DAVE: 'Course you bloody don't, why should you, you bloody like
to run a pet, don't you, your very own special deserving case.

SIMON: I swear to you, Dave, I've never once thought of you as
my pet or as a deserving case. If we'd wanted the former to
occupy our upstairs flat we'd have got a monkey, and if we'd
wanted the latter we'd have selected from among the
unmarried mothers or the dispossessed old age pensioners.
We thought quite hard about doing that, in fact.

DAVE: Then why didn't you?

SIMON: Because unmarried mothers mean babies, and babies
mean nappies, and crying. While old age pensioners mean
senility and eventual death.

DAVE: So I salve your bloody conscience without being a
nuisance, eh? Right?

SIMON: Wrong. You salve my conscience by being a bloody
nuisance. Your manners irritate me, your smell is unusually
offensive, you're extremely boring, your sex-life is both
depressing and disgusting, and you're a uniquely ungrateful
cadge. But you really mustn't mind, because the point is that
I don't, either. You have your one great value, that you run a
poor third to recent births and imminent deaths.

DAVE: I'm not staying – I'm not staying – I'm not staying in the
fucking top of your fucking house another fucking minute.
You – you – (*Makes as if to hit* SIMON.)
(SIMON *remains impassive.* DAVE *turns, goes out left. Noise of
door slamming.* SIMON *closes door left. As he does so* STEPHEN
enters right.)

STEPHEN: It's sugary and tastes of onions. And it's quite
revolting, just as you imagine.

SIMON: Well, I did imagine it would be revolting and probably sugary, but it never occurred to me it would taste of onions. But you can't have come back to report on its flavour already, you've only just left.

STEPHEN: I've been sitting in the car, thinking.

SIMON: What about?

STEPHEN: You, and your sneers. Oh, I don't altogether blame you, but I wish – (*sits down, looks at* SIMON) you'd had the guts to say it outright.

SIMON: Say what?

STEPHEN: That it's taken me twenty-four years to advance from Second Prefect of Wundale to Assistant Headmaster of Amplesides.

SIMON: (*Sitting down*) But that seems very respectable progress to me. At that rate you should make it to Eton, if it still exists, by your mid-fifties. And as that's what you want, why should I have a word to say against it?

STEPHEN: Nor against the way I'm doing it? My stuffing down nut cutlets, and herbal coffee and pansy wine. And then coming back for seconds.

SIMON: But you do rather more than eat the inedible and drink the undrinkable. You're among the best Junior Colts football managers in the country.

STEPHEN: You despise my job.

SIMON: You've a family to support.

STEPHEN: So you do despise my job, and despise me for doing it. Why don't you say it. That's all I'm asking you to do.

SIMON: But I don't want to say it! I can't remember when you were last as you've been today, or what I said then to make you feel any better. I wish I could, because that's what I'd like to say now.

STEPHEN: The last time I felt like this was eleven years ago, after Teresa had broken off our engagement, and you didn't say anything to make me feel any better. What you did say was that I was well out of it.

SIMON: Well, as you've been back in it for eleven years, you'll agree that it has little relevance now.

STEPHEN: It had little relevance then, either. As I was desperately in love with her.

SIMON: Good God, all I probably meant, and I don't even remember saying it, was that if she didn't want to marry you then it was better to be out of it before the wedding.

STEPHEN: Oh no, oh no, all you meant was that *you* were relieved to be out of it.

SIMON: Out of what?

STEPHEN: Out of having for your sister-in-law a girl you thought tedious and unattractive. And still do. And still do.

SIMON: Look Stephen, this is really rather eccentric, even in the English fratricidal tradition. First you hold it against me that I won't join you in abusing yourself, and then you hold it against me that not only did I fail to abuse your intended wife eleven years ago, but won't join you in abusing her now that she is your wife and has borne you seven children –

STEPHEN: Six children.

SIMON: Nearly seven.

STEPHEN: Nearly six.

SIMON: Well, straight after the sixth, it'll be nearly seven.(*He gets up.*)

STEPHEN: Teresa's absolutely right about you. She always has been. You're just indifferent. Absolutely indifferent!

SIMON: In what sense? As a wine is indifferent, or prepositionally, as in, say, indifferent to –

STEPHEN: Imbeciles like Teresa. Go on, say it!

SIMON: But I don't want to say it.

STEPHEN: Not to me, no. But that's what you tell your clever-clever metropolitan Jeff Goldings, isn't it? That Teresa and I are imbeciles.

SIMON: I swear to you, Stephen, I've never told a soul.

STEPHEN: Answer me one question, Simon. *One* question! What have you got against having children?

SIMON: Well Steve, in the first place there isn't enough room. In the second place they seem to start by mucking up their parents' lives, and then go on in the third place to muck up their own. In the fourth place it doesn't seem right to bring them into a world like this in the fifth place and in the sixth place I don't like them very much in the first place. OK.

STEPHEN: And Beth? What about her?

SIMON: (*After a little pause*) Beth and I have always known what we're doing, thank you Stephen.

STEPHEN: You think she's happy, do you?

SIMON: Yes, I do. And let's not let you say another word about her, because I don't want to hear it. Have you got that, Steve, *I don't want to hear it.* (*With low emphasis.*)

STEPHEN: No, I'm sure you don't. I'm sure you don't. The last thing you want to hear is how unhappy she is.

SIMON: Steve!

STEPHEN: Well, she is! So unhappy that last week she came around to Teresa and sobbed her heart out!

SIMON: Steve!

STEPHEN: She's having an affair, Simon. An affair with that Ned whom you so much despise. *That's* how unhappy your happy Beth is.

(*There is a long pause.*)

SIMON: With Ned. (*Pause.*) Beth's having an affair with Ned? (*Pause.*) Really? With Ned? Good God! (*Sits down.*)

STEPHEN: It's time you knew.

SIMON: No it isn't.

(*There is a pause.*)

STEPHEN: I had to tell you.

SIMON: Now that's a different matter.

(*There is the sound of a door opening left.* BETH *enters.*)

BETH: Hello. Hello, Stephen.

STEPHEN: Hello, Beth.

SIMON: (*Goes over, gives* BETH *a kiss*) You're back nice and early, aren't you?

BETH: Yes, I got an earlier train.

SIMON: Ah, that explains it. How was it, then, old Salisbury?

BETH: Old *Canterbury*, actually. Much as it ever was, except for the parts they've turned into new Canterbury.

SIMON: But the Cathedral's still there?

BETH: Although the French students were more interested in the new Marks and Spencers.

SIMON: And Ned?

BETH: Oh, he preferred the Cathedral.

STEPHEN: I really must be getting along. Headmaster will be wondering what's happening to me.

SIMON: Oh, but first you must tell Beth your news.
(*There is a slight pause.*)
The Assistant Headmastership, Steve.

STEPHEN: Oh. Oh yes. I got it.

BETH: Steve – how marvellous! (*Comes over, gives him a kiss.*) Congratulations – Teresa must be thrilled!

STEPHEN: Yes, she is. I've had some black moments since the interview, but she was absolutely sure – and old Si jollied me along a bit this morning. It's all a great relief, more than anything. Well, I really must dash – see you both very soon – (*goes towards the kitchen door.*) Oh, by the way, Si – I was a bit carried away just now, spoke a lot of nonsense, don't know why I said it.

SIMON: Don't you?

STEPHEN: Yes, well I suppose I meant to hurt, but I didn't mean harm, if you see.

SIMON: Well then that's fine, because no harm's been done. I didn't take it seriously.

STEPHEN: Good. (*Hesitates, turns, goes out.*)

BETH: What did he say? (*Sits and lights a cigarette.*)

SIMON: Actually I could hardly make out – he was in a post-success depression, I think, suddenly realizing that what he's got can therefore no longer be striven for. He'll be all right the moment he sets his sights on a full Headmastership. Or Amplesides is abolished. Triumph or disaster – you know, like a drug. What about tea or coffee?

BETH: No, I've had some, thanks.

SIMON: Where?

BETH: On the train.

SIMON: Oh, then you're probably still trying to work out which it was.

BETH: Did you enjoy your Wagner?

SIMON: I enjoyed some things about it, very much. The picture on its cover for example, its glossy and circular blackness when unsheathed, its light balance – and if the sound is any good it'll be quite perfect.

BETH: You haven't managed to play it then?

SIMON: Very nearly, very nearly. But what with Dave and Stephen, Jeff and Davina, the odd bod and sod, you know –

BETH: Oh, you poor thing, and you'd been looking forward to it all week.

SIMON: Still, one mustn't snatch at one's pleasures, nor over-plan them it seems. (*He puts the record away in its box.*)

BETH: (*Pause*) How was Jeff?

SIMON: Oh, in excellent form, really. He got drunk, threw his scotch in his girl's face, dashed off to Cambridge where he's been having it off with his ex-wife, Gwynyth. Did you know Gwynyth, or was she a little before your time?

BETH: Isn't it Gwendoline?

SIMON: Yes, yes, Gwendoline. Anyway, usual sort of Jeff saga, quite droll in its way.

BETH: And what's his girl like?

SIMON: She's got good tits and a nasty sense of humour.

BETH: And did she try to get you to bed?

SIMON: She did.

BETH: And how did you get out of it?

SIMON: Rudely, I'm afraid, as she's on to rather a good book, from the sound of it. Ah well –

BETH: Ah well, you can play your records now, can't you?

SIMON: Oh no. Wouldn't dream of it.

BETH: Why not?

SIMON: Well, for one thing, you hate Wagner.

BETH: Well, I'm going to have a bath.

SIMON: A four-hour bath?

BETH: Afterwards I've got to go along to the school – sort out the fares and docket them, that sort of thing.

SIMON: Ah! Well, in that case –

(SIMON *moves to hi-fi and takes out record.* BETH *rises,*

45

hesitates, and moves towards him.)

BETH: (*Stops, looks at* SIMON) Stephen told you, didn't he? About me. At least I hope he has.

SIMON: Why?

BETH: So I shan't have to tell you myself.

SIMON: You don't have to.

BETH: What?

SIMON: Tell me.

BETH: What?

SIMON: Tell me anything you don't want to tell me. Stephen said nothing of significance about anything.

BETH: But you see, I may not want to tell you, but I do want you to know.

SIMON: Why?

BETH: Because there's an important problem we shall have to discuss. And I want you to understand. (*Sits on sofa.*)

SIMON: In my experience, the worst thing you can do to an important problem is discuss it. You know – (*sitting down*) – I really do think this whole business of non-communication is one of the more poignant fallacies of our zestfully over-explanatory age. Most of us understand as much as we need to without having to be told – except old Dave, of course, now I thought he had quite an effective system, a tribute really to the way in which even the lowest amongst us can put our education (or lack of it, in Dave's case) and intelligence (or lack of it, in Dave's case) to serving our needs. He's done really remarkably well out of taking the metaphors of courtesy literally, as for example when he asks for a loan that is in fact a gift, and one replies, 'Of course, Dave, no trouble, pay it back when you can.' *But* this system completely collapses when he's faced with a plainly literal reply, as for example when he asks to borrow our coffee set, and he's told that it'll be lent with reluctance and one would like him to be careful with it. Weird, isn't it, he can take one's courteous metaphors literally, but he can't take one's literals literally, he translates them into metaphors for insults, and plans, I'm reasonably happy to inform you, to move out at once. So I've

managed one useful thing today, after all. When we come to
think of his replacement, let's narrow our moral vision
slightly, and settle for a pair of respectably married and out of
date homosexuals who still think they've something to hide.
They'll leave us entirely alone, and we can congratulate
ourselves on doing them a good turn. We'll have to raise the
rent to just this side of exorbitant of course, or they'll smell
something fishy, but we'll pass the money straight on to
charities for the aged, unmarried mothers, that sort of thing
and no one need be the wiser, what do you think?

BETH: In other words, you do know.

SIMON: In other words, can't we confine ourselves to the other
words.

BETH: What did Stephen tell you, please Simon.

SIMON: Nothing. Nothing, except for the odd detail, that I haven't
known for a long time. So you see it's all right. Nothing's
changed for the worst, though it might if we assume we have
to talk about it.

BETH: (*Long pause*) How long have you known for?

SIMON: Oh – (*sighs*) about ten months it would be roughly.
(*Pause*.) How long has it been going on for?

BETH: For about ten months, it would be. (*Pause*.) How did you
know?

SIMON: There's no point, Beth –

BETH: Yes, there is. Yes, there is. How did you know?

SIMON: Well, frankly, your sudden habit, after years of admirable
conversational economy on such day-to-day matters as what
you'd done today, of becoming a trifle prolix.

BETH: You mean you knew I was having an affair because I became
boring?

SIMON: No, no, over-detailed, that's all, darling. And quite
naturally, as you were anxious to account for stretches of time
in which you assumed I *would* be interested if I knew how
you'd *actually* filled them, if you see, so you sweetly devoted
considerable effort and paradoxically imaginative skill to
rendering them – for my sake I know – totally uninteresting.
My eyes may have been glazed but my heart was touched.

BETH: Thank you. And is that all you had to go on?

SIMON: Well, you have doubled your bath routine. Time was, you took one immediately before going out for the day. These ten months you've taken one immediately on return too. (*Pause.*) And once or twice you've addressed me, when in the twilight zone, with an unfamiliar endearment.

BETH: What was it?

SIMON: Foxy. (*Little pause.*) At least, I took it to be an endearment. Is it?

BETH: Yes. I'm sorry.

SIMON: No, no, it's quite all right.

BETH: You haven't felt it's interfered with your sex-life then?

SIMON: On the contrary. *Quite* the contrary. In fact there seems to have been an increased intensity in your – (*gestures*) which I suppose in itself was something of a sign.

BETH: In what way?

SIMON: Well, guilt, would it be? A desire to make up –

BETH: (*After a pause*) And did you know it was Ned, too?

SIMON: Ned *too*? Oh, did I also know it was Ned? No, that was the little detail I mentioned Stephen did provide. Ned. There I *was* surprised.

BETH: Why?

SIMON: Oh, I don't know. Perhaps because – well, no offence to Ned, whom I've *always* as you know thought of as a very engaging chap, in his way, no offence to *you* either, come to think of it, I'd just imagined when you did have an affair it would be with someone of more – more –

BETH: What?

SIMON: Consequence. *Overt* consequence.

BETH: He's of consequence to me.

SIMON: And *that's* what matters, quite.

BETH: What did you mean, when?

SIMON: Mmmm?

BETH: *When* I had an affair, you said.

SIMON: A grammatical slip, that's all. And since the hypothesis is now a fact –

BETH: But you used the emphatic form – when I *did* have an affair

– which implies that you positively assumed I'd have an affair. Didn't you?

SIMON: Well, given your nature, darling, and the fact that so many people do have them these days, I can't see any reason for being bouleversé now that you're having one, even with Ned, can I put it that way?

BETH: Given what about my nature?

SIMON: It's marvellously responsive – warm, a warm, responsive nature. And then I realized once we'd taken the decision not to have children, – and the fact that you work every day and therefore meet chaps – and pretty exotic ones too, from lithe young Spanish counts to experienced Japanese businessmen – not forgetting old Ned himself – it was only realistic –

BETH: From boredom, you mean. You know I'm having an affair because I'm boring, and you assumed I'd have one from boredom. That's why I'm in love with Ned, is it?

SIMON: I'm absolutely prepared to think of Ned as a very, very lovable fellow. I'm sure *his* wife loves him, why shouldn't mine.

BETH: You are being astonishingly hurtful.

SIMON: I don't want to be, I don't want to be! That's why I tried to avoid this conversation, darling.

BETH: You'd like to go back, would you, to where I came in, and pretend that I'd simply caught the early train from Salisbury, and here I was, old unfaithful Beth, back home and about to take her bath, as usual?

SIMON: Yes, I'd love to. (*Little pause.*) I thought it was Canterbury.

BETH: It was neither. We spent the night in a hotel in Euston, and the morning in Ned's poky little office at the school, agonizing.

SIMON: Agonizing? Good God, did you really?

BETH: About whether we should give up everything to live together properly.

SIMON: Properly?

BETH: We want, you see, to be husband and wife to each other.

SIMON: Husband *and* wife to each other? Is Ned up to such double duty? And what did you decide?

49

BETH: Do you care?

SIMON: Yes.

BETH: His wife isn't well. She's been under psychiatric treatment for years. And his daughter is autistic.

SIMON: Oh. I'm sorry. I can quite see why he wants to leave them.

BETH: But I could still leave you.

SIMON: Yes.

BETH: But you don't think I will. Do you?

SIMON: No.

BETH: And why not?

SIMON: Because I hope you'd rather live with me than anybody else, except Ned of course. And I know you'd rather live with almost anyone than live alone.

BETH: You think I am that pathetic?

SIMON: I don't think it's pathetic. I'd rather live with you than anyone else, including Ned. And I don't want to live alone either.

BETH: But do you want to live at all?

SIMON: What?

BETH: As you hold such a deeply contemptuous view of human life. That's Ned's diagnosis of you.

SIMON: But the description of my symptoms came from you, did it?

BETH: He says you're one of those men who only give permission to little bits of life to get through to you. He says that while we may envy you your serenity, we should be revolted by the rot from which it stems. Your sanity is of the kind that causes people to go quietly mad around you.

SIMON: What an elegant paraphrase. Tell me, did you take notes?

BETH: I didn't have to. Every word rang true.

SIMON: But if it's all true, why do you need to keep referring it back to Ned?

BETH: It's a way of keeping in touch with him. If I forgot in the middle of a sentence that he's there and mine, I might begin to scream at you and claw at you and punch at you.

SIMON: But why should you want to do that?

BETH: Because I hate you.

    (*The telephone rings.* SIMON *makes a move towards it. After the fourth ring, it stops.*)

SIMON: Oh, of course. I've put on the machine. (*Pause.*)

BETH: (*Quietly*) You know the most insulting thing, that you let me go on and on being unfaithful without altering your manner or your behaviour one – one – you don't care about me, or my being in love with somebody else, or my betraying you, good God! least of all that! But you do wish I hadn't actually *mentioned* it, because then we could have gone on, at least *you* could, pretending that everything was all right, no, not even pretending, as far as *you* were concerned, everything was all right, you probably still think it *is* all right – and – and – you've – you've – all those times we've made love, sometimes the very same evening as Ned and I – and yet you took me – in your usual considerate fashion, just as you take your third of a bottle of wine with dinner or your carefully measured brandy and your cigar after it, *and* enjoyed it all the more because I felt guilty, God help me *guilty* and so tried harder for your sake – and you *admit* that, no, not admit it, simply state it as if on the difference made by an extra voice or something in your bloody Wagner – don't you see, don't you see that that makes you a freak! You're – you're – oh, damn! Damn. Damn you. (*Pause.*) Oh, damn.

    (*There is a silence.*)

    So you might as well listen to your Wagner.

SIMON: I must say you've quite warmed me up for it. And what are *you* going to do, have your cleansing bath?

BETH: No, go to Ned for a couple of hours.

SIMON: Oh dear, more agonizing in his poky little office. Or is that a euphemism for Ned's brand of love-play? Excuse me, but what precisely has all this been about? You complain of my reticence over the last ten months, but what good has all this exposition served, what's it been for Beth? Ned's not going to leave his wife, I don't want you to leave me, you don't even think you're going to leave me – we have a perfectly sensible arrangement, we are happy enough together you and I, insultingly so if you like but still happy. We could go on and on, with Ned, until you've gone off him, why, why did you have to muck it up between you with your infantile agonizings.

BETH: Because there's a problem.

SIMON: What problem?

BETH: I'm going to have a baby.

SIMON: (*Stares at her for a long moment*) What? (*Another moment.*) Whose?

BETH: *That* is the problem. (*Goes out.*)

(SIMON *sits in a state of shock.* DAVE *enters left.*)

DAVE: (*Stands grinning at* SIMON) Well, I worked it out, you'll be unhappy to hear. Suzy put me onto you. She just laughed when I told her the stuff you'd said, she and her bloke had dealings with your type in their last place. You were trying to get me out, that's all. Well, it hasn't worked, see. I'm staying. See. And another thing, Suzy and her bloke are looking for a new place. I said they could move in upstairs with me. Got that? Got that? You won't like tangling with them either. (*Stares at* SIMON.) Having a bit of trouble sinking in, is it? (*Turns, goes out, leaving the door open.*)

(SIMON *remains sitting, dazed. Then he goes to the drinks table, pours himself a small Scotch. Looks at it. Frowns. Adds some more. Stands uncertainly, looks at the telephone, goes over to it. Remembers something vaguely, presses the play-back machine.*)

WOOD: (*His voice*) Hello, Hench, Bernard Wood, né Strapley here. I expect by now my little visit has passed entirely out of your consciousness, it was all of an hour ago that I left, and you've no doubt had any number of amusing little things to engage your attention. Your life goes on its self-appointed way, as I sit in my empty flat, my home. I've taken off my jacket, and I've lowered my braces so that they dangle around me – a picture, you might say, of old Wood, né Strapley, quite abandoned at the last. Imagine it, the jacket off, the braces down, thinking of you as I speak into the telephone, clasped tightly in my left hand as my right brings

up, not trembling too much – Hench – sweet little Hench –
and point the gun at my forehead – no, through the – no, I
can't do the mouth, the metal tastes too intimate – it'll have
to be – picture it – picture it – and as I – as I – Hench, as I
squeeze – squee . . .

(SIMON *switches off the machine, interrupting the message. He
sits motionless.* JEFF *appears in the doorway left.*)

SIMON: (*Sees him. Gets up slowly*) Ah yes. Jeff. All right, are we
then? Get back to – (*thinks*) Oxford, did you?

JEFF: I didn't get to the bloody corner.

SIMON: Oh really. Why not?

JEFF: There was a police car, Simon, right behind me, then right
beside me, then right on bloody top of me with the cops all
bloody over me, breathalysing me, shaking me about, and
then down at the station for the rest of it. That's why bloody
not. And you tipped the buggers off, friend, Christ!

SIMON: What? (*Vaguely*) What?

JEFF: No, don't deny it, don't deny it, please Christ don't deny it.
Davina told me when I phoned her. She told me – you tipped
them off. Christ!

SIMON: Oh. (*Thinks.*) That's what you believe, is it?

JEFF: That's what I bloody know, Simon.

SIMON: (*Calmly*) What sort of man do you think I am? (*He throws
his Scotch in* JEFF's *face.*) What sort of man do you think I
am?

JEFF: (*Sputtering, gasping*) Christ, Christ! My eyes! My eyes!
(SIMON *watches him a moment, then takes out his handkerchief,
gives it to* JEFF.)
Christ – (*Takes the handkerchief.*) Thanks. (*Little pause.*)
Thanks. (*Little pause.*) Sorry. Sorry, Simon. (*Pause, goes and
sits down.*) Can I have a drink? (*Pause.*) The bitch.
(SIMON *hesitates, then goes and gets him a Scotch, brings it to
him.*)
Thanks.
(*There is a pause.*)
Don't throw me out, eh? I've got nowhere to bloody go, and
I don't want to go there yet.

SIMON: I'm going to play *Parsifal*. Do you mind?

JEFF: No, lovely. Lovely.

SIMON: You sure?

JEFF: Christ yes. You know I adore Wagner.

SIMON: No, I didn't know that.

JEFF: Christ, I introduced you. At Oxford. I bloody introduced you.

SIMON: Did you really? (*Looks at him.*) Such a long time ago. Then I owe you more than I can say. Thank you, Jeff. (*Goes over to the hi-fi, puts on the record.*)

(*The opening bars of* Parsifal *fill the theatre. They sit listening as the music swells.*)

(*The light fades. Curtain.*)

Dog Days

To Ian Hamilton, in whose *The New Review*
this play was first published,
my thanks for many other things

Dog Days was first performed on 26 October 1976 at the Oxford Playhouse. The cast was as follows:

PETER	Charles Kay
HILARY	Gayle Hunnicutt
CHARLES	Richard Wilson
Three girls called JOANNA	Emma Williams
Director	Gordon McDougall
Designer	Saul Radomsky
Lighting	David Colmer

ACT ONE

SCENE I

JOANNA *is standing holding her folio under her arm. She puts it down next to the sofa, and tentatively begins to wander around the room. There are sounds of clattering from the kitchen. She wanders over to the desk and looks at the photos. She picks one up.* PETER *enters from the kitchen with two mugs of coffee.*

PETER: Only instant, I'm afraid. The trick is to pretend it's not coffee at all, but a quite other beverage. The next trick is to like the other beverage.

JOANNA: Sorry, I'm being nosy. I can never resist old snapshots – are these your parents, then?

PETER: That's right. It was taken in the garden of our house in Bromley, Kent.

JOANNA: Your dad is a fine figure of a man, isn't he? And I love his woollen cap – is it from the war or something?

PETER: Well, actually that's my mother, in her gardening gear. Though you're right, she was a fine figure of a man. That's my father there. On the edge of the picture, as usual. In the fine figure of the little drunk.

JOANNA: Do they still live there?

PETER: No. They're both dead. Killed in a car crash a few years back. And that's me, sitting on his shoulders, to give us both a mite of extra stature. And there's my brother Charlie, lurking between my mother's legs. He's still something of a homebody, with lots of children of his own now. I'm never sure how many, but it works on the opposite system to one's bank account – more than one expected. So there we are – a pretty typical suburban English family, eh? With its normal whiffs of incest, alcoholism and despair. (*He laughs and puts photo on desk.*) I'm so glad we decided to come back here. So much nicer than that dreadful pub, isn't it?

59

JOANNA: So you have this place all to yourself then, right?

PETER: Right. Oh, except for upstairs. That belongs to someone else.

JOANNA: Oh. Who?

PETER: My – um – landlady.

JOANNA: What does she do?

PETER: What – oh, she teaches English to foreigners. In one of those dingy academies off Oxford Street. And then she has to pick up her little boy from school, so she won't be back for ages, you see. So . . .

(*He gestures to* JOANNA *to sit on the sofa. She sits on the arm.*)

JOANNA: She's married then?

PETER: Mmm? Oh yes. Yes she is. But somehow one never thinks of him as one's landlord.

JOANNA: Why, what's he like?

PETER: Well, rather like most husbands in these parts. Not much on the surface, but probably simmering away, you know, beneath. But a decent enough chap . . . so why don't you tell me about yourself, it's your turn. (*He puts his hand on her knee.*)

JOANNA: (*Getting up*) Oh, there's not much to tell, really. Anyway, I'd rather get straight in and show you my work – I mean if you're really interested.

PETER: Of course I am. Indeed I am.

JOANNA: Right. (*She opens folio.*) These are just drawings and designs, you know, from my school portfolio – before it struck me to try to get into publishing.

PETER: (*Getting up and taking folio from her*) I'm so glad it did. (*He turns over drawings.*) Now that is lovely. What a marvellous colour-sense you've got. All those greys and reds. By God, you can draw too. That's super. Ah, nudes. I like nudes. The one on the left, though, the chap's a bit fat, isn't he – oh, they're both chaps. What's it for, a homosexual sex manual?

JOANNA: No, the idea is it's for one of those dieting books. Those blokes are before and after, you see.

PETER: Oh, I see. Before looks altogether nicer. I like that. I like that very much indeed.

(*He puts folio down and grabs her and kisses her.*)

JOANNA: (*Freeing herself*) Are you the slightest bit interested in
my work?

PETER: Yes, I am. Indeed I am. I've seen quite enough of it to
know you're very talented – in fact I've already made up my
mind – we've got a sociologist called Nuzek who delivered
his latest book only this morning. On Protestantism and
Pornography. I'm going to see what I can do to get you the
dust-jacket. And the paperback cover. If it goes into
paperback. Something on the lines of that dieting one might
do perfectly. I mean the thin nude could be Protestantism
and the fat one Pornography, or the other way around even.
I'm pretty sure I can get you lots of commissions.

JOANNA: In exchange for going to bed with you.

PETER: Well, it would have to be the sofa actually. But we could
plump up the cushions . . .
(*He kisses her again. She punches him. He doubles up in pain.*) I
gather the idea doesn't appeal to you.

JOANNA: No.

PETER: I see. Anything personal?

JOANNA: You're married, aren't you? To that landlady of yours!

PETER: Yes. So I'm very well trained.

JOANNA: And that little boy's your son?

PETER: Yes but he's very little. If you look straight ahead you
can't even see him. (*Little pause.*) You don't sleep with
married men, is that it?

JOANNA: Of course I do. It's just that I like to be asked first.
Politely. I don't put out every time somebody just clutches at
me.

PETER: Oh, I see. Well – in that case – would you do me the
honour of accompanying me to the sofa? We've got a good
hour.

JOANNA: No, thank you. Right now I'm interested in getting into
publishing and I have to meet someone on the other side of
London in an hour. But give me a ring when you have
something for me.

PETER: I'll do that.

JOANNA: Good. (*Nods, goes to door*) You know you're a bit of a prick, aren't you?

PETER: (*Angrily*) What!

JOANNA: I said you're a bit of a prick.

PETER: Oh. Thank God. I thought you said prig.

(JOANNA *laughs, exits.* PETER *runs after her exiting.*)

PETER: (*Voice over*) Hey – what's your number?

JOANNA: (*Voice over, very faint, calls out number*)
(*Lights down.*)

(*Lights up.*
The room full of sunlight. Outside the sound of children's voices at play. Toys and Sunday bits and pieces scattered around the room.
After a moment, PETER *enters, left, in weekend wear and very sloppy. He is smoking. He looks towards the window, winces, goes to the drinks table, pours himself a Scotch, squirts in soda water, turns, goes to the sofa.*)

CHARLES: (*Off, outside the window, right*) Nindy, what a clever girlie, did you do this just for Daddy, thank you darling, thank you. Now you go and watch the big ones play football while Daddy takes this in and looks for Uncle Peter.
(*There is a crashing sound from the kitchen.* PETER *listens to this, then rolls off the sofa, cupping his cigarette and drink.*
CHARLES *enters, carrying a plastic pot. He goes through and out, left. He is also in weekend wear, but neat, short-haired and springy of step.*
PETER *adjusts himself more comfortably, sips from his drink, puffs on his cigarette.*
Sound of tap running, lavatory flushing, left.
CHARLES *re-enters, carrying the pot. He hesitates, goes to the drinks table, then puts the pot down on it as he squirts himself an enormous soda water. He drains it off and then squirts himself a second glass.* PETER *coughs and* CHARLES *walks over to the sofa, and sees* PETER.)

CHARLES: What on earth are you doing?

PETER: Practising.

CHARLES: Practising what?

PETER: Secret drinking.

CHARLES: Oh, I see. Not feeling very sociable, are we?

PETER: On the contrary, but it's such a rare feeling I like to savour it on my own. (*Gets up, goes to the window.*)

CHARLES: (*Watches him*) I must say, you've been acting very strangely today. We've scarcely seen you except at lunch. Is something the matter?

PETER: No.

CHARLES: Frankly, some of your remarks were a bit off.

PETER: Really? Probably because I've kept them in too long. Did you know that Alison's joined the boys in football? Is that wise at seven months gone?

CHARLES: Oh, she'll be all right, you know how active she is during her pregnancies. Peter . . .

PETER: And between them too, to get to them so quickly. When do you intend to stop exactly? I realize Alison's a practising Catholic but this'll make six in five years . . .

CHARLES: Four, actually. In six years. As I'm sure you realize. And you also realize, because I've told you often enough, that we both happen to believe in letting them come as they please.

PETER: Well, you certainly do please them, from the speed at which they keep coming.

CHARLES: The important thing is that they please us. Anyway, now that you've chosen to raise the subject Alison and I sometimes wonder what you two have got against having more.

PETER: Contraceptives, and they work miracles.

CHARLES: Oh ha ha. But has it ever occurred to you that it might turn out a little hard on Jeremy himself? He'll be the one that'll have to cope with being an only child.

PETER: If I can cope with being an only father, when we need two or three, he can cope with being an only child when we don't need any more. (*He coughs.*)

CHARLES: Something's the matter, isn't it?

PETER: With what?

63

CHARLES: With you. For one thing you're smoking and drinking far more than usual.

PETER: Oh, that's quite usual with smoking and drinking.

CHARLES: But Pete, think of your health! I'm sure you would feel much better if you cut down.

PETER: Ah, but then I wouldn't have the Scotch and fags I need to help me endure it.

CHARLES: Endure what?

PETER: My health. (*Toasts himself.*) And yours. I notice you've cut down again though. The last time you were here you'd fought your way up to a five a day, wasn't it?

CHARLES: Only because I was under some stress.

PETER: What stress?

CHARLES: I was still waiting to hear whether I'd got it.

PETER: Got what?

CHARLES: The Assistant Headmastership at Amplesides.

PETER: And did you?

CHARLES: Not only did Alison phone Hilary as soon as I'd phoned her, but before lunch today Alison actually described a sort of informal interview she'd had with Headmaster.

PETER: Oh, that was with Headmaster!

CHARLES: Who did you think it was with?

PETER: Her gynaecologist.

CHARLES: That was during lunch.

PETER: She had an interview with her gynaecologist during lunch . . .?

CHARLES: Oh ha ha. She described her interview with the gynaecologist during lunch – I mean during lunch she described her interview – (*Stops.*)

PETER: Well anyway, Charlie, congratulations. I know how much you respect that headmaster of yours. It'll be wonderful to work so closely with him, won't it?

CHARLES: Yes, it will.

PETER: He's a great influence over your life, isn't he?

CHARLES: In some things, perhaps. I don't deny it.

PETER: How can you, when there's scarcely a decision, large or

64

small, on which you don't consult him – where he leads, you follow, eh?

CHARLES: I wouldn't go that far.

PETER: Really? How far has he gone?

CHARLES: It's no good, you won't get at me through Headmaster, you know.

PETER: Does he smoke?

CHARLES: He's got far too much sense.

PETER: Does he drink?

CHARLES: Yes, he does.

PETER: What does he drink?

CHARLES: The odd wine.

PETER: That wine you brought along for lunch was odd, was it one of his?

CHARLES: That was a retsina.

PETER: Home-made though, wasn't it?

CHARLES: How on earth would one home-make a retsina?

PETER: Exactly as the Greeks do, I should think. By boiling up some tree bark. They're vegetarian, aren't they, Headmaster and wife?

CHARLES: Yes, they are, so what?

PETER: And that's why you and Alison have given up meat, is it?

CHARLES: Given up meat?

PETER: You've got that smirk on, Charlie.

CHARLES: What smirk?

PETER: Your lying smirk.

CHARLES: Lying – what lie, for heaven's sake? Didn't you see me put Hilary's casserole away?

PETER: Yes, first into your handkerchief, then into your pocket. You used to employ the same technique with Mummy's Friday night fish stews – until she asked you to explain why your trousers smelt of haddock.

CHARLES: (*Long pause*) Yes, well I do apologize for that. The truth is, as we'd forgotten to warn Hilary that we'd turned vegetarian, and as we realized she'd gone to a lot of trouble to cook for us, we felt it a matter of common courtesy to go through with it. Frankly, we knew the children would more than make up for us. (*Little pause*.) I do hope she didn't notice, though.

PETER: Oh, you were as skilful as ever. The funny smile, the elaborate chewing, the dabs at your lips. You may have made her casserole look inedible, but you did look as if you were managing to eat it. Is it still in your pocket?

CHARLES: Yes.

PETER: Well, you can chuck it into the garbage now, I won't sneak.

CHARLES: Actually, I'd rather keep it.

PETER: Keep it!

CHARLES: Yes.

PETER: In your pocket?

CHARLES: For the time being.

PETER: (*After a pause*) Oh I see, no cloistered and fugitive virtue for you, eh Charlie? You like to carry your vice around with you, to fight every moment of the day. A handkerchief full of temptation! I just hope you don't spill it out in front of headmaster when you have to blow your nose. He might not believe your story.

CHARLES: (*Slowly*) Ha. Ha. Ha. I happen to want it for a dog.

PETER: You haven't got a dog.

CHARLES: No, but the school has. Alfonso – at least that's what I call him. He's a sort of stray that's always in and out of Headmaster's garden. Somebody's got to feed him.

PETER: And you've chosen my wife? Why can't Headmaster do the job, it's his garden. Or doesn't he like animals?

CHARLES: I'm sure he loves them. And I know his wife does. So I expect they do feed him. But I also expect he'd be grateful for any little tid bits. Does that clear that up? There can't be any further questions, Pete – now that you've managed to embarrass me, after all.

PETER: Well, just one.

CHARLES: I don't think I want to hear it.

PETER: OK. (*Goes and stands by the window*.)

CHARLES: (*Stands uncertainly, then goes to the soda water, takes a swift draught from his glass, looks at* PETER) All right, what is it?

PETER: Mmmmmm?

66

CHARLES: Your last question.

PETER: Mmm. Oh yes. Did you give up meat before your appointment as Assistant, to ingratiate yourself with Headmaster? Or afterwards, on orders from Headmaster? Or did you do it during the interview with Headmaster, in a dramatic renunciation?

CHARLES: I didn't give up, or have to give up, anything to get the Assistantship. Alison and I merely observed how well Headmaster and his wife looked on their regimen and drew the same conclusion. Which would doubtless have escaped you. Furthermore, far from feeling ashamed of it, I don't mind telling you that I, personally, feel absolutely marvellous for it. As if I were fifteen again!

PETER: I'm sorry to hear that. You were particularly ghastly at fifteen. Even Mummy thought so.

CHARLES: At least I see the world properly, in its vivid details. And most of what I see, I like. What do you see at the moment, Pete?

PETER: Nothing much to like, I admit, Charles. (*Little pause.*) Actually, from my recollection of Alison's gynaecological anecdotes, delivered during the lunch she was presumably pocketing in her pregnancy trousers, you don't have to give up anything to get the vivid details, Charles. As long, that is, as you don't give up your Alison.

CHARLES: Right! That does it! I've spent the whole morning trying to overlook your bloody nasty remarks –

PETER: Spoilsport.

CHARLES: But don't worry, I'm not going to overlook that one. You jeer at my feeling fifteen, but you have gone right back to the nursery to insult my wife like that.

PETER: You didn't have a wife like that in the nursery, Charlie. Or are you about to spring into the Freudian open by naming Mummy?

CHARLES: You little – (*Pulls himself together, and with dignity*) If it weren't for Hilary's feelings, and Jeremy's – I wouldn't set foot in this house again. (*Turns, goes towards exit kitchen, right.*)

PETER: Those are my own sentiments exactly. (*As* CHARLES, *unhearing, exits, he collapses on sofa.*)
(*There is a lighting change, to suggest time passing.* PETER *turns on lights. Much activity from the kitchen, right.*)

HILARY: (*Enters. Looks at* PETER, *and as she begins to clear up toys and bits and pieces*) Jeremy is in bed, I trust.

PETER: (*Not stirring*) Hours ago.

HILARY: And did you bother to get him to read to you?

PETER: Until we both realized he still couldn't.

HILARY: Of course he can.

PETER: Then we have a wunderkind who can read with his eyes shut. My own view is that he was reciting.

HILARY: You probably made him nervous.

PETER: Not as nervous as he made me. 'This is Janet. This is John. That is Janet. That is John.' (*In a sing-song.*) I thought he was trying to put me under a spell. I'd learnt to read by four. So had you. So had everybody in our day, except Charlie, and even he made it by five and a half.

HILARY: *And* except those who never learnt to read. Because they were never taught.

PETER: Oh, I recognize the modern system is more democratic. Now everybody gets taught but nobody reads.

HILARY: What would you know about the modern system? You don't even go to the lectures the school lays on to explain it.

PETER: I went to the first, if you remember, in which case you'll also remember that it was doubtful whether the lady who gave the lecture could read, she could scarcely speak. But don't worry, darling, it's all being attended to. We publishers are working hand in hand with the Department of Education. They're making it their job to ensure that our Jeremy won't read when he grows up, and we're making it ours to ensure that when he grows up there won't be any books around worth his reading. I promise you our son shall not feel deprived! The rest can be read by those foreigners you teach, most of whom seem to be writing them anyway, judging by the standard of the English I'm called on to edit.

68

(HILARY *has gone to the door, toys, etc., in her arms. Turns, glares at him.*)

PETER: By God, I believe that's what's known as a level look. Or would be if it weren't for your slight squint, now you're tired.

HILARY: (*Sees the pot, manages to pick it up*) Do you mean you've just lolled there, letting it stare you in the face?

PETER: I did try staring back, but it remained unmoved.

HILARY: Could you please open the door?

(PETER *gets up, saunters over, opens the door, swivelling at the same time to pick up the Scotch. As* HILARY *exits, pours himself a glass, lights a cigarette. Goes back to sofa.*
HILARY *off, calls something.*)

PETER: Wah — ?

(HILARY *continues to call, and* PETER *answers without listening.*)

PETER: Right, fine, fine. (*Goes back to the sofa, settles onto it.*)

HILARY: (*Enters, stage left*) God, I wish you'd at least answer me.

PETER: I did.

HILARY: And what did you say?

PETER: Wah? Right, fine and fine.

HILARY: And what sort of answer is that?

PETER: What sort of question was it?

HILARY: That typescript that's been lying in the lavatory since Thursday, how important is it?

PETER: To Nuzek, the Polish socio-prophet, very. Because he wrote it. To me, not at all. I'm merely its editor.

HILARY: So you won't have to read it then?

PETER: Nobody who buys it will read it, why should I?

HILARY: And those reviewers you used to worry about? Won't they notice if it's not edited?

PETER: Oh, they can write their reviews from my blurb.

PETER: And what will you write your blurb from?

PETER: Their last reviews. It's what's known in publishing as a benign circle. Nuzek's reputation depends on nobody reading him. His prose guarantees that nobody will. You're taking an unusual interest in the mysteries of my little trade, darling, how come?

HILARY: Because I want to find out whether wha–? right, fine and fine were reasonable answers to my question.
(*Goes over to the desk, picks up a briefcase beside it, takes out some papers.*)

PETER: And how did I do?

HILARY: All right, it appears. (*Beginning to sort through*) As it clearly doesn't matter that either Jeremy or one of your nephews blocked the lavatory with it this afternoon.

PETER: Christ, they didn't!

HILARY: I thought you said it didn't matter.

PETER: But he's coming to our six simultaneous publications party in a couple of weeks. It would ruin it if he finds out about this. He's very vain, you know, Nuzek. Ah well, I'll just have to explain that our son mistook it for a bottom copy. (*Gets up, goes to the drinks table*) Drink?

HILARY: No thanks.

PETER: (*Pouring himself a large one, adding soda water*) Ah, I've been looking forward to this all day.

HILARY: Really? What's so special about the fifth or sixth?

PETER: It's backed up by four or five others. By the way, how do you think your casserole went down with Charlie and Alison? (*Sitting down again.*)

HILARY: You needn't bother.

PETER: What?

HILARY: Alison confessed in the garden.

PETER: Oh. (*Little pause.*) In the garden she confessed, did she? She really does practise away at her Catholicism, in Church, in the open air, in bed – I must say, she's pretty swollen, even for seven months swollen older Alison. Do you think that gynaecologist of hers has taught her how to begin the next before delivering the last? She surely doesn't bother with such fripperies as labour any more – just a brief muscular spasm something like a hiccough. Oh, I remember when she was a mere slip of a lump of thing – studying Charlie and English at Reading University, who would have

believed – why even prophetic Nuzek will be a mite
perplexed to hear – that because my brother happened to
marry a lump of a slip whose reproductive organs might have
been plumbed by the Vatican itself, his master work on
Protestantism and Pornography is currently washing
through the sewers of London.

(HILARY *has got together her papers, and is on her way out.*)

(*Continuing*) What about some supper, I'm peckish. (*Taking
her by the wrist.*)

HILARY: Are you? Then you'll have to get it yourself.

PETER: Why?

HILARY: Because I've got to finish these tonight.

PETER: Why?

HILARY: So that I can brush up on some phonetics tomorrow
before taking Jeremy to school. Unless of course you take
him for once. Can you?

PETER: Darling, I don't drive, remember. You do.

HILARY: It's within walking distance. He could easily manage it.

PETER: But I couldn't. Besides, he'd use up my whole day's
supply of artless prattle, which I'm going to need for the
office. (*Little pause.*) Surely even in these glum days a wife
can rustle up a sandwich and cocoa for hubby, before
hurrying off to her diversions.

HILARY: Diversions! My diversions! Do you mean these! (*Shakes
essays at him.*)

PETER: (*Pretending to peer closely*) If those include the essay I
glanced at last night, on *Lady Windermere's Fan*. By some
Swiss or Swede or Frog. Or Hun or Finn or other Wog. He
concludes that Oscar Wilde was a bit of a humbugger. You
know, darling, they really shouldn't have to pay you for
reading, you really ought to pay them for writing, lines like
that. (*Reaches behind, pours Scotch into his glass.*)

HILARY: Is it any good telling you you'll be sorry in the morning,
if you drink that?

PETER: I'll be sorry now, if I don't.

HILARY: Not too nice though, for Jeremy, at breakfast.

PETER: Then I shan't let him have it for breakfast.

HILARY: (*Makes to go to door, stops, comes back*) Just because you've started being contemptuous of your work, don't you dare start showing me your contempt for mine. Because not only am I not contemptuous of it, no I'm not, but also –

PETER: Perhaps you should practise a little contempt for it. Taking it seriously is beginning to affect your conversational style. That last sentence was like the other half of a simultaneous translation.

HILARY: I started to tell you something and I'm going to finish.

PETER: OK. But keep your head. Now – 'not only do you have a job which not only are you not contemptuous of, no you're not, but also –' Can you pick it up from there? But also?

HILARY: But also I have this home to run, and I'm sick to death of your contempt for that too. It's a difficult enough proposition at the best of times, but it's virtually impossible since you've taken to sneering at me for trying to do it while refusing to make even a gesture towards actually helping.

PETER: Actually helping in what?

HILARY: Everything. As for instance taking Jeremy to school and fetching him. Every day. With four hours hard teaching between. Then there's the ironing, some of which you actually used to do at one time, remember, the twice-a-week drag through Sainsbury's now that you refuse to accompany me for one big load on Saturdays, then the cooking for Jeremy at tea-time, and preparing something for you later on, with tomorrow's teaching to get ready in the evening. On top of which I still do my best to look attractive –

PETER: On top of which on top of what, out of that assortment of recriminations and accolades? I know what else you've been doing, you sly boots you, you've been mugging up on the rhetoric of the new woman. A tirade in the form of a curriculum vitae. Wherever have you found the time? (*Pause.*) Actually, now you mention them, some of those meals you've been preparing recently were first prepared by Indians or Chinese, in those take-away restaurants. All you've had to do was to bring them home and then take them away. Usually uneaten. Before throwing them out. Why, if

Charlie's doggie knew about your catering arrangements, he'd give up headmaster's garden and lope straight up Muswell Hill.

HILARY: (*After a long pause*) Tell me – how long do you intend to keep this up?

PETER: What up?

HILARY: This – this pose of yours.

PETER: What pose of mine?

HILARY: I don't know what you're aiming at, but the result is somewhere between Falstaff and a spiteful woman columnist.

PETER: Falstaff. But I was only aiming for the spiteful woman columnist. (*Shakes his head effeminately.*)

HILARY: God, I wish you knew how you looked.

PETER: A wish you're about to make come true, from the look of you. (*Settles back as if comfortably.*) Well?

HILARY: You've got a – what? two-day stubble over your face, your eyes are blood-shot, you've got dandruff and a smoker's cough, which I've been hearing develop almost by the week. (*Pause.*) Like your paunch.

PETER: You've been hearing my paunch develop? So that's why you've been sleeping so far down the bed, eavesdropping?

HILARY: No, keeping away from your breath. Which reeks of nicotine and booze.

PETER: Now that's dandruff, bad breath, smoker's cough, stubble and paunch. (*Ticking them off on his fingers.*) But those details apart, do you find me as winsome as ever?

HILARY: I find you quite disgusting.

PETER: Careful sweetling, or in a second you'll say something you'll regret.

HILARY: I regret not having said it to you weeks ago. I don't know what's the matter with you, but I can't stand it any more. Not the sight of you, nor the nagging it provoked from me at first, nor the contempt I've felt for you recently. Because that's what *my* contempt has been for, you. We haven't been to a dinner party recently at which you haven't ended up drunker than anyone else, or any social occasion at which you haven't contributed to insult half the people in the room. I've been ashamed.

PETER: Well, some of those rooms were pretty large. Look at it this way, if they'd been half the size I'd have managed to insult the lot.

HILARY: But you haven't done it with style, Peter, don't delude yourself.

PETER: Quantity these days darling, a lot of those people I scarcely knew.

HILARY: But why? Why? Today, with your brother and his family around – I don't know what you said to him when he came in here, but he was in a dreadful state when he came out – and before that at lunch, the way you sat lolling forward, your eyes glassy with too much drink and too much food.

PETER: And too much boredom! Don't forget the too much boredom!

HILARY: The real bore was you! Stirring yourself only to bait Charlie, completely ignoring Alison –

PETER: Not fair! I tried to bait Alison too. She chose to ignore it.

HILARY: I can't go on like this!

PETER: Really? I thought you were just warming up.

HILARY: You're poisoning my life. And Jeremy's. He doesn't even want you to read to him in the evenings any more. He actually cried when I said tonight you might be doing it. Or does that make you pleased with yourself too? (*Pause.*) Neither of us can bear you as you are.

PETER: Well, neither of you will get me as I might have been, because that's over. And as for how I was –

HILARY: (*After a pause*) Well?

PETER: That's over too. So far over, I've forgotten how I did it.

HILARY: Very well. (*Turns, goes towards the door.*)

PETER: Oh, just a minute, darling!

(*Gets up, goes towards her, stands staring at her, then begins to unbutton her blouse.*)

HILARY: What are you doing?

PETER: Stripping you down. (*Stops, then puts his arms around*

HILARY, *pulls her to him, kisses her*.) Before having you off.
(HILARY *beats him off savagely*.)
Hey – hey – (*defending himself*) this is fun!
(*Advances on her again*.)

HILARY: (*Strikes out at him again*) Stop it, stop it, stop it!
(PETER *backs away. They stand, breathing heavily, staring at
each other*.)
How dare you!

PETER: How dare I what?

HILARY: Grab at me as if I were – were (*slight pause, then
witheringly*) like some dirty old man.

PETER: But you're not at all like some dirty old man. If you were
I'd grab him instead. (*Little pause*.) Well, it is Sunday, isn't
it? And therefore about the hour for our Sunday evening sex.
Distinguishable from our Wednesday evening sex by its
venue. Wednesday evening we have workday sex, upstairs in
bed after a dinner out. If we can arrange a baby-sitter and
you have no marking to do. Sunday evening we have
sabbatical sex down here on the sofa in a spontaneous tussle
after you've shyly removed the sofa cushion. (*Little pause*.)
At least so we used to not too long ago.

HILARY: Well, not any more.

PETER: Now let's see – that's no cooking any more and no
love-making any more –

HILARY: Love-making? You haven't made love to me for months.
You just use me as a stage towards one of your post-coital
cigarettes. That is, when you've been conscious. Otherwise
you merely roll on top of me yawning and away from me
snoring.

PETER: What do you do between my yawn and my snore, I
wonder, in the short period when I tend to be quite active?
Draw up your Sainsbury's shopping list. I recall catching the
odd murmur, though your limbs remain supine.

HILARY: It isn't a murmur. It's a mutter.

PETER: But what? Directions? Encouragement?

HILARY: Hurry up pig, or get it over with. That sort of
encouragement.

75

PETER: I see. Less of an effort then than actually resisting.

HILARY: At least quicker than all the rows and explanations that dragged on until dawn.

PETER: Which you now, you aging paradox you, seem bent on having. Well then, let's discuss your past bedtime froideurs – the ones that led to the rows, and for which everything from Victorian headaches to brutally contemporary ailments were offered in explanation.

HILARY: The most usual explanation was that I was tired after a day out at work and a day of domestic duties. A simple matter which you were incapable of understanding.

PETER: Which I suppose is why you had to put more effort into a normal marital fuck.

HILARY: Do you honestly mean that you're going in for all this – smoking and drinking and spite – to make up for your sex-life?

PETER: My lack of it, perhaps.

HILARY: How childish you really are.

PETER: Do you think it's been fun sharing a bed with you?

HILARY: Then don't. You can sleep down here.

PETER: Down here! (*Looks around him, laughs incredulously.*)

HILARY: I'll make up the sofa.

PETER: The sofa!

HILARY: Or on the floor, if you prefer.

PETER: If I don't sleep in our bed, I don't stay in this house.

HILARY: Very well. (*Exits, returns with blankets and pillow.*) Jeremy and I will go to my mother's tomorrow. I'll give you a week to find somewhere else.

(JEREMY's *voice:* 'Mummy, mummy.')

It's all right darling, nothing to be frightened of, Mummy's coming. (*Exits.*)

PETER: Sounds bloody frightening to me.

(*Lights.*)

SCENE 2

Lights up. Sofa covered in blankets and sheets. There is a suitcase packed but open on floor by sofa.

PETER *enters in socks, trousers and vest, wiping shaving soap off his face. Throws towel onto bed. Picks up shirt. There is a ring on the doorbell. He looks at his watch. Hurriedly buttons up shirt. Goes to front door, singing cheerfully. Sound of door opening.*

PETER: (*Off*) Oh.

CHARLES: (*Off*) May I come in?

(PETER *enters, continuing to dress, followed by* CHARLES.)

CHARLES: I didn't really expect to catch you in. I thought you'd be at work.

PETER: I didn't really expect you to catch me in. I thought you'd be at work.

CHARLES: Actually, I've got a free morning. At least until lunch, when I have to see Headmaster.

PETER: Have to, do you, Charlie?

CHARLES: That's right, Peter. It's a personal matter. What are you doing at home?

PETER: Dressing. To go to a party.

CHARLES: (*Shocked*) Party?

PETER: With a young lady friend.

CHARLES: Where's Hilary?

PETER: But Charlie, I told you when you phoned the other night. She's gone to stay with her mother while I look for a flat. Didn't you believe me?

CHARLES: You were drunk. I hoped it was one of your jokes.

PETER: Well, it may be a joke, Charlie, but it also happens to be true. I'm moving into a flat in Notting Hill Gate, as soon as it becomes free. Which it will be this evening at 6 p.m.

CHARLES: Is it any use asking you to explain?

PETER: Explain what?

CHARLES: Why you've left Hilary.

PETER: Certainly, as it's easily explained. She asked me to leave her bed and sleep down here but I've decided to keep on going right out of the house. All right?

CHARLES: No, it's damned well not all right. For one thing, what about Jeremy?

PETER: Oh, she won't be turning *him* out of her bed for some years yet, if then.

CHARLES: Look Pete – is it because of her job? You don't resent that, do you? Because you feel less important now that she's meeting new people – her colleagues –?

PETER: Oh, they don't sound particularly new. In fact, most of them sound old and weary, except for the students, who just sound foreign.

CHARLES: Oh come on, Pete, come on, I don't believe it's as simple as you make it seem. You can't tell me you're just going to walk out. Not just like that. There must be something really terrible between you suddenly, after so many years of happy marriage. What is it?

PETER: Oh, perhaps just so many years of happy marriage between us, eh, Charlie? And perhaps so many turned out to be more than our fair share.

CHARLES: So what now? A return to a bachelor pad and your old ways.

PETER: What old ways?

CHARLES: Your promiscuous old ways. Do you really think at your age you can just go back to a life of short affairs and what was that hideous phrase you used to use – easy lays. Well, you're not an Oxford undergraduate any longer, Peter, you won't find it easy with the Friedas.

PETER: Frieda? Who's Frieda?

CHARLES: Gerta, whoever she was, the German ballerina.

PETER: Oh, Gretal it was. Wasn't it?

CHARLES: (*Contemptuously*) And that Italian painter who was old enough to be your mother. Do you think it's going to be like that all over again? And that wretched business with André Gide's daughter.

PETER: André Gide's daughter! (*Laughs.*) Charlie, I assure you, André Gide never had a daughter.

CHARLES: Well, some French writer who was in vogue a dozen years ago. Well, you're a married man now, that's what you are.

PETER: Am I? Charlie, you know nothing about any of it.

CHARLES: Don't I? I remember the states you used to get into. It's a lucky thing for you you married Hilary when you did – your bachelor days nearly killed you.

PETER: Now I've got them back, perhaps they'll finish the job. You're not still jealous, are you, Charlie, of those old passions of mine?

CHARLES: Jealous? What should I be jealous of?

PETER: Well, you never slept with a woman before you married Alison, did you? You had no premarital sex at all, did you? Well, did you?

CHARLES: As a matter of fact I did, yes.

PETER: You didn't! Christ, who with?

CHARLES: Alison.

PETER: Why, you rascal! You used to boast that yours was a real wedding night, in the old-fashioned sense of the term. Which I always took to mean a disaster, by the way.

CHARLES: It only happened the once. One Sunday in my room in Reading we went – without meaning to – we went all the way. Afterwards we talked the whole thing through and decided that what with Alison's Catholicism and Mummy's desperation about your behaviour and my own – no doubt from your point of view – simple-minded principles, I'd have to control myself a little.

PETER: A little? That's not very flattering to either of you. Anyway, Charlie, you see how unqualified you are to judge other people's sexual lives. Your own having consisted of ten years of marriage to Alison, preceded by two or three years of light to heavy necking with Alison preceded by (*little pause*) Jane Russell, wasn't it? Into a jam jar.

(*There is a pause.*)

CHARLES: How did you know that?

PETER: What?

CHARLES: About the – the –

PETER: Jane Russell jam jar? Mummy told me you'd confessed.

CHARLES: When?

PETER: After she'd interrogated you about the jam jar and the

Jane Russells she found under your floorboards.

CHARLES: No, no. I mean when did she tell you?

PETER: Oh, immediately after *I'd* confessed. Which was after she'd interrogated me about the old sock and the Betty Grables she found on top of my cupboard. But why look so troubled, Charlie, everybody wanked at Wellington, including most of the staff, from a memory of their complexions. Do you remember that scandal when it was discovered that some of the older boarders had established it as a competitive sport and were awarding House Colours?

CHARLES: But she promised me she'd never say a word about it to anyone, especially you.

PETER: And I promised her I'd never tell you she told me. So now we're all square, two decades on. What exactly did she say to you?

CHARLES: That if I went on doing it, I'd never get into the Wellington First for football.

PETER: And she was quite right, you didn't. Although I suppose you didn't go on masturbating either?

CHARLES: What did she say to you?

PETER: That I'd ruin my eyes, lose my concentration, and wouldn't get a scholarship to Oxford. Of course I didn't know then what Oxford was like, or I'd have settled for spectacles and a job in a shoe shop.

CHARLES: You were bloody lucky to get into Oxford.

PETER: Really? Your line used to be that Reading was just as good.

CHARLES: Indeed it was. And is. You were lucky to get into Oxford because you'd never have got through the interview at Reading. (*After a pause*) Anyway, how dare you confuse my attitudes to sex with Mummy's. You wouldn't find a more enlightened attitude to masturbation than Headmaster's and mine at Amplesides. I'm not against sex, I'm very for it – good sex, that is. Which is what one has, lovingly, with those one loves.

PETER: Such as oneself?

CHARLES: Oh ha ha. Anyway, this is all a waste of time – as I take it you haven't left Hilary because she won't allow you to masturbate. You know why you're a bloody fool, Peter? Not for moral reasons, or conventional or unconventional ones, as they are nowadays, to do with the sanctity of family life and the squalors of easy sex – not those. But simply that you're on your way to losing your wife and your son both of whom you love. At bottom your nature is as affectionate as mine. So one day, probably very soon, you'll go back to Hilary, and it'll be too late. The damage will have been done. (*Pause.*) It's true, isn't it? You do love Hilary?

(*There is a ring at the doorbell, off.*)

PETER: Ah, excuse me, Charlie, can we leave that question hanging while I open the door.

(*Goes to open door.*)

(*Off*) Ah, here you are at last.

JOANNA: (*Off*) Hello. Sorry I'm late.

PETER: (*Entering with* JOANNA) Oh don't worry – I was in no danger of giving you up. This is my brother, Charlie.

JOANNA: Hello.

PETER: Joanna's one of our freelance cover designers. I've asked her to accompany me to the party.

JOANNA: It'll be the first real publishing do I've ever wormed my way into.

PETER: Then we mustn't miss a minute of it. Shall we go?

CHARLES: Just a minute – (*takes a photograph out of his pocket, hands it to* PETER) – something I was going to leave for you if you weren't in.

PETER: Ah, a memento mori. Well, as I was in, you can take it away again.

CHARLES: It belongs to you.

PETER: I don't want it, Charlie.

CHARLES: Why not? Does it upset you?

JOANNA: God, what's it of, anyway?

CHARLES: It's a photograph of my brother's wife and child.

(*Hands it to* JOANNA.)

JOANNA: (*Studies it*) Taken with an instamatic, right?

PETER: (*Takes the photograph back, hands it to* CHARLES) It

81

belongs to Alison, I believe we've established.
(*Holds the door open for* JOANNA.)
(JOANNA *and* CHARLES *stare at each other.* CHARLES *coldly,* JOANNA *puzzled.*)
(*To* JOANNA) Shall we go? (*They exit.*) Do stay, Charlie, if you want to and – (*gestures*) – help yourself to the soda water.

CHARLES: (*Stands trembling for a second, then goes to the soda syphon, squirts himself some*) The little – the little – (*Gulps down the soda water, pulls himself together, then goes over, places the photograph on the table, then changes mind and props it up in front of whisky. He exits through kitchen. Crashing sound.*)
(*Off*) Blast!
(*Lights half down.*)
(*Lights up.*)
PETER *enters, followed by* JOANNA. *They are both slightly drunk, and laughing.*)

JOANNA: Christ, no truly, you were devastating. I've never heard anyone put so many people down before. But then I've never seen so many intellectuals before. Are all publishing parties like that?

PETER: (*Who is lighting a cigarette*) It was a special occasion. We were launching a coffee table book on Virginia Wade's six greatest defeats in our 'Back Britain to the very bottom' series.

JOANNA: Virginia Wade, the tennis player? Was she the woman that made the speech?

PETER: No, that was the new Chairman of the Arts Council. He always wears drag for literary events, to give them a touch of style.

JOANNA: He doesn't!

PETER: No, he doesn't. I'm just fantasizing to distract our attention.

JOANNA: What from?

PETER: The party.
(*Pours himself a Scotch, squirts in soda water.*)

JOANNA: (*Laughs*) The way you put down that funny little

specimen with the glasses and the baggy trousers and the sandals.

PETER: Oh yes. Cyril. Our senior editor.

JOANNA: When he was praising up somebody or other's book.

PETER: Was it Nuzek's?

JOANNA: That's right, Nuzek's book. He said one thing you could be sure of with Nuzek, anything he wrote was bound to be full of pith and you said, 'Why Cyril, I didn't know you had a lisp'.

PETER: (*Puzzled*) But he hasn't got a lisp, old Cyril. Has he?

JOANNA: No, he hasn't, that's why you said it. Because he said full of pith and you –

PETER: Got it, got it, got it.

JOANNA: It took me two minutes to get it at the time.

PETER: Then Cyril was a mite quicker than you, if memory serves. Which it suddenly insists on doing, now you've set it in motion. Rather like some uncontrollably obsequious waiter . . . (*sits down.*)

JOANNA: And who was the little creep with the goatee and the beady eyes –

PETER: Oh, that was our chairman, his eyes aren't usually beady. They're usually twinkly. Famously twinkly, in fact.

JOANNA: Well, they were beady from the moment we arrived and you told that joke about Nu – Nude – what was it again?

PETER: Nuzek. Nu-zek.

JOANNA: (*Nods*) Nuzek. How the bottom copy was used to wipe a five-year-old bottom, so the paper hadn't been wasted after all. That one nearly brought the house down.

PETER: It still might.

JOANNA: God, people really enjoyed you, except those two and that little roly-poly bloke – the one with the foreign accent standing next to me. He really hated you. Who was he?

PETER: Mmmm?

JOANNA: That roly-poly bloke next to me.

PETER: Oh yes. A roly Pole called Nuzek. Nu-zek. Oh Christ.

JOANNA: What's the matter?

PETER: Nothing, nothing.

JOANNA: Hey, you're not sorry about those things you said or anything, are you?

PETER: Sorry! Why should I be sorry? (*Laughs.*) No, no, it's only that it is a long time since I struck out without making sure of hitting only air. Or a loved one.

(*Goes over to her, whispers in her ear, then looks at her, attempts a little laugh.*)

Look, we've got far better things to do (*lurches slightly*) than reminisce over my past before it's properly begun. I did say please this time. I don't know if you heard it.

JOANNA: (*Smiling*) I'd really like that. I really would.

PETER: Right.

(*Straightens up and takes jacket off.* JOANNA *begins to undress as well.*)

JOANNA: (*Who has been staring at the picture as she undresses*) How old's your wife anyway?

PETER: What? (*Sees the picture*) Oh. Um, thirty-one and a half.

JOANNA: Your boy's what, five?

PETER: Nearly six. That was taken a year ago.

JOANNA: (*Picks up the picture*) What's she look like? It's hard to tell because she's out of focus.

PETER: (*Going over in trousers and shirt*) Can we keep her that way, do you mind? (*Taking the picture from* JOANNA) To avoid pre- and even post-coital depression. (*Comes back with the picture, drops it on the floor*) I'm free now, you know. Absolutely free. (*They go on undressing, on opposite sides of the room. Lights.*)

ACT TWO

SCENE I

The sitting-room. Some time later.
JOANNA *is sitting on the bed in her underpants, doing up her bra.*
PETER *is on the chair, in vest and trousers, pulling on his socks. He stops, sits staring blankly ahead, then fumbles in his jacket pocket (which is slung over the back of the chair) for his cigarettes. Takes one out.*

JOANNA: (*Who has been watching him*) I've got some pot, if you want. (*Taking a small box out of handbag, beside the bed.*)

PETER: What? (*Sitting down, not looking at her.*)

JOANNA: Do you want a joint?

PETER: No, thanks. I find these altogether more exciting. (*Lights up, drags deeply, coughs.*) Don't need the police to be frightened of them.

JOANNA: (*Putting a joint between her lips*) Can I have a light then?

PETER: What? Oh, sorry. (*Half turns, tosses her the lighter without looking at her. It falls to one side.*) Sorry.
(JOANNA *lights up, also drags deeply into her lungs. They sit smoking for a short while.* PETER *coughs once or twice.*)

JOANNA: You've had a bad scene going recently, haven't you? I could tell that first time you brought me back and you were so desperate. And now it's got even worse, hasn't it? You're moving out, aren't you, or you've been thrown out. Is that it?
(PETER *grunts.*)
Look, if it helps, I am just getting over something too.
(*Pause.*) But I've learnt it's just a matter of time, that's all. I've got to the stage, you know, where I can tell myself it's over without even weeping. Dead. Terminado, finito. Finished. Not that anything ever finishes, right? Christ, we were even going to get married!

PETER: That would have finished it.

JOANNA: His name was Josh. Whitby.

PETER: Look, you really don't have to talk about it if you don't want to.

JOANNA: No, I want to.

PETER: Then I suppose it's irrelevant that you don't have to.

JOANNA: Thank you. You can't even bring yourself to look at me, can you?

PETER: Sorry. (*Turns, looks at her, looks away again.*) I am sorry. It must be that pre-coital depression I was worried about. It's struck.

JOANNA: But truly it doesn't matter. I don't mind.

PETER: Good. Unfortunately I do.

JOANNA: (*Comes over to him*) But you don't have to sit around like a sick dog, I mean the way you got out of bed and into your knickers – it was almost as bad as the way you got out of them – all doubled up and walking across the room in a crouch. You were ashamed before we even started, what of?

PETER: I think it must have been my paunch.

JOANNA: You know what you did while you were – I mean, you actually proposed to me.

PETER: Oh, you heard that, did you? I tried to make it sound like a love-cry. (*Pause.*) If you'd accepted on a pro-tem basis, things might have ended differently.

JOANNA: Perhaps, if you hadn't drunk so much, you'd have done it.

PETER: Perhaps if I hadn't drunk so much, I wouldn't have tried.

JOANNA: Thank you. Thank you. (*Grinds out her cigarette.*) Oh Christ, whatever has gone wrong between you and your wife isn't my fault, this is all a lot of balls.

PETER: You don't need a lot, actually one will do. Bull-fighters manage on even less, so they say.

JOANNA: This hasn't happened to you before then, never?

PETER: No.

JOANNA: Never with your wife, even?

PETER: Not even. Except in Paris on our honeymoon when I pretended for a fatal fraction of a thrust that we were on a dirty weekend.

86

JOANNA: Look, am I the only girl since you were married, apart
from your wife?

(PETER *says nothing.*)

JOANNA: Well, am I? (*Little pause.*) I am, aren't I? Right?

PETER: Right, right. You're the only girl I've had apart from my
wife. Right?

JOANNA: Wrong. You didn't have me. Right?

PETER: Right. Thank you. I'd forgotten your gift for instant
recall. Perhaps because I try so hard to lack it myself.

JOANNA: What were you doing, practising? Christ! (*Goes to the
rest of her clothes, begins to put them on.*) You know what you
are, you're the type . . .

PETER: Don't bother. I know the type. (*Gets up, puts on shirt, etc.*)
I gather all the other married men you've slept with managed
to come good.

JOANNA: But then they enjoyed it too.

PETER: Even the guilt?

JOANNA: Even the sex. You know, there was a time today when I
truly liked you – at the party, I thought you had something
then, but it was just words, wasn't it, just showing off and
then only because you'd got yourself drunk.

PETER: Yes, I think that's a pretty accurate summing up. Well
done.

JOANNA: I just hope you haven't given me anything catching,
that's all.

PETER: What? Oh, you mean my inhibitions? But they don't get
passed on by casual contact, only through an intimacy that
digs deep into tissues you seem to have been born without.
No, don't you worry, dear, you'll still be able to sleep
around, smoke pot, promote your new jargons, bury our old
language, and generally see our dying culture underground,
where my son . . . my son . . .

JOANNA: (*Looks at him. Laughs*) And I was only talking about
your dandruff. (*Goes out.*)

PETER: (*After a moment*) So was I.

(*Looks at shoulders, left and right, brushes futilely at them. He
goes over to suitcase, closes it. Picks it up, exits.*

Lights down.
Lights up.)

SCENE 2

The same. Several days later. It is evening, about eight o'clock. Lights on.

HILARY *enters, left.* JEREMY, *off, left, calls out something.*

HILARY: (*At the door*) No more cuddles tonight, you don't mean it anyway, sleep now. And no sneaking into my bed.

(*Listens, sounds of* JEREMY *off, complaining.* HILARY *smiles, goes across to the desk, picks up her briefcase, sits down at the desk, opens it. Takes out some papers, begins to look through them. Stops. Sits staring ahead.*

There is a sudden rap on the window.

HILARY *lets out a little scream. There is a crashing at the kitchen, and as* HILARY *rises in alarm,* CHARLES *enters.*)

CHARLES: Hello, I thought I'd come this way so as not to disturb.

HILARY: Thank you.

CHARLES: In case Jeremy was asleep.

HILARY: Yes.

CHARLES: Actually it's the pot. Nindy's pot. We left it here that Sunday – and Nindy's suddenly taken against the new one, after using it the last week. I don't know why, but she wants her old one back. Alison's had to use the sink ploy with the tap running – anyway I thought I'd just pop over and get it. You know? (*Little pause.*) I should have phoned.

HILARY: It's very nice to see you. I'll go and get it.

(*Goes off, left.*

CHARLES *goes to the drinks table. Makes to squirt some soda water into a glass. The syphon farts emptily.* CHARLES *studies the bottom of the syphon, then raises the syphon, bending slightly at the knees, puts the tube into his mouth, and squirts and sucks.* HILARY *re-enters with the pot, watches him.* CHARLES *not seeing, puts the syphon down.*)

HILARY: Here you are. (*Hands him the pot.*)

88

CHARLES: Thanks.

HILARY: (*After a pause*) Would you like a drink?

CHARLES: No, no thanks. Well, just some soda water, if there is any.

HILARY: I think it's empty.

CHARLES: There isn't another one in the cupboard? Peter – sometimes there's a spare in the cupboard.

HILARY: (*Goes to the cupboard, looks*) No.

CHARLES: Oh.

HILARY: Something else perhaps? There's some lime, or squash or Ribena . . .?

CHARLES: No, no thanks. I like soda water, you see. Its taste.

HILARY: But surely it hasn't got any taste.

CHARLES: Yes, that's what I like. And the way the bubbles shoot up against the roof of the mouth –

HILARY: Well, some coffee – or something to eat?

CHARLES: No, I had a nut and spinach cutlet before coming out. With boiled potatoes and blackberries. The blackberries were for pudding.

HILARY: Charlie – are we having this awkward conversation because you can't get into another awkward conversation you feel we should be having?

CHARLES: Well, I suppose I was wondering whether you'd heard from Peter yet.

HILARY: No.

CHARLES: But it's been almost a week now. Do you mean to say he hasn't even bothered to let you know where he's gone?

HILARY: I told you, Charlie, I don't want to talk about it.
(CHARLES *goes and sits down, evidently depressed.*)

HILARY: It's very sweet of you to take it all so badly, but really I think it would be more helpful if you tried to take it well.

CHARLES: (*Nods*) But I think he's a little – (*Checks himself.*) Sorry, Hilary. (*Sits in a sort of stupor.*)

HILARY: Is there something else the matter? Alison's all right . . .?

CHARLES: Oh yes, yes. She's fine. (*Little pause.*) Perhaps a touch of pre-natal depression.

HILARY: Oh dear. But that's unusual, isn't it? She's generally so exuberant just before.

CHARLES: No, I meant me. I always get a bit low – but I don't let Alison see, of course. Or anyone. But this time it's worse than usual – what with you and Pete – a double touch really. Appropriate as we're going to have twins.

HILARY: Twins! Why, Charlie, that's marvellous, twins! How wonderful.

CHARLES: I thought you knew.

HILARY: Yes, Alison did tell me, as a matter of fact. But she said she wasn't going to tell you. She wanted it to be a surprise.

CHARLES: Well, she couldn't resist after all. She told me this evening. I think to cheer me up over Pete and everything.

HILARY: But Charlie, you don't mind, do you? Twins, just *think*!

CHARLES: Oh, I'm sure once they're here. I wish she'd kept the surprise as a surprise though. Then I wouldn't have had time to prepare for it. Anyway I just used the pot as an excuse – I had to get away for a little, in case I couldn't cope. (*Little pause.*) It's monstrous of me to burden you with myself, isn't it?

HILARY: No, it isn't. I'm glad you came. It would be far more monstrous if Alison suspected – Charlie, you don't think a little whisky would help?

CHARLES: No, only a lot would. Sorry, Hil. I suppose really it's an inevitable progression. We've been turning them out in singles for eight years, we were bound to advance. Recently in class I've taken to saying everything twice. Perhaps it was an early warning –

HILARY: Is it a matter of economics, your depression?

CHARLES: Well, I have got used to pacing them out in my mind and planning ahead. But if they're going to start coming in clusters – ? What can I do?

HILARY: Couldn't you count this as two goes worth? Oh, of course, how silly of me. I'd forgotten Alison's Catholicism.

CHARLES: Her Catholicism's just a blind, Hilary. Lots of practising Catholics also practise contraception these days, while Alison scarcely bothers to practise Catholicism, except in her attitude to contraceptives. When it comes down to it, the Pope's just her fertility symbol. She likes babies, lots and lots of babies. She likes cuddling them, burping them, changing them, feeding them, preferably while bearing them. (*Pause.*) Oh, I don't blame her, of course. I always knew she was a natural homemaker, it's one of the reasons I wanted to marry her. It's just that the house I'm paying the mortgage on isn't big enough for the home she's making. I haven't dared tell her yet – (*Stops.*)

HILARY: What?

CHARLES: Well, there was a chance of getting a house that belongs to the school – much larger than ours and the rent would be nominal. Bursar was sure it could be arranged, but Headmaster said no.

HILARY: Why?

CHARLES: Oh, he was very nice about it, of course. He wants to start a new school house for boarders – perfectly sensible, really. But it's always a bit of a shock being turned down – (*little pause*) especially – (*lets out a little laugh.*)

HILARY: Charlie?

CHARLES: Can I tell you something? In great confidence.

HILARY: If you're sure I ought to know.

CHARLES: It's something ridiculous. Something very ridiculous. On the other hand it's not. You must try not to laugh, but I shan't blame you if you do. You see – I asked Headmaster about the house at lunch, but at tea I suddenly thought I'd look in on him, just for a cup and – well, I often do, you know, to talk about co-education or scholarships – but this time I also wanted him to see that I perfectly understood about not getting the house. Well, we had a very affable chat together, his wife was there and we always get along very well – it was very pleasant, I thought, very pleasant.

HILARY: Well, it sounds very pleasant.

CHARLES: Yes, it was. And when I left I decided to walk back to the car through their garden. I often go that way, especially if it's a fine evening. I wasn't at all depressed then, you know, of course I didn't know about the twins – well, perhaps I was a little depressed about Pete, thinking what a fool he was and why he couldn't count his blessings – and then I began to count my own, you know, the way one does – miscounting, as it turned out. But I began to feel rather happy. Rather happy, that's my point.

HILARY: And why shouldn't you be. You've got a great deal to be happy about.

CHARLES: Exactly, I know. And I wished I had Pete there because I was sure I could persuade him – when suddenly I heard Headmaster's voice. He was talking to his wife. They didn't see me – in fact, they must have thought I was long gone. I was just about to squeeze through some shrubs to let them know where I was, I didn't want them to think I was eavesdropping – when I heard Headmaster say 'But there must be some way of keeping the pest out of my house'.

HILARY: (*After a pause*) Oh Charlie!

CHARLES: And his wife said: 'Oh, I know he's an appalling nuisance, but I can't help having a soft spot for him'.

HILARY: Oh Charles!

CHARLES: 'That's because he grovels whenever he sees you!' And then he said –

HILARY: Oh Charlie, don't go on. Please. I can't bear it.

CHARLES: Said 'The other day I saw him peeing over the roses. He's always squatting in the path and fouling it. He leaves fleas over the carpet, you've said so yourself.'

HILARY: They were talking about that stray – Alfonso! At least I hope they were.

CHARLES: So what it comes to is this. You don't think I have the physical habits of a dog, just the moral temperament of one.

HILARY: I think no such thing!

CHARLES: Oh God, I admired him though, for a moment.

HILARY: Headmaster?

CHARLES: Alfonso. I wished I could pee over his roses, drop turds on his path and shake fleas over his carpet. But I wouldn't grovel to his wife, I'd bit her ankles.

HILARY: I thought you liked them!

92

CHARLES: So did I. Until I thought I heard them talking about me like that.

HILARY: But they weren't talking about you. They were talking about Alfonso.

CHARLES: I know, I know. But you see, the fact that I thought they were talking about me like that must mean there's something in my idea of them that expects them to talk like that about me. And something in me that expects to be talked about like that. It's just the sort of thing I know Pete's always – (*stops.*) Well anyway. But you know, almost the most shameful thing Hil – when I was in my car and well, trembling a little – a muddle of feelings, hate and anger for them, oh quite irrational, I realized it even at the time – but in the middle of all that I had this sudden very clear thought. Do you know what it was? Something really shameful?

HILARY: (*After a moment*) I think so. That you'd better stop feeding Alfonso, now you know what Headmaster thinks of him.

CHARLES: (*Nods, despairingly*) And a second later I imagined myself making some casual reference to the effect – that perhaps we ought to have something done about him.

HILARY: Put down, you mean? Oh Charlie!

CHARLES: If you met me now, for the first time, you wouldn't dream of asking me back to your house for dinner, would you?

HILARY: Of course I would.

CHARLES: No you wouldn't. Alison's very attached to you, you know.

HILARY: Yes, I do know.

CHARLES: Still, she thinks you're a conceited little turnip.

HILARY: Turnip?

CHARLES: Sometimes parsnip. She hates the way you prattle boastfully on about your job. That's the sort of thing she says about you, although she loves you. So what sort of things do you say about her, although you love her, if you do. About her constant pregnancies, for example, or her earth mother laugh – or her unattractiveness.

93

HILARY: I think she's *very* attractive!

CHARLES: What's so attractive about her?

HILARY: She's got a lovely, open face, a marvellous complexion.

CHARLES: And a dreadful figure.

HILARY: She has not!

CHARLES: Yes, she has. What isn't dreadful about it?

HILARY: (*Thinks desperately*) Well, for one thing, she's got absolutely beautiful breasts. So full.

CHARLES: Yes, well they usually are, aren't they? (*Little pause.*) What about her bottom?

HILARY: Charlie, this has gone on quite long enough.

CHARLES: Actually, her bottom isn't as baggy as it looks when she's wearing those pregnancy trousers she usually wears. (*Little pause.*) You don't think I hate her, do you?

HILARY: No. I know you love her.

CHARLES: But you hate hearing me say things like this about her.

HILARY: Yes. But I'd rather you said them to me than to her.

CHARLES: I'll stop in a minute. Honestly. But do you know what would make it all right for me, absolutely? If I could just go to bed some evenings, and stretch, and turn on the reading light, and sigh luxuriously, and open a book. An Arthur Ransome. I long to re-read all the Arthur Ransomes.

HILARY: Surely you can manage that?

CHARLES: Alison always goes up before me. Then when I come in she stretches, turns off the reading light, gives a luxurious sigh, and opens her legs. (*Little pause.*) No, that's not true. We have a long cuddle first, which I need. But that's how it ends. Every night. We have this joke, that she can't get to sleep without it. And recently since we've gone macrobiotic there's been a joke about not being able to get up without it, either.

HILARY: But not every night, Charlie, it's not possible.

CHARLES: Yes, every night. Even when there are bottles to warm up, nappies to be changed, midnight wee-wees and six week cholic. Every night, Hilary. You see, she loves everything to do with babies, but especially the way they're made.

HILARY: But couldn't you, well, just hint that you need a rest sometimes?

CHARLES: Of course I can't. Our marriage is constructed on our triumphant sex life, as you know. That, and our shared love of children.

HILARY: But you do like children. Don't you?

CHARLES: Nobody likes children these days. Why should I? They don't even like each other. But I love them, if that's what perpetually counting them and fretting for them and planning because of them amounts to. But I don't want to look at them, or hear them, let alone watch them eat, empty their pots and nappies –

HILARY: You sound just like Peter.

CHARLES: Oh God, I wish I were just like him, or even better be him! (*Little pause.*) Sorry, Hilary, I wasn't referring to – to his current behaviour. But you see he's always been the younger one, the brighter one, the indulged one – the anarchic one. While I've just been the conventional one, the slow and loving and responsible one. The one-girl one. All those affairs he had before you –

HILARY: What? What affairs?

CHARLES: But surely he told you about them?

HILARY: No.

CHARLES: I shouldn't have spoken.

HILARY: No, I want to hear.

CHARLES: Are you sure?

HILARY: I want to hear.

CHARLES: But how could he have not confessed! The German ballerina, the Italian painter, Gide's daughter –

HILARY: Gide's daughter!

CHARLES: No, it wasn't Gide's, it was – I can't remember, a French writer. His daughter. The affair of his life until he met you. And he never said a word?

HILARY: I'd forgotten. It was all so long ago.

CHARLES: I suppose it was. But it still makes me angry to think of them. Because, you see, secretly, I wanted them, and if I couldn't have them, I wanted him to. Just as – just as – well, although I've always loved Alison, but was never actually in love with her, so I've – I've always been in love with you.

Though now I love you too as my sister-in-law. From the first moment he showed you off to me. But you know that, don't you?

(HILARY *nods*.)

But you belonged to Pete, of course. Just as I did to Alison. All four of us were perfectly matched. You had lots of affairs too, didn't you, before you married Pete?

HILARY: Lots?

CHARLES: Well, quite a few.

HILARY: I suppose quite a few, yes.

CHARLES: How many?

HILARY: (*After a pause*) Five, actually.

CHARLES: (*Whistles*) Five! Alison's always said – (*Pause.*) So you see, you were perfectly matched. Almost mathematically. While I was always the sort of chap to meet the sort of chap that Alison is, without having anything before – and that was that. (*Little pause.*) You've never been the slightest bit in love with me, have you?

(HILARY *shakes her head*.)

And perhaps that's why I can't help being a little glad that you and Pete have broken up. Oh, not only because of being in love with you, but also – this is my very last confession, Hil.

HILARY: Thank God!

CHARLES: Because it's easier for me to bear being what I am, a loving family man, an obsequious Assistant Headmaster in a minor Public School, a bit of an old-fashioned Puritan, if he's behaving despicably. I want him to live my destructive life for me, while I go on living my decent life, for myself. Oh God, how shameful! I do want him to come back, I do, I do.

(HILARY *puts her face to one side. She is in tears*.)

Hil – Hil – oh, I am sorry, I've been selfish. I'd no right – oh, don't cry, please. (*Comes over, puts an arm around her.*) Did I make you?

(HILARY *shakes her head*.)

Because of Pete and you?

HILARY: No, not especially, a little.

CHARLES: Because of Alison and me.

HILARY: A little, but not only.

CHARLES: Ah, Lacrimae Rerum. Tears within things. I felt them rising in me when Alison was laughing over the twins, and I was trying to laugh with her. Pete will come back to you, Hil. I know he loves you.

HILARY: So do I.

CHARLES: So you know he'll come back to you?

HILARY: Yes, I know it.

CHARLES: Then nothing's really too bad, is it?

(*Lights down.*)

(*Lights up.*

Muswell Hill. CHARLES *is sitting on the sofa, eating a carrot and holding the pot. There is the sound of the front door closing, left, then* PETER *enters. He is carrying his suitcase, has a monstrous hair-cut, is neatly and newly suited. He is also carrying flowers and chocolates. He puts down suitcase and presents himself to* CHARLES *with a flourish.*)

PETER: Well, Charlie, I'm back. Where's Hilary?

CHARLES: Gone to have a bath.

PETER: Ah! What are you doing here?

CHARLES: I came to collect the pot. I was just leaving.

(*There is a pause.*)

And how's your girl?

PETER: Did you mention her to Hilary?

CHARLES: No.

PETER: Thank you.

CHARLES: For Hilary's sake, not yours.

PETER: Naturally. (*Looks towards the door, then at* CHARLES.) Oh, for God's sake don't look so censorious. My tail is back between my legs, where it belongs. Isn't that what you wanted?

CHARLES: But should you be smirking?

PETER: Am I? Well, it's a family trait in moments of embarrassment. As you should know.

CHARLES: Embarrassment? Is that what you call this mess? You

walk out on your wife and son after weeks of the most
repellent behaviour all for the sake of some heartless little
creature – and then you turn up with a hair-cut and in a new
suit and refer smirkingly to embarrassment. Well, let me tell
you, Peter –

PETER: No, please don't, Charlie. Please don't tell me anything. I
know.

CHARLES: (*Biting angrily at the carrot*) What do you know?

PETER: Well, for one thing, I know that you couldn't just go off,
could you, and have a casual affair with some heartless little
creature, just like that, after weeks of the most repellent
behaviour. Could you?

CHARLES: No, I damn well could not!

PETER: Well, nor could I. (*Sinks into the chair.*) I could manage
the repellent behaviour, but not the heartless little creature.

CHARLES: You mean nothing happened?

PETER: Nothing to speak of. Although I expect she'll speak of it,
all right.

CHARLES: So you haven't betrayed Hilary after all?

PETER: Oh yes. I betrayed them both, given their different
expectations. But incompetently. Neither a successful
adulterer nor a faithful husband. Something between the
two.

CHARLES: I did warn you that you couldn't go back.

PETER: To what?

CHARLES: To your old promiscuity. Your Gertas, your Friedas,
your – (*gestures.*)

PETER: My André Gide's daughters. (*Laughs.*)

CHARLES: Oh, I've remembered since. It was Cocteau's daughter.

PETER: You can't honestly believe Cocteau had a daughter either?

CHARLES: I don't honestly care whose daughter it was. Whose
was it anyway?

PETER: Cocteau's.

CHARLES: You just said he didn't have a daughter.

PETER: Exactly.

CHARLES: (*After a long pause, tensely*) What do you mean?

PETER: Isn't it perfectly obvious?

CHARLES: There isn't any famous French writer's daughter?

PETER: I'm sure there are lots. But I've never slept with them.

CHARLES: And the Gertas, the Friedas, the Italian painters, the ballet dancer who was old enough to be your mother.

PETER: I think it was the Italian painter who was old enough to be my mother. Unless it was a retired ballet dancer.

CHARLES: You made them all up?

PETER: We made them all up, really, Charlie. The two of us. Your indignation gave substance to my fantasies. Without your help they'd never have existed for me – and they seem to have gone on existing for you. They died for me years ago, isn't that funny?

CHARLES: So Hilary was the first girl you went all the way with.

PETER: The only anything I've ever been all the way with, except of course for that old sock.

CHARLES: (*Sits staring ahead*) You lied to me, all these years.

PETER: You seemed to expect that sort of thing from me. It seemed a shame to go on letting you down. Besides, you were so righteously convinced that I wasn't at all like you, it helped me to believe the same thing. I knew that we were both sheep, but my seeming a black one added a bit of colour to our joint self. (*Pause.*) But aren't you glad that underneath we're both such decent chaps? I've never done anything of which you'd really disapprove – at least not until after I left Hilary and even that – well, here I am after all.

CHARLES: We're not the same. We're not.

PETER: In what are we different then, except in Alison's fecundity. And I've frequently longed for more children. It's Hilary who's against that – since she started going back to work.

CHARLES: Well – well you and Hilary, you made love long before you were married. Before you were engaged, even. Or was that a lie too?

PETER: Not quite. The first time we went to bed we didn't manage to get quite all the way. The second time we weren't engaged for most of the way, but we were by the time we'd gone all of it. It was a package deal. She insisted.

CHARLES: On your getting engaged?

PETER: On my going all the way. The engagement was my solution for getting there. Brothers, Charlie, you see, under the skin. (*Gets up, shows his hands to* CHARLES.) What do you see?

CHARLES: Your hands. (*Studies them*) Nicotine stains, otherwise – (*shakes his head*) – just your hands.

PETER: Not mine any longer. Daddy's. I never noticed them while he was alive but I recognise them now he's dead. Living heirlooms, without the liver spots. Doubtless they'll come.

(CHARLES *looks at his own hands*.)

You have Mummy's, to the very cuticle. As you don't smoke either. The rest of us, of course, the usual hodge-podge of inherited characteristics, some too far back to be traceable. I wonder whose hands Jeremy will recognize when he gets to our age . . . (*Pause.*) Anyway, we're on our way, you and I.

CHARLES: On our way where?

PETER: Just on. And on. Through these early middle into the late middle, the late late middle or the early late – and so on and on, until pegging out. If not before. Somebody's father, somebody's husband, somebody's editor in my case, some Headmaster's Assistant in yours, somebody's brother in both our cases, eh, Charlie? All relationships and no self. Not even our own hands.

CHARLES: (*After a pause*) But we're not the same in our attitudes to our work, are we? The way you've always sneered at my getting ahead. Virtually accused me of ingratiating myself –

PETER: Now there it's true I thought there was a difference. I really despised some of your ploys, Charlie. But not any longer. I've since found out that in a crisis we're identical there, too.

CHARLES: Identical in what?

PETER: At that party – the six simultaneous publications party – I made some remarks. At the top of my voice. Which I subsequently regretted. Actually I regretted them a second before I made them.

CHARLES: Then why did you make them?

PETER: So as not to waste the regret. Anyway, my job hung in the balance, and I thought, as I set out to save it, that if you could do it with Headmaster and wife, I could do it with my lot.

CHARLES: Do what?

PETER: Grovel. With telegrams at first – I thought I might get a cheap deal with the post office. Apology cables on the lines of Greeting Cables. But I had to stop after the first two, I couldn't bear the operator's tone as he read them back to me. In the end I used taxis and grovelled direct. It was surprisingly easy.

CHARLES: (*Goes over to the drinks table*) You found it so, did you?

PETER: Absolutely. Thanks to you, Charlie. At first I pretended to myself I was you, you see, and in no time at all I was grovelling happily away in my own identity. You'd have been proud of me. You know, I think that with a little bit of luck we're going to make it to the top together, just as Mummy would have wished, on all fours so to speak, and side by side. As you consult oilily with Headmaster over your next raise or house move, I'll be fawning my way up the publishing ladder.

CHARLES: Did you know you were out of soda water?

PETER: Then I shall order some more. (*Pause.*) Now I'd better go up and do some grovelling to my wife, eh? (*Looks at* CHARLES) Charlie, what is it? You don't look yourself, and I've given you such a chance to be, only more so. You've skimped dreadfully on the I-told-you-sos. Haven't I earned them? (*Pause.*) Is everything all right at home? (*Pause.*) Alison all right? The kids?

CHARLES: Fine. Fine.

CHARLES: (*Hesitates, then brightly*) By the way, something occurred to me about that dog.

CHARLES: Dog?

PETER: Dog. Your adopted dog. Alfonso, wasn't it? Hadn't you better make sure that headmaster really doesn't mind him hanging about the garden before feeding him? Some people hate strays –

(CHARLES *leaps across the room, seizes* PETER *by the lapels, shakes him vigorously.*)

Hey – hey –

(CHARLES *lets him go.*)

Christ, what was that for? Haven't I grovelled enough, even for you.

CHARLES: (*Hits him on the upper arm, sharply and spitefully*) You little –

PETER: Ow, you sod!

CHARLES: Bastard!

(*Turns, walks off, stage left. Sound of door slamming.*)

PETER: Christ!

(*Rubs his arm, goes across to the flowers and chocolates. Picks them up. Turns to the door, left.*

HILARY *enters in a bathrobe. Looks at* PETER.

PETER *turns. After a moment*) Good evening.

HILARY: Charlie's left then?

PETER: Well, first he shook me half senseless, clouted me on the arm, and called me little bastard. *Then* he left. What was interesting is that he chose the place where he used to get me, day in and day out, up to twenty years ago. It's soft and painful, doesn't do permanent damage, and leaves no bruise for a parental eye.

HILARY: Were you baiting him?

PETER: On the contrary. I was simply pointing out that we were brothers under the skin, and offering him some practical advice. Perhaps that's it – now I've shown him how my life is run, I've released all his sibling rivalry. (*Laughs nervously. There is a pause.*) Anyway, I've come – (*hesitates*) – home. Groomed for the occasion. What do you think of my hair-cut, by the way? Executed by a great traditionalist in Holborn. He was so delighted to get back to old-fashioned hair-shearing that he tried to do it for nothing. I had to insist. (*Pause.*) But I didn't charge him much. (*Laughs.*) Well, the last time we spoke, you seemed to be hankering for what I'd once been. No other part of me is so immediately susceptible to backwards change. And look – (*holds out chocolates and flowers*) more memorabilia from our wooing past.

(HILARY *makes no move.*)

Am I smirking?

HILARY: Not noticeably.

PETER: Oh, well I ought to be. I'm very embarrassed. Not to say frightened even. (*Little pause.*) Surely you knew I'd come back.

HILARY: Yes.

PETER: And that I'd apologize for – well, you know.

HILARY: Yes.

PETER: Well – (*Puts the flowers and chocolates on the table.*) How's Jeremy?

HILARY: He's asleep.

PETER: Oh good. And how's school? His, I mean?

HILARY: All right.

PETER: Still not reading, I suppose?

HILARY: Since the weekend he's moved on to the second Janet and John.

PETER: Well, let's hope the narrative is beginning to gather pace. And how are you?

HILARY: Perfectly well, thank you.

PETER: Look Hil, I've missed you and him and everything – perhaps it was worth my going to find that out – not that I didn't know it. But now the fact is it makes me happy, as it did when we first lived together. (*Pause.*) I know the fault was mine, entirely mine. I was taking my frustrations out on you and was being altogether childish. I had no right to do it, no right to walk out – (*This very quickly.*)

HILARY: But I asked you to really – didn't I?

PETER: Well, because I forced you to, didn't I? A fairly familiar marital ploy. I expect, so that when one gets tired of playing the role of culprit one can have a go at being the victim. I promise I shan't do that anyway. I abjectly admit that it was all my fault.

HILARY: No, it wasn't.

PETER: Oh yes it was, Hil, I drove you past the point of tolerance, I know that. But now what I desperately want is to put this whole mess behind us, with the understanding of course that you can put it in front of me during any healthy little marital spat of the future. (*Smiles.*) I've brought you something else, by the way. (*Takes a sheet of paper out of his pocket, hands it to* HILARY.) The first items I've already had a go at putting into effect – the hair-cut is, I admit, a little excessive, but at least it takes care of the dandruff, for which there's no longer any room. I've also gargled my throat raw, my present huskiness isn't all emotion, you know, and as for items two and three, I haven't smoked since three this afternoon, and the Scotch I needed before facing you I didn't actually swallow. Now you'll see that I've been able to give a firm commitment on Sainsbury's shopping for Saturday mornings but that any weekday treks would, of course, be subject to various career responsibilities. (*Little pause.*) Both our careers, that is. I admit that the way I've shared the business of taking Jeremy to school seems a trifle inequitable on a quick glance, but then I had to take into account that you drive and I'll have to walk. Three mornings for you and two for me therefore seems reasonable, but I am, you'll note, prepared to renegotiate as particular weeks make particular demands. (*Pause.*) The clause on sex at the end was, of course, the trickiest and required several draftings, but you'll see that the only emphatic stipulation is a shared bed. The declaration with which I precede my signature is true. Where it says I love you and always will. (*Pause.*) I've kept a second copy for myself as a memento mori – I mean, aide memoire – but I thought of doing a third and circulating it to the registry office. They may feel it's worth incorporating into the official exchange of vows. Thus bridegrooms could make an immediate start on inflating into husbands. Of eight years standing.

(HILARY *finishes reading the paper*.)

You don't seem very interested. Have I left something out?

HILARY: Nothing really.

PETER: But you don't want to make a fresh start?

HILARY: But we're not very fresh any more, Pete. Either of us.

PETER: Well, what about an advance then, from where we used to be at our best. (*Pause*.) Hil. I'm not asking you for anything except the most precious thing in the world for me. To say that it's all right really.

HILARY: But it isn't.

PETER: But surely you can say – well, you know. That you love, and always will, whatever.

HILARY: That's for children, not grown-ups.

PETER: (*After a pause*) That's Jeremy taken care of. Oh, Hil – (*Steps towards her.*)

HILARY: Don't! (*Crying out.*)

PETER: (*Stops*) Because – just because – Charlie has been talking, has he?

HILARY: Almost non-stop. But not about you.

PETER: But then what is it? I mean, all right, all right, I've conceded that I deserve punishing –

HILARY: That's for children too.

PETER: Surely not these days. I thought that was why adults had to settle for punishing each other. (*Pause*.) All right, let me put it another way, I'm back in my own maisonette, what are you going to do about it?

HILARY: Ask you to leave.

PETER: Are you going to explain?

HILARY: I'm trying to avoid an ugly scene.

PETER: This is your idea of a pretty one, is it?

PETER: Would you please leave, Peter, I'll tell you everything in a letter.

PETER: In a letter! (*Incredulously*) A letter! Well, darling, I promise you I shall receive it at my own front door. Because I'm bloody well not going. I've discovered I'm too young to leave home. I'm sticking, upstairs, downstairs, in the kitchen, in your way. I'm your husband, Jeremy's father. And what are you going to do about that? Call in the lawyers and the policemen.

HILARY: If I have to. (*Pause*.) Anyway, now you know I really want you to go, and that I shall go on wanting you to go. And until you do – you stay down here. I'm going to bed.

PETER: No, you're not. (*Takes her arm.*) Do you really think you can get out of it after eight years of my love and devotion because I've given you a few bad times recently? Well, what about my bad times, the ones I can't escape from though I've just tried – and I'm not talking about your neglect of me for your work, your increasing frigidity and those calculated little aloofnesses that you started practising even before I started practising going to seed.

HILARY: Is that why you did it? So that I'd take a little notice of you?

PETER: I'm talking about the real – the true – bad times, the ones that have come every day of my life since I first began to love you. When the telephone rings in my office and before I answer it I think of you in a car crash or of Jeremy ill or maimed in some idiotic accident at school or the sudden hopeless questions, such as 'But what should I do if anything happened to either of you?' As I know it's bound to, to both of you in the end, and that all I can really pray for is that it happens to me first, after a decent interval, and then that there are further decent intervals between your going and his. Except that life doesn't work according to decent intervals, which are anyway formulated by types like you and me out here in Muswell Hill.

HILARY: Shut up, shut up, this isn't fair.

PETER: Precisely my point. But it's true.

HILARY: Of course it's true. Do you think I haven't thought the same about Jeremy?

PETER: But not about me?

HILARY: Yes. But it doesn't matter.

PETER: Doesn't matter!

HILARY: Because I'm still going to live my own life. (*Pause.*) Oh God, Peter, it's not the beginning when we were in love with each other. Or the end, when we could have cried over each other, and probably still will, both those parts are easy, anyone can do those. It's the stretch in between, that's our married life, that I can't stand.

PETER: Because for a short time, a matter of months, what, three months –

HILARY: Oh longer. Much longer.

PETER: Four then, at the most. Before that I was a model husband, father, the lot! Second only to Charlie.

HILARY: I wouldn't want to be married to Charlie either. But he's found himself an Alison, why couldn't you?

PETER: What!

HILARY: Did you sleep with anyone, while you were away?

PETER: Is that what you think?

HILARY: Well, did you?

PETER: I certainly did not!

HILARY: Why not?

PETER: Because I couldn't – it's not in my nature – perhaps I tried, I won't deny it – we went to bed together, yes, all right – but we didn't make love! You know I couldn't!

HILARY: Why not?

PETER: You wouldn't let me! When it came to it I didn't want a foreign body next to mine in bed. I felt clumsy and awkward and dirty, and that's the truth too. So you can't make anything out of that, Hilary. I may not be so in law, but you know I'm a faithful husband.

HILARY: Yes, I know. And that's what I can't stand.
(PETER *stares at her*.)
Pete – you're married to a faithless wife.
(*There is a pause*.)
Oh why didn't you come back as you left – drunken and sneering. You look so – so clean!

PETER: You mean there's somebody else?
(HILARY *nods*.)
In ten days you found a replacement – well, send him back.

HILARY: Not in ten days. A long time ago! I wanted you to go, I wanted you to go, I want you to go. I can't bear your wretched innocence, your oppressive faithfulness. It's been like deceiving a child.

PETER: It's not – (*blankly, after a second*) – fair. At that bloody school of yours, is he?

HILARY: Yes.

PETER: Well what is he – some damned – foreigner? What? A Turk, an Arab, a Spanish monk, a Frenchman – how low have you sunk?

HILARY: He's a teacher.

PETER: To the very bottom then! What's his name?

HILARY: What does it matter?

PETER: What's his name!

HILARY: Please, you'll wake Jeremy. George Green.

PETER: George Green. You've never mentioned any George Green. Nothing. Nothing. No passing references to any George Green, no murmurings in your sleep of George Green, no smiling by-the-ways-have-I-told-you-about-George Green. Nothing, I don't believe it.

HILARY: It's true, Peter, I love him.

PETER: Love George Green! Well, come on, come on, what is he? Married, widowed, divorced, one of these fashionably converting homosexuals, he can't be single unless he's a mere boy, is he a mere boy, George Green?

HILARY: No. He's older than us, actually.

PETER: How much older?

HILARY: By ten years.

PETER: Divorced, eh? How many times?

HILARY: Twice.

PETER: A bit of a specialist then, but not versatile. Or has he just been practising until the right married woman, my wife, came along? How many children?

HILARY: Two by his first wife, one by his second.

PETER: But is he trained in children over five? Or does he pass them on at an early age? I'm speaking for Jeremy now.

HILARY: He sees a great deal of them.

PETER: And he sees a great deal of mine?

HILARY: Not yet. (*Pause.*) Peter, I –

PETER: Shut up!

HILARY: At least he's a grown-up. I want you to move out straight away.

PETER: Oh, but just a minute, darling, isn't it slightly

unconventional to see me from our bedroom to the drawing-room sofa to the pavement, back again and out again all within ten days? Most marriages conclude at a slightly more leisurely pace. We're skimping on the niceties. After all we've been complacent witnesses to a lot of break-ups in our time, we must owe returns to newly re-weds and divorcees all over London. So for God's sake let's stick to form. By your own admission we haven't even begun to make Jeremy miserable. What about the heart-searchings followed by the heart-rendings, yours and mine – (*He sits, shaking on the arm of the sofa.*)

(HILARY *makes to leave the room, stops, comes back. Makes to put hand on his head.*)

Don't do that! (*Sharply, then*) They still stock period Brylcreem in Holborn. My period anyway. (*Pause.*) Go to bed, Hilary, leave me alone.

(HILARY *hesitates, then turns, goes to the door, left.*)

After all you'll have another of your hard days tomorrow, won't you, with all its explanations, caresses, half-plans, avowals and pronunciation classes, not to speak of collecting Jeremy from school.

(HILARY *goes out.*)

Then buying me a Chinese throw-away and facing me over it – (*Looks, sees Hilary has gone, remains sitting on the arm of the sofa. Takes out cigarettes from pocket, studies Government Warning on package, takes cigarette out, lights up. There is a crashing noise from the kitchen.*)

CHARLES: (*Enters. He is carrying a syphon of soda water*) I got you some. (*Holds up the syphon.*)

PETER: Thanks.

CHARLES: Well, I do drink so much of it – (*Carries it across to the table, puts it down.*) Um, may I –?

PETER: Help yourself.

CHARLES: (*Squirts some into a glass*) I'm sorry about before. Drink?

PETER: Please.

CHARLES: (*Pours him a very small Scotch, brings it over*) That's the first time in twenty years I've hit you.

PETER: (*Looking at the Scotch in dismay*) At least it was evocative.

CHARLES: No hard feelings.

PETER: No. But I don't know why you did it.

CHARLES: Nor do I really. (*Pause.*) By the way, I don't know if Hilary told you, we're going to have twins.

PETER: You and Hilary?

CHARLES: (*Laughs*) Alison is, I should say.

PETER: Twins, Charlie. Congratulations.

CHARLES: Thanks. (*Little pause.*) Is everything all right between you two?

PETER: Oh yes.

CHARLES: Well, you said it would be. You told her everything, did you?

PETER: I think we're much clearer about each other, Charlie, thanks.

CHARLES: Even about that girl, eh, and going to bed with her, even though you didn't –

PETER: She knows everything, even about Cocteau's daughter.

CHARLES: But I realized afterwards that she'd never known about her. Them. I mean, how could you tell her about affairs you've never had?

PETER: I didn't have to tell her, she always knew I didn't have them. After all, she virtually had to give me directions on our engagement night.

CHARLES: She's very understanding. (*Little pause.*) You know, I'm sorry they didn't exist.

PETER: So am I. So, probably, is she. But then if they had, I'd have been a different sort of person and –

CHARLES: And she wouldn't have wanted to marry you.

PETER: Yes, a bit of a conundrum, that. (*He smiles.*)

CHARLES: Anyway, I'm glad you're back, Pete. I missed you. I mean, the great thing is, isn't it, to love one another in spite.

PETER: In spite? Yes, I'll drink to that. (*Raises his glass.*)

CHARLES: ⎫
PETER: ⎬(*Toasting each other*) In spite.

CHARLES: Good-night, old Pete.

PETER: Good-night, old Charlie.
   (CHARLES *exits. Crash. 'Drat'.*
   PETER *picks up bags, looks around, exits. Door slams.*)
   (*Curtain.*)

Molly

Molly was first performed in November 1977 at the Watford Palace Theatre. The cast was as follows:

MOLLY	Mary Miller
TEDDY	Raymond Francis
OLIVER	Anthony Allen
EVE	Barbara Atkinson
GREAVES	Arthur Cox
POLICE CONSTABLE	Stephen Enns
Director	Stephen Hollis
Set design	Christopher Morley
Costume design	Ann Curtis
Lighting	Brian Harris

ACT ONE

SCENE I

The play is set in the 1930s.
Living-room of a house. It has three doors: one stage right, which leads
into the conservatory, part of which is visible on the stage; one back,
that leads into the kitchen, dining-room etc.; and one left, that leads to
the hall, front door, and other offices and stairs. In the room is a
cocktail cabinet, new and of the thirties, amply stocked; an armchair;
a large sofa; tables, chairs, all in the style of the twenties and thirties.
The curtain rises on the room, empty. Light beginning to fade. There is
a pause, and then MOLLY, *wearing a light coat, a silk scarf, enters*
slowly through the conservatory. She takes off her scarf, drops it onto
the sofa. She stands listless, then takes from her coat pocket her
cigarettes and a lighter. She lights a cigarette, draws on it deeply, then
stares around her with an air of desperation, goes to radio, turns it on,
listens for a moment to music, makes an irritated expression, turns the
radio off, goes to drinks table, pours herself a drink, takes a sip as,
above, sound of door opening.

TEDDY: (*Off, up*) Moll! (*Calling*) Molly!

MOLLY: (*Hesitates*) In here darling.

    (*There is another call of 'Moll', then a door slams. The sound of*
    footsteps, coming down. MOLLY *puts down glass, walks swiftly*
    out through the conservatory, vanishing exactly as the door, left,
    opens and TEDDY *enters, saying irritably 'Moll' as he does so.*
    Sees the room empty, makes an irritable exclamation, goes over to
    the conservatory, shouts 'Moll!' He is in his mid-sixties, has a
    deaf aid, elaborate and visible and of the thirties, and an air of
    slightly bogus physicality. Shouts again: 'Moll-ly'.

      EVE *enters from the back. Looks toward the conservatory. She*
    is a woman in her mid-fifties, severely dressed and severe of
    expression; spectacles; and an air of brisk efficiency.)

TEDDY: (*Off*) Damn it! (*He comes back from the conservatory, sees*

EVE.) Oh, hello Evie, where's Moll?

EVE: (*Speaking loudly*) She's gone for a walk.

TEDDY: When?

EVE: About an hour ago.

TEDDY: Then why didn't she ask me. (*Goes to cocktail cabinet.*) I could have just done with a walk.

EVE: You were taking a nap.

TEDDY: But I didn't want to. I wanted to go for a walk. I spend the whole afternoon waiting for her to make up her mind whether she wants to go or not –
(*Pours himself a large Scotch.*

EVE sees Molly's scarf, goes over to it and deftly and surreptitiously picks it up, and puts it on one of the tables, where it is unlikely to be noticed.)

– and then I go upstairs to get a book and sit down on the bed with it for a moment and – (*Adds soda water to his Scotch, splashes it.*) Damn, damn! (*Looks at* EVE.)

EVE: I'll get a cloth –

TEDDY: Oh sit down Evie, sit down. I can manage – (*Mops up the soda with a handkerchief.*) Sorry Eve, I'm always a grump if I doze through the afternoon – like a bear with a headache – what'll you have, one of your dry as dust sherrys?

EVE: Oh, no thank you, Teddy, I really ought to get back to the kitchen –

TEDDY: (*Pours* EVE *a sherry*) Tell me, Evie, do you think Moll wants to stay? We've been here a month now but she makes me feel as if we only just moved in yesterday, or we're going to be moved out tomorrow, but we're never going to have the part in between, has she said anything to you? (*Brings her the sherry.*)

EVE: Thank you. Well, she's said she likes it here.

TEDDY: What about you?

EVE: Oh yes. Very much.

TEDDY: That's good, because we need you, Evie. Your hitching on to us was real luck, you keep us orderly. Don't you think of abandoning us.

EVE: That's very kind of you, Teddy.

TEDDY: Well, it's her England, that's what she said she wanted. And it'd do for me if she settles for it. Wish I didn't sleep so much, that's the only thing. Never slept like this in Canada. Never had time to. But then I had a business to run, bills of lading to get out, had to meet the ships at sometimes two in the morning, did you know that, Evie? (*Pause*.) Funny thing is I miss the smell of fish. The whole town smelt of it, the uptown streets, it got into the stores. I didn't notice it until I'd left. Hey, it's getting dark. That's something else I'm not used to, your English springs. We don't have springs in Canada, just a sort of wink between winter and summer. But then we have our falls, you don't have falls, do you?

EVE: No, we only have autumns, I'm afraid.

TEDDY: What? Well, I don't like her out in the dark. Wandering about. She used to tell me England's got the best climate in the world, you know what I think now I've seen it, it may be the best climate, but the weather's terrible. (*Laughs*.) Not my idea of friendly either. (*Goes back to cocktail cabinet*.) Now in Nova Scotia, move into a village they'd be right round asking what they could do to help, inviting us over, but we've been here two whole weeks, and who do we know, Dr Gracey, when I need him to look after my ears.

EVE: More people know Tom Fool than Tom Fool knows people.

TEDDY: Who?

EVE: Tom Fool.

TEDDY: Tom who?

EVE: Fool.

TEDDY: Well I don't know him, somebody in the village?

EVE: It's a saying.

TEDDY: (*Not having understood*) Oh. Ready for another? (*Coming across with the bottle*.)

EVE: No I won't, thanks –
(TEDDY *pours sherry*. EVE *just manages to catch it*.)

TEDDY: You know what woke me up? I thought I heard her singing, that one about the seals of Nanaimo, and playing the piano – I heard it quite clear, every note, so it must have been a dream – she was going to try and write more songs

once she got back here, that's why she wanted a place with a
piano in it, but she hasn't played it yet – I'm going to get on
to her about that, this evening. Did you know I got that seal
song played over Station RCVX – knew the owner – he put it
out across the whole of Nova Scotia. Bob Hoskins. He was a
good friend of mine. In hardware. You ever been married,
Evie?

EVE: No.

TEDDY: Why not?

EVE: I'm afraid no one ever asked me.

TEDDY: That's the girl. (*Laughs.*) Hey, Evie, mind if I ask you a
delicate question?

EVE: No.

TEDDY: You sure?

EVE: Well, as I'm living in your house, you have a perfect right to
know anything about me you want. Within reason, of
course.

TEDDY: Am I paying you enough.

EVE: Yes, quite enough, thank you, Teddy. No thank you.
You're more than generous. Now if you'll excuse me I really
must go and have a look at the dinner. (*Gets up and goes out.*)

TEDDY: Oh.

(*Sits for a moment, then gets up, goes to the cocktail cabinet, adds
a dash of Scotch, squirts soda water, splashes it slightly, makes as
if to mop it, gestures irritably, goes over to the conservatory,
stands looking through.*)

What the hell's she playing at?

(*There is a ring at the door-bell, left.* TEDDY *makes no move.*)

EVE: (*Appears from back*) Somebody at the door.

(TEDDY *still makes no move.* EVE *makes to speak again, instead
goes off, left.*)

TEDDY: (*Turns, walks to the door, back, stands at it*) Hey Evie, I'm
getting really worried –

(EVE *re-enters from left, accompanied by* OLIVER.

OLIVER *is a boy of about seventeen, awkward and not
particularly attractive. Dressed in his Sunday clothes, as for an
interview.*

TEDDY *turns away from the door, sees* OLIVER *and* EVE.)

EVE: (*Coming over to* TEDDY) It's a boy from the village.

TEDDY: What? Is Moll all right?

EVE: He says something about a job.

TEDDY: What job?

EVE: I've no idea.

TEDDY: (*Goes over to* OLIVER) Well hello boy, what can we do for you?

OLIVER: Sir. They said at Sprinkley's there was a job.

EVE: That's the garage in the village.

TEDDY: What's your name, boy?

OLIVER: Oliver, sir.

TEDDY: What?

OLIVER: Oliver, sir. Oliver Treefe.

TEDDY: Oliver?

OLIVER: Yes sir.

TEDDY: Oliver what, Oliver?

OLIVER: Oliver Treefe, sir.

EVE: You'll have to speak up please, Oliver.

TEDDY: Sorry Oliver, I'm not picking you up.

OLIVER: (*Realizing*) OLIVER TREEFE, SIR. (*In a bellow.*)

TEDDY: Oliver Treefsir, well Oliver Treefsir, what can we do for you?

OLIVER: They said (*in a bellow*) at Sprinkley's Garage a lady had been in to inquire about a boy, sir.

EVE: (*To* TEDDY) It must have been Molly. (*To* OLIVER) When did she come in?

OLIVER: This afternoon (*bellowing at* EVE) they said. They said she said there was a car needed looking after. Mr Goldberg's Alvis.

TEDDY: What?

EVE: Mr Goldberg's Alvis, Teddy.

TEDDY: Mr Goldberg hasn't got an Alvis. I've got it. Part of the deal for the house. He left it for me for what he called a consideration, he's probably bought himself a new car out of the consideration, eh boy? Quite a businessman, your Mr Goldberg. (*Laughs.*)

(OLIVER *laughs*.)

Quite a businessman. It doesn't go, boy. Needs a lot of tinkering. Can you tinker?

OLIVER: Yes sir.

TEDDY: Can, eh? That's right, don't undersell yourself, what about a drink, we got some of that stuff you English call beer somewhere and you look to be at the beer-guzzling age, eh Evie? Like one? (*Goes to cocktail cabinet.*)

OLIVER: Well, no thank you very much, sir.

(TEDDY *begins to wrestle with a bottle of beer*.)

EVE: Did the lady mention any special time to call, Oliver?

OLIVER: They said she said the evening would be best, Missus.

EVE: I see. And was it only about the car?

OLIVER: Well, they said she said it would be a bit of driving and helping about the garden and odd-jobs. They said it was a proper job, Missus.

EVE: Well, I'm afraid Mrs Treadley isn't here at the moment, but I'll take down your details and let her have them. Who can give you references, Oliver?

OLIVER: Well, there's Sprinkley's.

EVE: And anyone else?

TEDDY: (*Pours beer, which foams up over cabinet*) Damn! (*Mops at it with handkerchief.*) First thing you've got to do is make her go, second thing is to break me into her ways. I'm not used to cars like your Mr Goldberg's Alvises, especially now my balance's gone, so you'll have to show me how to handle her, whether she needs coaxing or bullying, a car's like any machine, a man's made her so she's going to have something wrong with her. I used to do a lot of driving – ever heard of the Breton Trail, that's in Nova Scotia. (*Bringing* OLIVER *his beer*) Here, get yourself outside of that –

OLIVER: Thank you, sir.

TEDDY: That's in Nova Scotia, where the roads go straight ten yards before they turn around and go back five. In a Manson. By God I loved that car. Always knew where to tinker when she gave me trouble. Think I could get to love

a car that used to belong to your Mr Goldberg, eh, that he
left to rot and rust for a consideration? Eh?

EVE: I was just getting down some references, Teddy.

TEDDY: Oh.

EVE: Now who else besides Sprinkley's, Oliver?

OLIVER: I done some gardening with my dad –

TEDDY: Who?

OLIVER: My dad, sir.

TEDDY: Your dad – a reference from your dad? We could all get
references from our dads, boy. (*Laughs.*)

OLIVER: No, I only meant –

EVE: Where else have you worked, Oliver?

(MOLLY *enters the conservatory, stands watching for a moment,
unseen by the others.*)

Where else have you worked, Oliver?

OLIVER: Well – (*Pauses*) – well I did some for Mrs Shepherd,
Missus, but I stopped after a bit.

EVE: Indeed, why?

MOLLY: (*Enters*) Of course, you're the boy, aren't you, that
Sprinkley's promised to send. I'm so sorry I wasn't here
when you arrived, please forgive me.

OLIVER: That's all right, Miss.

MOLLY: (*To* TEDDY *and* EVE) I popped in as I was passing the
garage, when the thought struck, and then it slipped my
mind, sorry darlings.

TEDDY: Where you been, Moll, old Evie was getting worried
about you, out there in the dark.

MOLLY: (*To* EVE) Were you, darling? There was no need, it was
all quite friendly and above board. Well, what have you fixed
up, between the three of you?

EVE: We're just sorting out the question of references.

TEDDY: Drink, Moll. (*Going to cocktail cabinet.*)

MOLLY: Thank you, darling, I'd love one.

TEDDY: We've just been trying to make out from your Oliver
Treefsir here whether he's the sort that kills us.

MOLLY: (*Smiling at* OLIVER) Are you the sort to kill us, Oliver?

OLIVER: No, Miss.

MOLLY: There we are, what more could we ask. You see, my
husband's the sort that likes to drive very fast himself, but
when he's being driven he likes it to be by the sort that
drives very slow, don't you darling? But I can't drive at all,
so I like everybody to drive fast, even the people in other
cars.

(TEDDY *comes over, hands* MOLLY *a drink*.)

Thank you, darling. Now what about the gardening, are
you going to do that for us too?

OLIVER: Well, yes Miss, I mean if you want –

MOLLY: Because we need a gardener to garden for us as well as a
driver who won't kill us, Oliver, it's all in the most terrible
tangle out there, some of the spring whatsits look quite
alarming. What are your fingers like, can we see them?

OLIVER: Miss?

MOLLY: Can we see your fingers?

(OLIVER *shows his fingers*.)

Mmmm – yes, they look as if they could be green, you see
we met a lady on the boat coming over from Canada who
talked every lunch time and dinner time about gardening,
and she said – do you remember, darling? –

TEDDY: What?

MOLLY: The herbaceous border lady, darling, she said that for
gardens green fingers were quite essential, of course, and
that the best way to make flowers grow was to talk to them
and sing to them and even to recite to them, now would you
be willing to talk and sing and recite poems to our flowers,
Oliver? (*Looks at him seriously*.)

OLIVER: Um, well – (*Gives a little laugh*.)

MOLLY: Oh well (*smiling*). What about pulling up weeds and
mowing the lawn instead?

OLIVER: Oh yes, Miss. I could do that. I mean, my dad does the
gardening for some of them in the village in the evenings,
and I've helped him.

MOLLY: There you are then. You meet our requirements
exactly, doesn't he darling?

TEDDY: What?

EVE: Excuse me, Moll, but I haven't quite found out how you can get hold of Mrs Shepherd.

MOLLY: Why do I want to get hold of Mrs Shepherd?

TEDDY: Hey, that boy's been standing there with a mitt full of beer and you ladies haven't let him take a sip of it – you have your drink, boy. Go on.

(OLIVER *hesitates, then raises his glass, drinks.*)

EVE: (*To* MOLLY) Oliver used to work for Mrs Shepherd until she let him go.

(OLIVER *finishes his drink.*)

TEDDY: That's the boy!

MOLLY: Why did Mrs Shepherd let you go, Oliver?

OLIVER: She – well, she just said she didn't need me any more, that's all.

MOLLY: Oh. And if she had needed you any more we wouldn't be able to have you now, would we, so you see, Evie, Mrs Shepherd was only acting for the best, wasn't she Oliver, if we *can* have you now, that is? But omigod, how much are we to pay you?

OLIVER: Well, Miss, whatever – I don't know.

MOLLY: How much did Mrs Shepherd pay you?

OLIVER: Two pound a week, Miss.

MOLLY: Two pounds a week!

EVE: That would be the normal rate.

MOLLY: But it seems a mere trifle for chauffeuring us about and not killing us and keeping our weeds down and our flowers up and general handymanning, you would do a little handymanning wouldn't you, Oliver? I really think a minimum of four pounds a week, wouldn't you, darling?

EVE: Four pounds!

TEDDY: What?

MOLLY: Four pounds a week for Oliver, darling, includes handymanning.

TEDDY: Give him four and a half.

MOLLY: Four pounds ten, Oliver, there we are. Will you come to us for that?

OLIVER: Yes, Miss! I mean, I'll have to talk it over with my dad –

MOLLY: Of course you will. But even so, I think we've got you, haven't we?

OLIVER: Yes Miss.

MOLLY: Well then, Dad willing, when can you start, tomorrow?

EVE: Tomorrow's Sunday.

MOLLY: Monday then.

OLIVER: Yes Miss.

MOLLY: All settled darling, I had to use my wiles but I've brought him to it.

TEDDY: Another beer, boy?

OLIVER: Um, no thanks –

MOLLY: Oh, we mustn't keep him any longer (*taking the glass from* OLIVER, *winks at him*) he's got important matters to discuss with his Dad. Haven't you?

OLIVER: Yes Miss.

EVE: I'll see you out, Oliver. (*Leads him to the door.*)

MOLLY: See you Monday, Oliver.

TEDDY: Bye there, boy.

OLIVER: Sir. (*Shouting.*)

TEDDY: I like the look of him.

MOLLY: Did you really, darling? Can't say I did, pale, spotty and slightly furtive, I thought. But just the sort to know all about engines and lawn-mowers and things – (*taking off her coat*) and one never does know how to turn people down – (*Drops coat in chair.*)

TEDDY: Where did you go?

MOLLY: Further than I meant.

TEDDY: (*Sits down, looks at her*) Why didn't you take me with you?

MOLLY: (*Goes over to him, rumples his hair*) You were snoozing, my sweet, I hadn't the heart to wake you – (*kisses the top of his head, goes over to the cocktail cabinet with his glass, pours them both a drink*) – and it really wasn't very nice anyway, you'd have found me a terrible bore. I kept thinking I heard a tune I could write down and make into one of my silly songs, it was as if I were following it, through one field, then another, right to the river where the bridge is, I was sure it was there somewhere, like a person I was going to meet, but nobody came (*brings him his drink back*) nobody at all.

TEDDY: What? I missed all that.

MOLLY: I was just chattering.

(EVE *enters, from left.*)

Well darling, you got it all out of him, I take it.

EVE: What?

MOLLY: Mrs What'sit's address and the rest of it.

EVE: Mrs Shepherd's. Yes, I did. I hope you don't mind. I think she might be that lady we saw in the post office the other day, having a parcel weighed.

MOLLY: With a ridiculous hat and false teeth?

EVE: I didn't really notice her teeth.

MOLLY: What about her ankles, did you notice those?

EVE: Notice what?

MOLLY: Weren't they very thick?

EVE: I'm afraid I didn't notice her ankles, either.

MOLLY: Then it can't have been Mrs What'sit, darling, in the post office.

EVE: You've met her then?

MOLLY: Who?

EVE: Mrs Shepherd.

TEDDY: Who are you two nattering about?

MOLLY: Mrs Shepherd, darling.

TEDDY: Who's she?

MOLLY: We haven't the slightest idea, but Eve's got her address and she's determined to find out, aren't you, darling?

EVE: I'm sorry, Molly, I know it wasn't my place to interfere –

MOLLY: Oh Eve!

EVE: It's just that I don't think you should take people on without knowing anything about them, except what they tell you themselves.

MOLLY: Really, darling? I don't agree, we took you on without knowing anything about you except what you told us yourself, and that's worked out quite well.

EVE: I gave you three references!

MOLLY: Yes, darling but you don't think I read them. They were far too long, and bound to be flattering, which wouldn't have been fun, so I hired you in lieu.

(EVE *picks up Molly's coat and scarf, takes them out to hall, left.*)

Omigod! (*Sinks into a chair.*)

TEDDY: What?

MOLLY: I've offended Eve again.

TEDDY: What?

MOLLY: She really is the most humourless –

(EVE *enters, from left.*)

TEDDY: (*Not seeing her*) When's she going to feed us, that's what I want to know.

EVE: I'm on my way to the kitchen now.

MOLLY: Oh darling – (*To* EVE) I was only teasing, of course I read your references, they were divine, one from the two ladies in Richmond, one from the Doctor in Kingston and one from – from – wherever, but I remember it quite well, said you were scrupulous in violet ink and couldn't manage without you and no more could we, and you were right to insist on Mr What'sit's address, and I did rush us into the youth quite fecklessly, it was just that I felt funny about having forgotten him entirely, but I know he won't get away with anything, darling, with you to keep an eye on him, and if you ever bump into Mrs Shepherd again you can quiz her to your heart's content, all right, darling, all forgiven? Please. Pretty please with sugar on it?

EVE: (*Smiles*) Oh Moll. Now you're teasing me again.

MOLLY: No I'm not, darling. I mean it. Every word almost.

EVE: (*Still smiling*) It'll just be a few minutes, Teddy.

TEDDY: No rush, Evie, have another drink!

EVE: Then you'll never eat. (*Goes out back.*)

MOLLY: Omigod! (*Wearily. Lights a cigarette.*)

(TEDDY *watches her. There is a pause.*)

TEDDY: Hey you, come here! (*Pause.*) Come on, come here, I said.

MOLLY: (*Concealing irritation, clearly knows what is to happen, gets up, goes over to* TEDDY) Sir?

TEDDY: Now my girl, how many's that since lunch?

MOLLY: Only one, sir.

TEDDY: Come on, Moll, the truth now. All the time you were gadding about out there.

MOLLY: Well, three. (*Pause.*) Four. (*Pause. Holds up five fingers.*) Ten. Twenty.

TEDDY: (*Not hearing*) Five, eh? Well, add on another four and one on top of that makes – one – two – three – four – five – six – seven – eight – nine – (*Slapping* MOLLY *on the bottom, laughing.*)

(MOLLY *giggles, cries ouch.*)

Now get us another drink, girl.

MOLLY: My Lord.

(*Makes a little curtsy, takes his glass, pours him a drink and one for herself.*)

TEDDY: And another thing, girl, what about getting to the piano, all your talk about your songs and you haven't touched a key since we moved in, that was another of Mr Goldberg's considerations – he can hire himself a whole band out of that one – I was telling Eve all about your seal-song and Bob Hoskins transmitting it over RCVX – (*takes her hand as she brings him the drink*) play it now, eh, Moll.

MOLLY: But darling, she's getting the dinner on the table.

TEDDY: What? Don't want to?

MOLLY: Not very much, darling. For one thing the piano's out of tune. And so am I. (*Looks at him from above, sadly.*) You come and sit here then.

(*Takes him by the hand, leads him to the chair nearest the piano, then goes to the piano, begins to play uncertainly. The piano is out of tune.*

MOLLY *makes a face. After a moment she begins to sing, very loudly, but nicely, 'And did those feet'.*

EVE *enters from the back, stands listening.*

TEDDY *is evidently straining to hear, his foot beating out of time to the music.*)

TEDDY: (*As* MOLLY *is fading out*) There. There Evie. She wrote it herself. What do you think of it?

EVE: I think it's lovely.

MOLLY: Why Evie, you're tone deaf!

EVE: Perhaps I am. But I know a nice voice when I hear one. Dinner's ready.

(MOLLY *comes over, takes* TEDDY's *hand; they go through back, and as* EVE *closes the door behind them: Lights.*)

SCENE 2

A week or so later. Mid-afternoon. The room is full of sunlight, the conservatory door is open.

OLIVER *enters through the conservatory, furtively. He is wearing an open-necked shirt, baggy gardening trousers. He looks towards the kitchen, back, then towards the door, left, then goes to the sofa, on which is Molly's handbag. Opens the handbag, takes out a package of cigarettes and the lighter. Quickly extracts a cigarette, puts it in his pocket, then another, which he lights. Puts the lighter back in the handbag, closes it. Stands smoking, looking around.*

EVE *enters from the back. Stands watching* OLIVER.

OLIVER, *suddenly conscious of another presence, turns. They stare at each other.*

OLIVER: I've finished digging up them weeds around the garage, Missus.

EVE: And have you done the hedge?

OLIVER: No, Missus, I – I don't know where the shears is.

EVE: We don't keep them in the sitting-room, Oliver. Perhaps they're under the potato sacking on the second shelf in the conservatory where I told you to put them the last time you used them, have you looked?

OLIVER: No Missus.

EVE: Have you put the weeds in the compost?

OLIVER: No Miss.

EVE: Then do that first. Then the hedge. And oh, Oliver – (EVE *gets an ashtray, comes towards* OLIVER, *holds it out.*) In here, please.

(OLIVER *stubs out the cigarette.*)

Now here are two things for you to understand, Oliver.
Firstly, we don't like you wandering into the house
whenever you feel like it, and secondly we don't like you
smoking in the house, you left a saucer full of stubs in my
kitchen after your lunch today. All right?

OLIVER: Yes Missus. (*Sulkily.*)

EVE: And by the way, I'm not Missus, I'm Miss. Miss Mace.
(*Attempts a more friendly tone. Little pause.*) Is anything the
matter?

OLIVER: Well, Missus – Miss. The only thing – well, I mean, I
was told it was going to be fixing the Alvis and driving it
mainly, that was my work, and there was a bit of gardening
on the side, but I mean I've got the Alvis fixed, but I've only
got to drive it twice in two weeks, it's been gardening all the
time, and even painting the inside of the garage.

EVE: I see. Well, Oliver, if you're not satisfied with the conditions
of your employment, you're quite at liberty to leave. Is that
what you want to do?

OLIVER: No Missus.

EVE: Miss.

OLIVER: No Miss.

EVE: I'm sure you don't. So you'd better get on with it, hadn't
you?

OLIVER: (*After a pause*) Yes, Miss. (*Turns to go.*)

EVE: (*Looks into the ashtray*) Oliver. What cigarettes do you
smoke?

OLIVER: Any sort, Missus. Miss.

EVE: Including the sort that Mrs Treadley smokes?

EVE: (*Shrugs*) I don't know what sort she smokes.

EVE: She smokes this sort. (*Holding up stub.*) Did you take one of
hers?

OLIVER: No Miss!

EVE: I think you did, Oliver. That's what you were doing in here,
wasn't it?

OLIVER: No Miss, I never!

EVE: Please don't lie, Oliver.

OLIVER: (*As* MOLLY *enters*) I'm not lying, Miss!

MOLLY: (*Looking from one to the other*) What's going on, it sounds thrilling!

EVE: I'm just trying to find out whether Oliver's been helping himself to your cigarettes.

OLIVER: I didn't, Miss.

MOLLY: Oh, I do hope you didn't, Oliver, I'm terribly low and I do hate to be caught without one. Shall I check and see how I'm off? (*Goes over to handbag, opens it, looks into the cigarette package.*) About a dozen, I suppose that'll do, could you remember some, Evie, if you're going shopping. (*Little pause.*) Are you doing something in the garden, Oliver?

OLIVER: I've got to put weeds in the compost and then clip the hedge, Miss.

MOLLY: Such a nice day for being outside.

OLIVER: Yes, Miss. (*Smirks at* EVE, *goes out.*)

EVE: Molly, I know he helped himself.

MOLLY: (*Lighting a cigarette*) Yes, darling, I expect you're right.

EVE: Well, if there's one thing I hate it's a pilferer. And a liar.

MOLLY: Well we all have our pet aversions, I detest ghastly scenes and boys getting shrill all over something extremely trivial, darling.

EVE: I see. (*Turns, goes out, back.*)

MOLLY: I see. I see. Pretty please with sugar on it. (*Imitating first* EVE, *then herself.*) Oh God – (*She gets up.*) Evie! (*Makes to go back.*)

TEDDY: (*Enters, left*) Hey Moll, you nearly let me fall asleep again, you ready?

MOLLY: What? What for, darling?

TEDDY: Our walk.

MOLLY: What walk?

TEDDY: Aren't you coming for a walk?

MOLLY: But darling, we worked it all out at lunch, now we've got the piano tuned at last I was going to try and settle to some song writing, and you were going to go for a walk.

TEDDY: We're going to Gwyllup, it's five miles.

MOLLY: No darling, we were going to *drive* to Gwyllup another day –

TEDDY: No, no, walk.

MOLLY: Anyway, not this afternoon –

TEDDY: You're smoking again.

MOLLY: So I am, I am.

TEDDY: If you don't want to, you'd better not.

MOLLY: But I do. I do.

TEDDY: Then we'd better get started.

MOLLY: No, I mean smoke – (*Stubs the cigarette out irritably.*)

TEDDY: Do you or don't you, I can't make it out.

EVE: (*Enters back*) I'm just going to do the shopping.

TEDDY: What?

EVE: I've got down tomatoes, oranges, cauliflower, the beef to be collected, four skewers –

MOLLY: Oh darling, do come in properly, it can't be any good for your throat – baying at me from over there.

TEDDY: I'm going to walk to Gwyllup. The question is whether you are.

EVE: I'm sorry. I didn't mean to bay at you. (*Frostily.*)

TEDDY: I can perfectly well go by myself.

EVE: I just wanted to know if you wanted to add anything.

MOLLY: Add anything? To the skewers and the four cauliflowers?

EVE: To the shopping list.

TEDDY: When you two have sorted it out, whatever it is that's so important to you, I'll be upstairs in my room. I don't want to keep interrupting you ladies when you're nattering about something important – (*Going out, slams the door, left.*) (*There is a pause.*)

MOLLY: Omigod! We go to all the trouble of getting that little man over from Guildford so that I can play the piano properly at last, and perhaps even, who knows? compose a song, and when I actually at last arrange to spend an afternoon at the piano, I find myself harassed with tales about youths stealing cigarettes, and grown men demanding to be taken for walks – it's too much, it's too, too much! (*Takes out a cigarette, lights it.*) (EVE *turns away, her face working.*) (MOLLY *looks at* EVE, *looks away angrily, draws on her*

cigarette.) Sorry darling. Didn't mean to be ratty. Forgive
please. (*Little pause*.) Pretty please, with sugar on it.

EVE: I expect it *is* all my fault. *I'm* sorry, Molly. The truth is, I've
got a bit of a headache, this weather's a little close for me.
(*Attempts a little laugh*.) That always means it's going to rain.
Sorry Moll.

MOLLY: Oh poor darling, can I get you an aspirin?

EVE: No – nothing does any good until it rains.

MOLLY: Anyway, you mustn't think of going to the shops – why
don't you have a nice lie-down?

EVE: Oh, I'll be all right. Really. I shouldn't have made such a
fuss over Oliver.

MOLLY: Someone's got to make fusses for us, darling, and as
you're the only grown-up in the house, it'd better be you.
We are childish, aren't we, Teddy and I?

EVE: Of course you're not.

MOLLY: Yes we are.

EVE: Well – I've always liked children.

MOLLY: Really, darling? I wouldn't have thought you'd much to
do with them before.

EVE: Oh yes. I helped to look after some once. A long time ago.

MOLLY: Did you? (*Abruptly*.) I'd like a child. Do you think it's
too late for me?
(*Little pause.* EVE *looks embarrassed*.)
I mean adopt one, of course. Now that I'm back in England –
home again. One could easily adopt one, couldn't one? What
do you think?

EVE: I think it's the most marvellous idea!

MOLLY: After all, if we keep this place on, we've lots of room. He
could have the small room as a bedroom, and the room
opposite as a play-room and I could move across the hall to
be next to him – and even if we don't stay here we could find
somewhere else just as big – you see how I've been working it
out?

EVE: Oh Moll!

MOLLY: And you wouldn't run away if we did?

EVE: I'd love it! And what does Teddy think?

MOLLY: Oh, I haven't mentioned it to him yet. One thing at a time for the poor darling – first England, then a child, then if we get on with that one perhaps another to go with it and so on, we may end up with a flock of them – (*laughing*) – we'd have to keep some out in the fields!

EVE: (*Laughs*) Oh Moll!

TEDDY: (*Enters left*) I'm not going to doze through the afternoon, have you two fixed it all up between yourselves, yet?

MOLLY: Oh yes, darling, completely. Haven't we, Evie?

EVE: (*Smiling*) Yes.

TEDDY: Then you're ready to hike to Gwyllup? Or do I go on my own?

MOLLY: Oh darling, do you mind if I try out the lovely piano you've had fixed up for me? Do you?

TEDDY: You're saying no?

MOLLY: Darling, I will, if you like.

TEDDY: I'm going anyway, as that's what we arranged.

MOLLY: Besides, Evie says it's going to rain, and you know how bad that can be for your ears – why don't you take a little local stroll.

TEDDY: I'm going to Gwyllup. (*Pause.*) I'm going to Gwyllup.

MOLLY: (*Hesitates*) Then at least take your raincoat and your mackintosh hat.

TEDDY: What?

MOLLY: Your raincoat and mackintosh hat.

TEDDY: What for? It's not going to rain. Bye. (*Stamps out through the conservatory.*)

MOLLY: Oh damn, damn, what shall I do, if it rains into his ears – and he *will* go to Gwyllup too, he's so stubborn – and if I go after him now he'll just stump angrily along –

EVE: (*Getting up*) I'll take them to him. (*Runs to door, left, returns at once with hat and coat.*)

MOLLY: Oh thank you, darling. But really somebody ought to go with him, I know it's a lot to ask – will you?

EVE: (*Hesitates, then smiles*) Of course, Moll.

MOLLY: You are a darling – and they say Gwyllup's very beautiful.

EVE: (*Runs through the conservatory, with hat and coat. As she does so, she calls*) Oliver – Oliver – run after Mr Treadley, tell him to wait a minute, hurry, hurry!

(MOLLY *stands listening for a moment, then goes into the conservatory, stands watching, still visible to the audience, then returns. Goes to the cigarettes, picks one out, lights it, puffs on it. Sits down to smoke. After a moment gets up, stands uncertainly, kicks off her shoes, then wanders over to the piano, picks out a tune, tries to play, then crashes a discord, sits puffing on her cigarette. Gets up, paces about restlessly, then goes to the cocktail cabinet, pours herself a gin, walks determinedly back to the piano, sits down, gets up, goes over, lights another cigarette, sits down with the drink.*)

MOLLY: Alone at last. (*Pause, then in a desolate voice.*) Omigod!
(*Pause, suddenly shakes her head from side to side, stops, puts her fingers to her forehead.*) Omigod! (*Collapses back into the sofa.*)

(OLIVER *appears in the conservatory. He is carrying the coat and the mackintosh hat.* MOLLY *doesn't notice him.* OLIVER *clears his throat.*)

(*Looks at him*) Oh hello. He sent them back, did he?

OLIVER: Yes, Miss. He said to say he doesn't need them. And he says thank you, um, for –

MOLLY: What?

OLIVER: Well, Evie, Miss.

MOLLY: (*Smiles wryly*) Thank you. Well, sling them – sling them over there somewhere, would you?
(OLIVER *puts them on the end of the sofa.*)
And how's everything in the garden?

OLIVER: I got the weeds on the compost, I'm going to start on the hedge.

MOLLY: How lucky – to have something you've got to do.

OLIVER: Yes Miss.
(*Slight pause.* OLIVER *goes into the conservatory, clatters about, just in sight.* MOLLY *looks towards the conservatory, watches.*)
Just getting the shears, Miss. (*Holds them up.*)

MOLLY: Come in for a moment, Oliver, please. (*With authority.*)

(OLIVER *enters, carrying the shears*.)

Two, Oliver.

OLIVER: Miss?

MOLLY: (*Holds up two fingers*) You took two of my cigarettes, Oliver.

OLIVER: I didn't! Miss, I swear –

MOLLY: Oh Oliver, don't, please. It makes you sound like a goose when you protest – you honk.

OLIVER: But – (*Stops*.)

MOLLY: (*Gets cigarettes, holds package out to* OLIVER) Here, have another one.

OLIVER: No thank you, Miss.

MOLLY: Oh go on. You mustn't mind my knowing about you being a liar, I lie all the time, all the time, about lots of things, about cigarettes too. I promise I won't smoke more than five a day, my husband thinks it's bad for my health, but of course I sneak extra ones, like now with you, he'd have a fit if he could see me puffing away. Do you know what he'd do? He'd put me across his knee and spank me, Oliver. Yes, he would. What do you think of that?

OLIVER: Well Miss – (*Gives a strange half laugh*.)

MOLLY: Now I've told you all that, you've got to take one, haven't you?

(OLIVER *hesitates, then takes one*.)

I bet your Dad doesn't put you across his knee and spank you, at least not any more, does he?

OLIVER: No Miss. (*Laughs again*.)

MOLLY: You did take them, didn't you?

OLIVER: Yes Miss.

MOLLY: There, now we've both confessed. But I'm very sorry Oliver, now I shall have to punish you. You do realize that, you can't pinch my cigarettes and then lie and bluster about it and not expect punishment, can you? (*She allows a long pause*.) Sit down please, Oliver.

(OLIVER, *after a moment, sits*.)

Do you know what I'm going to do to you?

(OLIVER *shakes his head*.)

I'm going to teach you a lesson, Oliver. I'm going to make you sit here and talk to me. (*Laughs.*) Just for a little, do you mind?

OLIVER: (*Smiles*) No Miss. Except there's the hedge and she goes on at me.

MOLLY: Oh, *her*! Don't worry about her, Oliver, I'll protect you from her! (*Pause.*) Tell me, do you think it's going to rain?

OLIVER: Yes Miss.

MOLLY: Oh don't say that, why?

OLIVER: Because it feels like rain. And my dad said it would.

MOLLY: And is your dad always right?

OLIVER: Usually Miss.

MOLLY: About everything, or just about the weather?

OLIVER: Well, about the weather, anyway, Miss.

MOLLY: How does he know, by sniffing the air, or holding his finger up or rising at six for shepherds' warning?

OLIVER: No Miss.

MOLLY: How then?

OLIVER: He listen to the radio Miss, at breakfast. (*There is a pause.*)

MOLLY: Well, clever old Dad. (*Laughing.*) I bet you don't dare lie to him.

OLIVER: Oh no, Miss.

MOLLY: What about?

OLIVER: Miss?

MOLLY: What do you lie to him about?

OLIVER: I said I didn't, Miss.

MOLLY: Yes that was a lie to me. What do you lie to him about? Come on, Oliver, do tell me. Please, pretty please. Because I know you do.

OLIVER: How, Miss?

MOLLY: Because if we didn't lie to people we love and live with, we wouldn't be able to love and live with them. See.
(*Gets up, goes to cocktail cabinet, pours herself a gin, studies* OLIVER.)

OLIVER: (*After a pause*) Well, only about Guildford. What I do over at Guildford. That's all.

MOLLY: And what *do* you do over at Guildford?
  (*During this scene, and by imperceptible degrees, the stage darkens to suggest the sky darkening.*)
  Oh of course, you've got a girl there. (*Drinks.*)

OLIVER: Well – (*Shrugs.*)

MOLLY: Haven't you?

OLIVER: Not any more. There was a girl. I used to have tea with her sometimes.

MOLLY: Only tea?

OLIVER: Yes. She worked in a tea shop.

MOLLY: (*Drinks again*) And is that all you did with her?

OLIVER: We went to the films sometimes.

MOLLY: Were you lovers?

OLIVER: What?

MOLLY: Lovers.
  (*There is a pause.*)
  Here – (*pours a drink of gin, brings it to* OLIVER) have a sip of this.

OLIVER: What is it?

MOLLY: A truth drink. To help you tell me whether you were lovers. It's all right, I swear I won't tell your dad if you promise not to tell mine. Husband. Sip and tell, Oliver.

OLIVER: (*Sips*) Well – (*Sips again.*) No Miss.

MOLLY: No, won't tell, or no, weren't lovers?

OLIVER: Weren't – um, lovers.

MOLLY: Oh dear, oh dear, why not?

OLIVER: (*Laughs embarrassed.*) Don't know anything about any of that.

MOLLY: Any of what? (*Goes over to him, takes the shears off his lap, puts them on the floor.*) There. Any of what?

OLIVER: My dad wouldn't stand for any of that. He'd kill me if I did anything like that.

MOLLY: (*Standing close to him*) Then what happened between yourself and this girl, what was her name?

OLIVER: Rosie. Rosie Hitchens. Well – just one day she turned around when I went over and said her mum didn't want her to see me any more.

137

MOLLY: And she didn't?

OLIVER: (*After a pause*) No.

MOLLY: (*After a pause*) Poor Oliver. Poor Rosie Hutchings, come to that.

OLIVER: Hitchens. Her name was.

MOLLY: Is your mother dead?

OLIVER: Yes Miss. When I was born.

MOLLY: You're terribly fond of your dad, aren't you? Tell me, what do you do together? I mean in the evenings, or the weekends?

OLIVER: Well – we go shooting.

MOLLY: Do you, oh, dear, what do you shoot?

OLIVER: Only rabbits.

MOLLY: *Only* rabbits? Oh Oliver. And do you kill many of them?

OLIVER: Quite a few. My dad's a good shot. I'm not bad.

MOLLY: What do you think, when you see them dead?

OLIVER: That they're dead, Miss. Dead rabbits. For pie.

MOLLY: Have you got a dog?

OLIVER: We had one once, Miss.

MOLLY: What happened to it?

OLIVER: It got run over.

MOLLY: And what did you think, when you saw it dead.

OLIVER: It was in the middle of the Guildford road, where all the lorries run. My dad took me down to see it, lying there squashed, I was only six about.

MOLLY: Why did he do that?

OLIVER: To show me what happened if I was careless on the road.

MOLLY: Omigod, Oliver! And what did you say, when you saw it there?

OLIVER: I said (*thinks*) were we going to have it for lunch.

MOLLY: You didn't!

OLIVER: No Miss. We had it for supper.

MOLLY: (*After a moment, laughing*) You're making fun of me! That's nice. (*Pours more gin into* OLIVER'S *glass*.) There! You see how it helps. And me. (*Pours some into her own*.) Because now I'm going to tell you why I hate to think of shooting only rabbits even, and you mustn't laugh at me, promise?

OLIVER: Miss.

MOLLY: You see, I hate anything being killed by people. Ever
since I heard about something very dreadful – about how
these great Canadian men with their red necks and tartan
caps on their heads drive down to the beach in the trucks and
they catch the seals, the mother seals and the baby seals, and
they beat their heads in with clubs and hammers. (*Sits down
beside him.*) Yes they do, Oliver, and sometimes the mothers
stay a little way out in the sea, watching, while these – these
men! – skin their babies while they're still alive often, skin
them for their furs. Dreadful. Dreadful. They have such big
eyes and they stare at their babies – D'you see, Oliver. (*Looks
at him intently.*) I wrote a song about it. It was broadcast on
the radio over there, and played right across Novia Scotia.
But it didn't stop them. That's when I knew I couldn't live in
Canada any more, amongst people like that. So don't shoot
any rabbits ever again. Please don't, Oliver. Pretty please.
With sugar on it. (*There is a pause.*) Oh I know, you've got
to, for your dad's sake. You'll just have to try to miss them,
that's all. For my sake. Aim – (*raises her arm at* OLIVER, *jerks
at the last second*) sideways. (*Laughs.*) But don't hit your dad.
For his sake. Are you happy with us?

OLIVER: Oh yes, Miss.

MOLLY: I watch you sometimes, Oliver. Did you know that?
When you're in the garden. As busy as bees. Mowing the
lawn yesterday. I watched you from an upstairs window.
And then on your knees weeding this morning. But I haven't
seen you recite poetry to the flowers. No. And sometimes
you even look a trifle – sulky. There. I've said it. As if you
weren't truly and really deeply happy with us. Why not,
Oliver?

OLIVER: I am, Miss. (*Pause.*) Well.

MOLLY: No, go on. On.

OLIVER: She gets at me a lot, Miss.

MOLLY: Oh, she gets at us all a lot, pay her no mind, we don't.
When she gets at me I pay her out my very best smile and say
forgive me, Evie, pretty please, with sugar on it. You can try

that. Because then you can ignore her and be rude to her or whatever you want. What else is wrong?

OLIVER: Nothing, Miss. Well.

MOLLY: Oh, Oliver. On.

OLIVER: Well, only about the car, that's all. I mean I was taken on to do the car, but now I've got it fixed up I've only taken it out twice, the rest of it's been gardening and painting the garage, and the other day it was sash cords even she made me do.

MOLLY: I'm so glad you've told me this, Oliver. I'll have a word with Teddy when he gets back. (*Pours herself another drink.*) I promise you more outings in the car. I never break my promises you know.

OLIVER: Oh, I don't really mind. It's just that that's what I thought I was being taken on to do mainly and, well, they make jokes about it at Sprinkley's and up at the pub, because my dad told them all I was going to be a chauffeur and they say if you're a chauffeur where's your uniform. My dad doesn't like that.

MOLLY: If your dad doesn't like it, that settles it. Although I don't know about a uniform – I don't know if I'd like you so much in a uniform. Will you teach me to drive, Oliver, and keep it a secret from my dad. Will you?

OLIVER: Yes Miss.

MOLLY: And then when you've taught me I'll show him I can. Eh? Oliver? (*Laughs.*) If you promise to teach me then you shall have a uniform – even though I like you just as you are, Oliver. I like you very much. You do know that, don't you? (*They stare at each other.*)
Do you like him?

OLIVER: Who?

MOLLY: Teddy.

OLIVER: Yes, Miss.

MOLLY: So do I. Even though he calls you boy and Ollie and Oliver Treefsir?

OLIVER: Oh, I don't mind that. It's just his way.

MOLLY: Because he's deaf, you see. It's so sad. Because people when they're deaf can't have normal friendly conversations with each other, as we're having, so they have to find little tricks of their own to show normal friendliness, and to hide their deafness too. And he's very friendly. More than normally.

OLIVER: He doesn't really –

MOLLY: What?

OLIVER: (*Hesitates*) Put you over his knee, does he?

MOLLY: (*Stares at* OLIVER) D'you mind?

OLIVER: Miss. (*Laughs.*) He doesn't! Does he?

MOLLY: I'm so worried, Oliver, about his getting his ears wet. And your saying it's going to rain – (*Goes over to the window, looks out.*) It's darker, getting darker. It *is* raining a little. Oh damn! Oh, poor Teddy. But it's delicious, too, isn't it, the two of us snug inside, talking and drinking, while outside – (*shivers*) delicious. (*Takes a gulp of gin.*) Do you like me, Oliver?

OLIVER: Miss?

MOLLY: Or do you think I'm just a silly old vamp, do you?

OLIVER: No, Miss.

MOLLY: What then? Say it. You must say it. I said it to you.

OLIVER: Like you, Miss.

MOLLY: But I don't frighten you, do I?

OLIVER: No, Miss.

MOLLY: We'll have another cigarette, shall we?

(*Goes with cigarettes, offers one to* OLIVER, *lights it for him. She is staring at him. Takes a step around the side of the sofa, puts her foot on the shears, stumbles, cries out.*)

OLIVER: (*Gets to his feet*) What is it, Miss, what is it?

MOLLY: I've cut myself – my foot – (*Tries to see the sole of her foot.*) Can you see?

(OLIVER, *bending some yards away, stares.*)

Look properly – take it – (*Stretches out her leg.*)

OLIVER: (*Takes her foot gingerly*) I can't see any cut, Miss.

MOLLY: But it's wet – I can feel the bleeding –

OLIVER: No Miss – that's your drink – I can smell it – that's all –

MOLLY: But it hurts, oh God, it hurts – (*Loses balance, hops.*)

OLIVER: Miss – Miss – (*Lets go of* MOLLY's *leg.*)

    (MOLLY *stumbles towards* OLIVER, *who puts out his arms to catch her.*)

MOLLY: Oh Oliver – (*clinging to him*) it did hurt – it did –

OLIVER: Miss. (*In alarm.*)

MOLLY: Oliver – don't be frightened. Don't be.

OLIVER: Miss?

    (MOLLY *begins to kiss* OLIVER, *ravenously.* OLIVER *clumsily responds. Lights down to sound of rain. Rain continues through the darkness.*)

SCENE 3

About an hour later. Lights up to greyness. Still raining heavily.
OLIVER *is sitting on the sofa, putting on his socks. He has already put on his underpants. The raincoat is spread under him, across the sofa, the waterproof side up, there are cushions on the floor.* MOLLY *is in her underpants, doing up her bra. She is standing some way from*
OLIVER. *She is dressing quickly.* OLIVER *stops dressing, watches*
MOLLY. *His face works. He turns, rolls into the sofa, puts his arm over his face.*

MOLLY: (*Not noticing*) Oh that rain, that bloody rain – but they'll have found somewhere in the village – or a tree – the poor man – next time I'll check the weather with your dad or the wireless – (*Dressing through this, turns, looks at* OLIVER.) Oliver – (*Goes over to him.*) Oliver, darling, what is it? (*Sits down on the sofa next to him, tries to remove* OLIVER's *arm from his face.*) Oliver – don't – you mustn't – here, here – (*Pulls his arm away.*) Why are you? Is it because you're unhappy? Are you unhappy?

OLIVER: (*Shakes his head*) No, Miss.

MOLLY: Because you're happy then?

    (OLIVER, *crying, turns his face away.*)

    (*Taking his face in her hands*) Because you're happy?

OLIVER: Miss. I don't know, Miss.

MOLLY: (*Cuddles him*) There Oliver, nothing to cry for, nothing to cry for. I'm glad, I am, yes I am, and I want you to be happy, but you mustn't cry –

OLIVER: (*Embraces her with sudden and desperate passion*) Please Miss please Miss please Miss –

MOLLY: What, darling? What?

OLIVER: You won't send me away, Miss.

MOLLY: No, no – of course not – just for now – just for a little while – but there'll be other times. I promise you. Lots of other times, but we mustn't let them find out, must we? They wouldn't understand, and I wouldn't want to hurt Teddy, he loves me, you know, and I must care for him too, mustn't I, and not let him be hurt, so now I've got to put everything right and you must finish getting dressed, darling, and help me by being as quick as you can, darling, before they come back – do you understand, darling? Do you?

(OLIVER *nods*.)

Go on then. Go on, my darling – (*Gets up, finishes dressing*.)

(OLIVER *goes on dressing, sniffing*.)

(MOLLY *comes over, buttons his shirt*) Now you go now, my darling – (*leads him to the door left*) there's a good boy – (*Kisses him*.)

(OLIVER *goes out left, there is a pause. He comes back, rushes over to* MOLLY, *throws his arms around her*.)

(MOLLY *strokes his head*.) I'll see you soon. I promise. And I never break my promises.

(*They separate.* OLIVER *stands looking at* MOLLY.)

Go, Oliver. (*Gently, leads him out left and sounds of her saying goodbye quickly at the front door. Front door closes, off,* MOLLY *enters left as* TEDDY, *followed by* EVE, *enters the conservatory, right.* TEDDY *is soaking, mud-stained. Followed by* EVE, *also soaking*.)

(MOLLY *stares, shocked*.) Omigod – darling, what happened?

TEDDY: Well, here I am, Moll, back from a stroll in your nice quiet countryside, right in the middle of the fields, eh Evie, then wham, right from out of your nice quiet clouds, wham, wham, wham! (*Laughs*.)

MOLLY: Darling, you must get into some dry clothes. (*Getting up, going to him*.)

EVE: And a hot bath!

> (TEDDY *has gone to cocktail cabinet, pours himself an enormous Scotch.*)

TEDDY: And there we were, Evie and me (*gulping the Scotch*), licking across the field in the dark, sheets of it coming down, and there was this tree Evie saw, on a bank and a ditch running under it, anyway wouldn't pass in Novia Scotia for a river (*laughs*) and I swayed on the edge, eh, Evie?

MOLLY: Darling, tell me afterwards, get changed now!

TEDDY: Felt like minutes, rocking and swaying, and Evie had hold of my arm pulling me back, but a hand shot out of nowhere and down I went.

MOLLY: A hand?

TEDDY: And down I went, right Evie?

MOLLY: You were pushed?

TEDDY: And down I went, right, Evie, Evie almost coming with me. (*Laughs.*) So don't you two talk to me about your friendly English countryside again, we've got bob-cat, bear and skunk in Nova Scotia but we don't have anything you can't see or hear or understand come up behind you and tumble you into the mud for no damn reason – (*gulps again*) raining inside my skull – (*pulls out the hearing aid*) damn thing, damned thing, battery soaking – get it fixed, fixed tomorrow – (*Takes another gulp, stands staring at MOLLY.*) Hey, Moll!

MOLLY: He's trembling – darling! He's feverish – come on, darling, we must get you to a bath and bed – come along. (*Pulls TEDDY towards the door.*)

TEDDY: I'm all right – I'm all right – (*Goes out.*)

MOLLY: (*Before she closes the door, turns, stares at EVE*) I told you to make him take his raincoat and his mackintosh hat! I *told* you! (*Goes out.*)

> (EVE *stands for a moment. Then bends, automatically. Picks up Teddy's hat.*)

EVE: (*In an emotional voice*) It's jolly well not fair! (*Suddenly takes in the chaos of the room, glasses, cushions, etc.*)
> (*Lights. Curtain.*)

ACT TWO

SCENE I

A week or so later. The sun is shining. It is mid-afternoon.
EVE is sitting with some knitting on her lap. She is staring ahead.
There is the sound of a door closing, off, up left. Then quick footsteps,
EVE starts knitting.

MOLLY: Hello darling, seen my handbag?

EVE: On the sofa.

MOLLY: You are clever. (*Going to the handbag.*)

EVE: You usually leave it on the sofa. Have you got Teddy's
    drops?

MOLLY: Oh yes, here they are. (*Fishes them out of the handbag,*
    puts them on the table.)

EVE: He always needs them first thing, when he wakes.

MOLLY: I know, poor darling. Isn't that growing – Teddy'll be so
    thrilled. I wish I could knit.

EVE: Do you? It's not difficult.

MOLLY: No, I suppose it can't be, as so many dolts can. It's one
    of those activities I always thought I'd find myself doing
    when I grew up – like putting on grey hair and wrinkles.

EVE: Indeed?

MOLLY: Oh darling, I didn't mean – (*Laughs.*)

EVE: (*Smiles coldly*) Are you going out?

MOLLY: Yes, I've got an appointment with Oliver for a driving
    lesson. What about you?

EVE: Oh no. I don't think Teddy should be left alone at the
    moment.

MOLLY: But darling, he's asleep, I've just checked.

EVE: Yesterday when you were having a driving lesson and I was
    down here he woke up and thought he was alone in the
    house. He was quite fretful for a good half hour.

MOLLY: I must say, darling, that doesn't sound like a good half hour to me. (*Hesitates.*) In that case why don't you go out and I'll stay in, it's your turn.

EVE: No. I'd as soon get on with this. Besides, Oliver will be expecting you.

MOLLY: Oh, I can always find something else for him to do.

EVE: I'm glad he's settling down so well. Since you moved him into the house.

MOLLY: Hasn't he been a godsend.

EVE: Yes. Mrs Shepherd says he's funny in the head. She came around yesterday morning. She'd heard he was living in so she came around especially to warn us. She said he was funny in the head. That's why they dismissed him. Her husband caught him in their bedroom, going through her underwear drawer.

MOLLY: Oh, don't worry, darling. Your underwear drawer is quite safe. Oliver's told me all about it.

EVE: I see. You don't think it peculiar even then?

MOLLY: Nothing like as peculiar as Mrs Shepherd, trekking all the way up here to tell us about it.

EVE: Oh well, as long as *you* don't mind –

MOLLY: No, I don't mind, darling. Not at all. And if you're not keen to go out I'll get some fresh air. (*Gets up, goes towards the conservatory.*)

EVE: (*Watches her, and as* MOLLY *gets to the conservatory door*) Oh by the way, Molly, as soon as Teddy's better I shall be leaving. (*Little pause.*) I thought I should tell you now, so you'd have time to find someone more suitable.

MOLLY: (*Takes out a cigarette, lights it*) More suitable to what, darling?

EVE: To what's going on in this house.

MOLLY: What *is* going on in this house?

EVE: Wasn't Oliver in your room last night?

MOLLY: Yes, he did look in to say goodnight and to ask how Teddy was.

EVE: He stayed the whole night.

(MOLLY *makes to exclaim.*)

Please don't lie to me, Moll, I couldn't bear it. I heard Teddy

146

stumbling down the hall at midnight. It was only by the grace of God that I managed to stop him opening the door on the two of you. He'd had a nightmare, and wanted comforting. Thank God *he* couldn't hear what I heard. (*There is a honk from outside, right.*)

MOLLY: Omigod! Thank you, Evie!

EVE: Oh it wasn't you I was thinking of, it was Teddy.

MOLLY: I know. Thank you. Teddy and I don't sleep together, surely you've realized that.

EVE: But – but he's still your husband. You married him.

MOLLY: Yes. And I do my best to make him happy, haven't you noticed? I get drunk with him, and cuddle him, and let him slap me on the bottom – all – all that. It's enough for Teddy. It's not always enough for me.

EVE: You mean – you've done this before?

MOLLY: From time to time. Though not as often as I want to.

EVE: Oh, you sound so hard – so hard.

MOLLY: Do I, darling? Sorry. You've been companion-housekeeper to a wicked woman, darling, you see. I need my sex. There. I've said it.

EVE: Then you had no right to marry Teddy.

MOLLY: Hadn't I? He wanted me to.

EVE: But what did you marry him for? His money?

MOLLY: I admit I wouldn't have if he'd been an impoverished – (*Gestures.*)

EVE: Garage hand. Like Oliver Treefe, you mean?

MOLLY: Well, unlike Oliver, Teddy would have been a sixty-year-old impoverished garage hand when I married him, so I probably wouldn't have married him, no.

EVE: I don't understand.

MOLLY: What, darling? What don't you understand?

EVE: You who could have married anybody –

MOLLY: Not when I married Teddy. Don't forget he *was* sixty, and I was *all* of thirty – and he was quite a dynamic Halifax businessman and I was one of those, you know, glamorous English divorcees that end up in countries like Canada on spec.

EVE: I didn't know you'd been married before.

MOLLY: Gets worse and worse, doesn't it, darling. Yes. Married before. Sorry. There were no children though, other than the two of us. Then he began to grow up, and left me for someone who would look after him properly. I've never been very good at getting meals on tables and organizing homes and curtains and housekeeping – all the things you're so good at doing. He's a solicitor in Harrow now, I think it is, with no doubt children and all the rest of the things – (*gestures*) he couldn't imagine me providing him with. (*Pause.*) Actually, I did almost manage a child, but it miscarried. He blamed me for that – my fecklessness – because we'd been to a party and I drank a mite too much and slipped and fell down the stairs. He rather hated me – (*Pause.*) So after I'd set him free I took a plunge, and went off to Canada, where I just managed to keep my head above water doing lady-like little jobs and being glamorous and English – all the right things to be if one wanted one of those ghastly Canadian men as a lover, you know, balding and fattening, but no good for husbands, because they were already. Until Teddy came along. I was working as a part-time receptionist sort of person who did a little piano playing and drinking in the hotel and he was the first eligible male I've infatuated. Except there is just this little thing wrong with him, I don't know what, but he doesn't have sex, I don't believe he ever has. But apart from that and already beginning to deafen he was quite dynamic and infatuated. There. Now do you understand, Eve?

EVE: I suppose I might, oh I wouldn't approve but I might understand if it were some – some man you'd – you'd – but Oliver Treefe! Can't you see what he is?

MOLLY: What is he, darling? Other than peculiar in the head?

EVE: Well, for one thing he's – he's twenty years younger than you.

MOLLY: Is that worse than being almost thirty years older?

EVE: But he's – he's completely uneducated. He's not even particularly nice to look at. Even I can see that. He's a common, loutish –

MOLLY: Stop it, Evie. Please. The truth is, Ollie and I –

EVE: Ollie and you! Ollie and you! No, I can't stop it, I jolly well think it's disgusting. Disgusting!

MOLLY: (*In a sudden scream*) We're all disgusting!
(*There is a pause.*)

EVE: (*Gets up*) Well *I'm* not, Molly Treadley. No, *I'm* not!
(OLIVER *enters through the conservatory. He is wearing a chauffeur's uniform, carrying a cap and gauntlets.*)

OLIVER: Oh, excuse me, Miss, I've been honking for you outside.

MOLLY: Honking for me?
(EVE *exits, left.*)

OLIVER: She in one of her bad moods?

MOLLY: A touch edgy, perhaps. (*Little pause.*) Look darling, I'm sorry, but I'd better not come this afternoon, after all.

OLIVER: Why not?

MOLLY: Why don't you give your dad that ride you've been promising him. He's scarcely seen you this last ten days.

OLIVER: He's working.

MOLLY: Well darling, anything you want to do – do. (*Smiles at him.*)

OLIVER: I want to go out with you. You promised me, Moll. To make up for all that hanging about outside Gracey's this morning.

MOLLY: I know darling, I'm sorry, but really I can't.

OLIVER: It *is* because of her, isn't it?

MOLLY: I suppose so. Because of her and him and you and me – it's all very complicated and I'm not up to explaining it and you wouldn't like it if I did, darling, but what it comes down to is that it would make everything worse if we skipped off right now.

OLIVER: It's not fair. I've been sitting out there, honking and waiting and honking and waiting and I've changed the oil even, and now you tell me you can't come out and won't tell me why, but it's because of her and him – I know it is.

MOLLY: Oliver!
(OLIVER *makes to say something else.*)
No, don't say another word, Ollie. Not now. Just go. For your sake, darling.

OLIVER: (*Looks at her, turns, makes as if to exit through the conservatory, stops*) It's true what they say, isn't it? That you hooked him for his money and car and that. That's what Sprinkley said from the beginning, the first time he saw you, and my dad said something about you and him, he thinks it's wrong, and Bob Howells making jokes in the pub, if he pays you for every go or how many times a week you have to let him do it, they were all laughing at his jokes in the pub about him and you. All of them. That's what I have to sit and listen to.

MOLLY: (*Goes to* OLIVER) Who is Bob Howells, darling?

OLIVER: He's Sprinkley's cousin, he –
(MOLLY *slaps* OLIVER *across the face.* OLIVER *stands for a moment, then runs over to the sofa, falls onto it.*)

MOLLY: (*Looks at him, goes over to him*) If you ever – ever – talk to me like that again, it's back to Bob Howells and Sprinkley's for you, my boy.

OLIVER: You wouldn't. (*In a whisper.*)

MOLLY: Yes, I would, my lad. You can add some jokes of your own and lead the laughter, but you'll never see me again, except from a great distance.
(*There is a pause.* OLIVER *sits upright, staring at* MOLLY.)
Oh Oliver, why do you get like this?

OLIVER: But I love you, I love you.

MOLLY: That's all right, darling. You may love me. I want you to.

OLIVER: But I can't stand it when I'm not with you, when you're in here talking to her, or go into his room to talk to him, and I don't know what's going on, but I think of you and him touching you and I don't know, what am I to do, Moll. You see, before it was like – it was like I was stuck somewhere underground and – and you took me out – and now I want to be out all the time, but when you're not there it's like being stuck back down again. (*Little pause.*) Last night you said I was your husband even. But I'm not, am I? He is, isn't he? He has you most.

MOLLY: But you have far more of me, especially now. He

doesn't kiss me where you kiss me, he doesn't hold me as you hold me – we mustn't grudge him anything, Ollie. Not anything. (*Little pause.*) Darling.

OLIVER: (*Looks at her*) I'm sorry for what I said. I didn't mean it.

MOLLY: I know. (*Puts her arms around him.*) Oh my Ollie.

OLIVER: You still love me then don't you?

MOLLY: Of course I do.

OLIVER: You won't ever send me away, will you?

MOLLY: When Rosie Hitchins from Guildford comes to claim you back.

OLIVER: Never!

MOLLY: Well, not if I can help it.

OLIVER: Then I've got you, then, haven't I? (*Jubilant.*) Got you! (*They embrace.* MOLLY *kisses him tenderly, as if he were a child. She wipes his cheeks with her fingers, then kisses him again. The kiss becomes passionate.* OLIVER *puts his hands on* MOLLY's *breasts, sighs.* MOLLY *responds.*)
Please Moll. Come out.

MOLLY: (*Steps away*) You're quite impossible, Oliver Treefe. (*Laughs.*)

OLIVER: You will, won't you?

MOLLY: (*Hesitates*) Oh why not – yes – let's – (*There is a knock on the door, left.* MOLLY *looks at the door. Another knock.*)
Come in.

EVE: (*Enters*) Excuse me. I wasn't sure whether you'd gone.

MOLLY: Oh, that's all right, darling. We're just off.

EVE: I wondered if I could have a few words with you.

MOLLY: Of course. Oliver, wait in the car, would you. I won't be a minute.
(OLIVER *glances suspiciously at* EVE, *exits.*)

EVE: I think it would be better if I left as soon as possible. So I'd be grateful if you got back by five. I'd like to catch the six o'clock train.

MOLLY: Would you like Oliver to drive you to the station?

EVE: No thank you. I'll call for a taxi, if I may.

MOLLY: Where are you going?

EVE: To Gosport.

MOLLY: I didn't know you had anyone in Gosport.

EVE: A niece.

MOLLY: And does she have children?

EVE: Yes.

MOLLY: You'll be able to help her with them, I suppose.

EVE: They're quite grown up.

MOLLY: Those are the ones that really need your help. (*Smiles.*)

EVE: If Teddy wakes I shan't say anything, I'd rather you explained.

MOLLY: He'll miss you dreadfully. So will I, of course.

EVE: I'll pack now. (*Goes towards the door, left.*)

MOLLY: (*Hesitates, then*) Evie.

> (EVE *stops, turns.*)
> Evie, please don't go! (*Runs across to her, embraces her.*) I need you so. I do.
> (EVE *stands stiffly for a moment, then turns, embraces* MOLLY.)

EVE: Oh Moll!

MOLLY: You won't leave me, Evie. Will you?

EVE: (*After a moment*) No Moll. Not if you really need me.

MOLLY: Oh thank you, darling. Thank you. Thank you.

> (*There is a sudden thumping from above. There is a pause. There is a honk from off, right.*)

TEDDY: (*Off, above*) Hey, Mollie, Eve – hey!

> (MOLLY *looks at* EVE *appealingly.*)

EVE: You'd better go. But I can't tell lies for you, Molly Treadley. I can't do that.

MOLLY: No, darling. I know.

> (*Goes out through conservatory.*
>
> EVE *watches her go through conservatory, stands for a moment. Puts her hand to her forehead.*
>
> TEDDY *enters, left. He is wearing dressing-gown, slippers, but is without a hearing-aid.*)

EVE: (*Turning*) Teddy – you shouldn't be up.

TEDDY: Where's Moll?

EVE: (*Slowly and loudly*) She's gone out.

> (*Sound of the car screeching down the drive.*)

TEDDY: She went out this morning – where's she gone to this time?

EVE: (*Hesitates*) Oh, just for a drive.

TEDDY: What?

EVE: To get your drops. Teddy, you mustn't stay down here – (*Goes over to him.*)

TEDDY: What? (*Irritably, pulling his arm away.*) Did she forget them this morning, then?

EVE: They had to make up a fresh batch – it's too cold for you down here, Teddy.

TEDDY: Not going back to bed with a stuffed nose – like being in a damned prison. (*Goes over, pours himself a Scotch, slops the drink, pays no attention, takes a gulp.*) Can't taste the taste, only the heat. (*Sits down.*) Go in the car?

EVE: Yes. (*Goes back, sits down.*)

TEDDY: (*After a pause*) Saw them coming around the side of the house the other afternoon. Looked out of my window and there they were, around my side of the house, right beneath me. Like a pair of ghosts. (*Attempts to sniff.*) Don't worry, not delirious, Evie. Like ghosts because I couldn't hear them. Couldn't have smelt them either, come to that. Lost my hearing, now I lost my smelling, what goes next, eh? (*Laughs.*) She was laughing. He had his mouth open. Maybe shouting a joke or something. Anyway, his mouth was open.

EVE: I think he has adenoids.

TEDDY: Great sense of humour?

EVE: No, adenoids.

TEDDY: Knocked on my window, but they didn't hear. Went right on round. A moment later they were back again, on the other side, gravel showering every which way. Too damned fast. (*Pause.*) Too damned fast. God knows what he gets up to when I can't see him. (*Pause, sniffs.*) Why didn't you tell her yesterday I was running out, you could see I was, couldn't you?

EVE: I'm sorry.

TEDDY: What you knitting there, a coloured ladder?

EVE: A scarf.

TEDDY: What?

EVE: (*Explosively*) A *scarf*! It's going to be a scarf.

TEDDY: Like having him around the house all the time?

EVE: Who?

TEDDY: What's he like?

EVE: Oh, I expect he's a normal boy.

TEDDY: What?

EVE: A normal boy.

TEDDY: (*After a pause*) Hey Evie – (*pause*) last night – (*sniffs*) you tuck me up in bed? Or was it a dream?

EVE: I made your bed comfortable for you. The covers had slipped.

TEDDY: Oh. (*Little pause, then vaguely.*) What? (*Attempts to blow his nose.*) Damn! Damn! (*Sits, sunken in misery.*)

EVE: (*Looks at* TEDDY, *goes on with her knitting, looks at* TEDDY, *then suddenly*) Get rid of him, Teddy!

TEDDY: (*Looks at her. Pause*) What?
   (EVE *gets up, goes over to him, takes out the bottle of drops, hands it to* TEDDY.)

EVE: I can't bear to see you suffering like this.

TEDDY: That's all right, Evie, anyone can make a mistake.
   (*Takes the bottle, administers the drops, two to each nostril.*
      EVE *goes back, sits down.*)
   Tell me something, Evie – that scarf. Is it for me?

EVE: Yes.

TEDDY: Thank you, Evie.
   (*There is a pause.* TEDDY *sits staring ahead.* EVE *goes on with her knitting.*)
   What? (*Dimly.*)
   (*Lights.*)

SCENE 2

A couple of hours later. TEDDY *is sitting, staring ahead, as before.* EVE *is knitting.* TEDDY *gets up, goes with his glass over to the cocktail cabinet, pours himself another large Scotch.* EVE *looks up towards him then goes on with her knitting.*

MOLLY *enters through the conservatory, followed by* OLIVER.

MOLLY: (*Stops, stares at* TEDDY, *looks at* EVE) Darling, should you be up, Gracey said a few more days in bed –

TEDDY: Got tired of being stuck up there in bed – thought I'd come down, I'm fine – hello there boy, how are you?

OLIVER: Sir.

TEDDY: What?

OLIVER: All right, thank you, sir.

TEDDY: What about a drink? Moll? (*Dashes some gin into a glass, hands it to her.*)

MOLLY: But darling –

TEDDY: Where you been?

MOLLY: Oh, just out for a little drive –

TEDDY: What?

MOLLY: For a little drive.

TEDDY: Get my drops?

MOLLY: No, I got you a fresh bottle this morning –

TEDDY: Don't need them anyway, Evie had a bottle all the time – nice drive?

MOLLY: Except for a horrid little scene on the way back.

TEDDY: What?

MOLLY: A horrid little scene.

TEDDY: You and him?

MOLLY: No darling, two louts shooting in the field past the bridge. I made Oliver stop the car and when we went over there was a rabbit, they'd only wounded it and tied its legs, can you believe? and a beastly little dog –

OLIVER: A terrier.

TEDDY: What?

OLIVER: A terrier, sir.

TEDDY: No good boy, yours is the voice I'll never catch.

MOLLY: Anyway, they just stood there while Oliver had to kill it with a stick.

TEDDY: Killed the dog with a stick.

MOLLY: No, a rabbit, darling –

TEDDY: Rabbit, eh? Bet she didn't like that, eh boy?

OLIVER: No sir.

TEDDY: Doesn't like animals being hurt, do you Moll? Ever told you about the seals at Nanaimo, she wrote a song about it, got done across Nova Scotia because Bob Hoskins was a friend of mine, I asked him to do it for her. A good friend. (*Laughs*.) Eh Moll? But she'd never ever been to Nanaimo, eh Moll, but somebody told her about the seals and she made up a song out of her head, and that's how it got heard right across Nova Scotia. Nanaimo's in British Columbia, four thousand miles away – What do you think of that, eh Ollie – these ladies, seals, rabbits, songs – all the same to them, hey boy? Out in Nova Scotia we only shoot rabbits when we can't find any Catholics. We like to shoot Catholics. (*Laughs*.) Ever told you about that, Moll? When some damned fool out hunting saw the bushes move, fired into them, wounded another damned fool hunting. Nova Scotia paper headlined the story, 'Father of Nine Shot. Mistaken for rabbit.' Hey. Nine kids, that's how we knew he was a Catholic. (*Laughs*.) Wish we'd had you around, boy, to beat him to death with a stick.

(MOLLY *has lit a cigarette*.)

Hey girl, come over here. Come on.

(MOLLY *looks at him*.)

Come on, girl. Here, I say.

(MOLLY *goes over to* TEDDY.)

How many's it been, eh? How many seen her smoke, boy? Two hundred, three hundred, since I was laid up – say five, let you off with five, Molly, eh – one – two – three – four – five – (*Smacking at her bottom*.) There, letting you off lightly, eh girl.

(OLIVER'*s face is set*.)

MOLLY: (*Seeing* OLIVER'*s face*) Evie, is there some tea for Oliver?

EVE: (*Gets up*) Come with me, Oliver. (*Goes out, back*.)

TEDDY: Hey boy, something I've been meaning to ask you – that hedge you started, remember seeing you at it on my way to the ditch I fell into – how's it going, got it level?

OLIVER: Well, I've been doing a lot of driving. Haven't had a chance to get back to it yet.

TEDDY: Don't know what you're saying, boy, but I can see from
    your face it's an excuse, where's Mr Goldberg's Alvis, put it
    away?

OLIVER: Sir.

TEDDY: Where?

OLIVER: In the garage, sir.

TEDDY: Give me the keys, boy.

MOLLY: Darling, I did say Oliver could give his dad a run later this
    evening –

TEDDY: The keys. (*Holds out his hand.*)
    (OLIVER *takes the keys out of his pocket, glaring at* TEDDY.)
    That's the boy. Now why don't you go trim the hedge until the
    sun sets – eh? (*Gives him a friendly cuff on the shoulder.*)

MOLLY: But he hasn't had tea –

TEDDY: What? (*Turns around, gives her a malevolent stare.*)

MOLLY: He hasn't – (*Stops.*)

TEDDY: Well? (*Looks at* OLIVER.)
    (OLIVER *turns, blunders into the conservatory.*)
    Hey, just a minute –
    (OLIVER *picking up shears.*)
    There's another thing, don't need you around the house at
    night any more, you can go back to your daddy now, best if
    you move out this evening, eh?
    (OLIVER *stands staring at* TEDDY, *then turns, goes off.*)
    (*Turns.*) Tell you the truth, Moll, don't like him. Foxy little
    face. Have you noticed his foxy little face?

MOLLY: No.

TEDDY: Just what you said when we took him on – furtive, pasty,
    crooked –

EVE: (*Appears at the back*) Oliver's tea is ready.
    (*There is a pause.*)

TEDDY: Oh, hey Eve, that boy, he's not going to be around at night
    – just told him to go home to his daddy.

EVE: Oh.

TEDDY: Come and have one of your dry-as-dust sherries, Evie.
    (*Goes to the cocktail cabinet.*) Things are getting back to rights
    here, going to get Moll to play us one of her tunes in a minute –

EVE: That'll be nice – (*Advancing.*)

MOLLY: (*To* EVE) Would you please leave us. (*Low.*)

TEDDY: What?

> (EVE *goes towards door, left.*)
> Hey, Evie, where are you going?
> (EVE *exits.*)
> What's the matter with her?
> (*There is a pause.*)
> Hey Moll? Hey?
> (*They stare at each other.*)

MOLLY: Why did you do that?

TEDDY: What?

MOLLY: I've never known you humiliate a child before.

TEDDY: What?

MOLLY: Never known you humiliate a child before. (*Loudly, fiercely.*)

TEDDY: Oh. (*Pause.*) Never had one to humiliate before. (*Laughs, then turns, goes and sits down.*)

MOLLY: (*Watches him, then runs to him*) Oh Teddy – what is it, what is it?

> (TEDDY *looks at her, turns his head away, mutters something.*)
> (*Kneels, takes his hand*) You're still not well, you shouldn't be up, darling – please come to bed –

TEDDY: What? What? What? (*Pause.*) Faces are different when they shout at the deaf. Ever thought of that, what I have to see in your faces – swelling, with effort and – contempt. And a little trickle of noise comes out I have to make sense of. Most often I get it wrong. I can see that in your faces too. Bellowing, contempt and boredom. That's all I see on your faces, all there is to see, isn't anything else, I see what's there. Everything. All I have of my own is – is the smell of fish. Fish. Know what's ahead of me – think I don't. I've seen old men. Hate this country of yours. Small and damp like a prison. Shambling, shambling about – cocktail cabinet to armchair, armchair to cocktail cabinet, pyjamas bagging out around the arse, crutch stained with pee dribble, cocktail cabinet to lavatory to armchair, to – to – Eve tucking me in, like I was a kid – teeth out in a glass – and all the time your faces swelling and bellowing, boredom and contempt, hate it, hate it, hate you all – what you've done to me – why didn't you leave me alone, never needed you, don't need you, natter, natter, natter – (*Sits staring ahead*.) Brought me here to die. Know you. Know what you are. (*Sits staring ahead, shrunken and malevolent*.)

MOLLY: Omigod!

TEDDY: What? (*Laughs*.) Ha! Look – there he is – back – look at him – little – (*Gets up, goes over to the conservatory*.) Get up! (OLIVER *rises. He is holding the shears*.)

Hah! You're fired boy! Fired! Mine. Belongs to me. Mr Goldberg's Alvis too – do what I like with her – everything – you're fired, fired – (*Spits into* OLIVER's *face, laughs, turns, goes to chair, sits down with his back to* OLIVER, *looks at* MOLLY, *laughs*.)

(OLIVER *stumbles towards* TEDDY.)

MOLLY: Don't, don't, omigod – don't – don't –

(OLIVER *thrusts the shears into* TEDDY's *neck, again and again.* TEDDY *lurches back, blood spouting*.)

Omigod – omigod – (*Goes to* TEDDY.)

OLIVER: Didn't mean it, didn't mean it, Miss – he made me – made me – what'll I do – (*pause*) Miss!

(OLIVER *drops the shears, turns, runs out through conservatory*.)

MOLLY: (*Looks at* TEDDY) Poor Teddy. Poor old man. (*Pause*.) Omigod! Omigod! (*Goes to him, puts her arms around him*.) Eve! Eeee-eeve! Eee-ve!

(*After a pause,* EVE *enters*.)

Eee-eeve! (*Sees her*.) He's alive, he's still alive, get help you fool! Get help!

(*Lights*.)

SCENE 3

About an hour later. TEDDY's *body has been removed.* GREAVES *and a* PC *are standing, whispering.*

EVE: (*Enters, left*) It's just as I said. She's asleep. Dr Gracey gave her a very strong sedative. There's not the slightest chance you'll be able to see her until the morning.

GREAVES: Then perhaps you'll answer a few questions, Miss Mace.

EVE: I'm afraid I can't. I must get back to Mrs Treadley.

GREAVES: But if she's asleep?

EVE: Dr Gracey asked me to sit by her. She was in a state of shock. And if she wakes –

GREAVES: Miss Mace, I don't quite understand your position in the household.

EVE: I'm – the companion-housekeeper.

GREAVES: I see. And are you the only staff?

EVE: Well, there's a boy from the village, to help with the gardening and drive the car from time to time.

GREAVES: And was he here when the accident happened?

EVE: No. He'd gone home.

GREAVES: So there was just you, and Mr and Mrs Treadley?

EVE: Yes.

GREAVES: And did you see the accident?

EVE: No. I was in the kitchen.

GREAVES: So Mr and Mrs Treadley were alone in here?

EVE: Yes. Now I really must –

GREAVES: Where are the shears?

EVE: The shears?

GREAVES: Dr Gracey said the wound had been caused by gardening shears.

EVE: Oh. Oh yes – they're in there. On the second shelf under the potato sacking.

GREAVES: Why?

EVE: Because that's where they belong.

GREAVES: But they must have been covered in blood.

EVE: Of course they were. I washed it off.

GREAVES: But that was important evidence.

EVE: Evidence of what? It was an accident. Now I really must go to Mrs Treadley – you can come back tomorrow.

MOLLY: (*Enters, in night-dress and dressing-gown*) Ee-eeve – (*Stops.*) Oh, who are you?

EVE: (*Crosses to her*) Molly – you shouldn't be up, you must get back to bed.

MOLLY: Who are they?

GREAVES: Police, Mrs Treadley, I wonder if we could –

EVE: They were just leaving. Now come along –

MOLLY: The police. Oh I'm so glad you've come, I want to make a complaint.

EVE: Molly –

MOLLY: No, darling, I'm going to. About those ambulance men. They were rough – far too rough – I told them to be careful, but one of them pushed me away, yes, actually *pushed* me, didn't he Evie, when I was trying to help them lift him – and then they said he was dead but he wasn't, not until they came and heaved him about and wouldn't let me – he was alive, wasn't he Evie. I know because I held him to see, and I could feel something pumping under his blood, quite strongly, there was life in him and then they came – it must have been them, something they did – and they were very rude too, weren't they, Evie, do you know they refused to let me ride to the hospital with him, my own husband and they refused – so I want to report them, will you report them for me?

GREAVES: I shall certainly question them, Mrs Treadley.

MOLLY: Will you? Oh thank you – thank you, you're very – would you like a drink?

GREAVES: No thank you, Mrs Treadley.

MOLLY: What about you, I'm sure you'd like one, wouldn't you?

GREAVES: We're not allowed to drink on duty, Mrs Treadley.

EVE: Now come my dear – back to bed –

MOLLY: No, no, just a minute, Evie, I'd like a – I can't sleep you know – it's no good – I've tried and tried – you're sure you're not allowed – will you excuse me if I just have a little, teeny weeny – (*Goes to drink.*)

EVE: You really mustn't drink – Dr Gracey gave you a sedative –

MOLLY: Well, it hasn't worked darling, has it, I mean here I am full of beans, God knows what he gave me, unless it was beans of course – (*laughs*) and wasn't he so incompetent, he really was, not that I want to get him into trouble, he's old

and easily upset, all he could do was shake those dreadful
wattles of his, he had no idea, no idea at all. I can't help
thinking if we'd got a younger man Teddy might still be –
someone who could stand up to those ambulance bullies and
– but all poor Gracey could do was shake his wattles and try
to get me to bed, oh – (*laughs*) I don't mean – of course not –
(*stops*) but I don't want to get him into trouble. Certainly not.
He was very good to Teddy's ears. (*There is a pause.*) Oh, I
do feel – feel – drinking by myself – do excuse me, but it's
been a bit of a – a bit of a –

GREAVES: Would you mind telling me how it happened, Mrs
Treadley.

MOLLY: What?

EVE: You can't possibly ask her questions – you can see the state
she's in. Now come, Molly, I insist –

MOLLY: Oh tush tush, Eve, tush, I'm perfectly all right,
perfectly. And I want to – to help these men – now what is it
you – ?

GREAVES: How did it happen, Mrs Treadley?

MOLLY: What?

GREAVES: How was Mr Treadley killed?

EVE: Molly, don't –

MOLLY: But it was an accident. Surely you know – haven't you
told them, Evie, it was nobody's fault – except those men
who were rough and poor old Gracey, it just – just happened
you see, didn't it, Evie?

GREAVES: But Miss Mace wasn't in the room at the time.

MOLLY: What? Oh – no, no, you weren't were you darling, she
generally comes in later, to clean up our messes for us, don't
you darling? (*Laughs.*)

GREAVES: You and Mr Treadley were alone.

MOLLY: What?

GREAVES: There was just you and Mr Treadley.

MOLLY: Oh, yes. Yes, that's right. Me and Mr – Teddy. And the
cocktail cabinet, of course, that's always there, to make a
third.

EVE: Molly – (*goes to her*) don't talk now. Don't talk now.

MOLLY: What, why darling, there's nothing to be afraid of, is there?

GREAVES: No, Mrs Treadley.

MOLLY: You see, it was just an accident. They understand that. That's all there is to it. (*Turns on radio. There is music playing.*)

EVE: Now Molly you're going to come with me –

GREAVES: (*Goes to* EVE, *and very quietly*) Miss Mace! Mrs Treadley has offered to help us in our enquiries. If you persist in interrupting, I shall have to ask you to leave the room.

MOLLY: What? (*Looks at* EVE.)

GREAVES: You were telling us what happened, Mrs Treadley.

MOLLY: Well, it was – something ghastly happened, you see. He had an accident. I – I didn't really see it, my back must have been turned or I was looking away for a moment but – but then there he was. Spurting – spurting – do you see?

GREAVES: One moment he was alive, and the next he was dying?

MOLLY: Yes – well, he had these sudden changes of mood recently, didn't he Evie? (*Laughs.*)

(GREAVES *looks at* MOLLY. *There is a pause.*)

Just a minute – need to – another little – a truth drink so you'll know I – (*Laughs, going to pour herself another drink, unsteady on her feet.*)

EVE: (*Goes over*) No, Molly – no – (*Attempts to take the bottle from her.*)

(*There is a short, absurd wrestle.*)

MOLLY: Bugger off, bitch!

(EVE *recoils.*)

Sorry Evie – sorry. Forgive please. Pretty please with sugar on it. (*Laughs, pours, then to* GREAVES.) That's all I have to say –

EVE: (*To* GREAVES) This is disgraceful, disgraceful. I'm going to phone Dr Gracey and tell him –

GREAVES: That's your privilege, Miss.

MOLLY: What, she's got a pash on me, haven't you, Evie – (EVE *exits, left.*)

MOLLY: Yes, she has, do you know about the pashes ladies have on ladies, ladies like her on ladies like me, are you married?

GREAVES: Yes.

MOLLY: Is she pretty, your wife?

GREAVES: (*Crosses to the radio, turns it off. Silence, then intimately*) You were going to tell me the truth, Mrs Treadley.

MOLLY: What?

GREAVES: The truth.

MOLLY: What about?

GREAVES: Your husband's death. He was murdered, wasn't he?

MOLLY: Murdered? (*Pause. She yawns.*) I'm sorry – sorry – what?

GREAVES: Did you do it?

MOLLY: What?

GREAVES: You did, didn't you?

MOLLY: What – what do you do to people, when you – you catch them?

GREAVES: That's for the courts to decide.

MOLLY: But if they're children?

GREAVES: But there aren't any children, are there, Mrs Treadley?

MOLLY: Oh yes. Yes. We're all children in this house, all of us. That's what caused it, you see. But nobody meant – oh please believe – it wasn't meant. He – he brought it on himself! He did! He did! An old man, come to the end, he wanted to die, he wanted to – full of hate – I couldn't bear his hate – and he knew – you see he knew – he was right, about his old man's smells, his deafness and the boredom, the boredom and the bellowing and the contempt and the pee-dribble and his pyjamas arsing – and – and –

GREAVES: And is that why you killed him, Mrs Treadley?

MOLLY: What?

GREAVES: Did you kill him?

MOLLY: I –

(*Pause.*)

EVE: (*Enters*) I've spoken to Dr Gracey. He's coming over –

MOLLY: It was her! She did it! She did it! (*Pause.*) No, no, sorry Evie, sorry darling – it was me. Yes. I killed him. I killed him. I took the things and I – I – (*Makes thrusting movements,*

stops abruptly.) And now you all hate me, don't you, like the ambulance and Gracey and all – all hate me – well, here I am, look at me you – you – (*runs to* PC) what do you see, an old vamp, is that what you see, but you'd roger me, too, wouldn't you, I could make you love – I'm still – look – look (*Makes to lift her night-dress to him.*)
(EVE *strides across, grips* MOLLY *by the arm, pulls her away.* MOLLY *collapses against* EVE.)
Bed now, Evie, bed please. Bed darling –
(*Lights.*)

SCENE 4

Some months later. Afternoon. The room fills with light, steadily, to bright sunlight. There are dust sheets over the sofa, the chairs. On the sofa, Molly's scarf, handbag. The door, left, is open.
EVE *enters from the left, wearing a light raincoat. She goes to the handbag, begins to go through it.* MOLLY *appears at the door, back. She is also wearing a light coat. She stands watching* EVE, *then comes across, takes the handbag from her.*

MOLLY: Thank you, darling. I do wish people would stop rummaging through it, it's been emptied and refilled by so many different ladies recently, police ladies, prison ladies, hospital ladies, (*takes out a cigarette*) it doesn't feel mine any more. (*Lights cigarette.*) What were you looking for, darling? The sleeping pills?

EVE: I couldn't remember whether we'd brought them.

MOLLY: Do you need them, though? Surely we don't mind being awake on an August afternoon? (*Takes a bottle out of the pocket.*) Do you want to look after them?

EVE: No, of course not, Moll.

MOLLY: Oh, you might as well, darling. I'm not going to try again. For one thing, I don't seem to be very good at it, and I do hate the way they drag one back, with stomach pumps and sermons. Do take them, darling. There.

EVE: (*Takes them*) I'll make up a bed if you still want to lie down.

MOLLY: Lie down?

EVE: You said you had a headache.

MOLLY: Did I? Well then it's gone.

EVE: Oh. Oh good! Well, what about our walk then?

MOLLY: Our walk?

EVE: You were looking forward to a walk.

MOLLY: I think I'll leave it until tomorrow. (*Pause.*) To tell you the truth, darling, I'm a bit confused at finding everything so familiar.

EVE: It's my fault. I shouldn't have agreed to let you come back – at least so soon.

MOLLY: So soon? But I haven't been here for a long time. After such an eventful spring, and a summer wasted in – in institutions – I'd have hated to have missed the old haunts in their autumn colours. I long to see them.

EVE: You do want a walk then?

MOLLY: What do you want, Evie?

EVE: (*Intensely*) I want our old Moll back again.

MOLLY: Do you really? Our old judge found the old Moll a trifle too degenerate for his taste. Quite disgusting, in fact. Quite disgusting. Disgusting.

EVE: He had no right – no right to say those things. They had no right to make you go through that trial, not after – after the truth had come out. I shall never believe in British justice again.

MOLLY: Poor Eve! Still, think what we would have lost. The sight of old Treefe, for example, touching his forelock to thank everyone for all the trouble they were putting themselves to, to hang his son. Who's only just come of hangable age. (*Pause.*) Can I have a drink? No – no more drinks for me.

EVE: You must stop blaming yourself, Molly. You stood by him right to the bitter end.

MOLLY: Not quite, darling. His bitter end comes on Monday week, at six in the morning, isn't it? He's going to that without me. (*Pause.*) Looking across as if he believed I could just come out of my box and into his, and cuddle him through it. His peaky face, and the spot blooming on his nose. Do you think he'll expect me on Monday week, too, right to the very last, as a child expects his Mummy to come and take him away. (*Turns away.*) I'd have made a good mother, wouldn't I?

EVE: He did do it, Moll.

MOLLY: Of course he did. (*Pause, makes a violent gesture.*) So hang the little beggar! By the way, darling, I haven't thanked you properly for bringing him to book. Thank you. If it hadn't been for you –

EVE: I couldn't let you sacrifice yourself. I couldn't, Moll.

MOLLY: No. No. I don't suppose you could.

EVE: We have to do right by those we care about.

MOLLY: Yes. Yes we do. You love me Evie, don't you?

EVE: Yes.

MOLLY: Thank you.

EVE: Oh Moll – (*Gives a sudden shy smile.*)

MOLLY: It *is* a lovely afternoon, isn't it? Would you like a walk?

EVE: I'd love one.

MOLLY: Right. Off you go then.

(*They stare at each other.*)

Darling, we really must start doing our separate wants, or how shall we two live together? Please go darling. (*Pause.*) Please.

(EVE *exits through conservatory.*)

(*After a pause*) Pretty please (*pause*) with sugar on it.

(*Lights. Curtain.*)

Pig in a Poke

Pig in a Poke was first shown on London Weekend Television in 1969. The cast was as follows:

GRIEG	Colin Blakely
WENDY	Jennifer Hilary
STEPHEN	John Steiner
MRS WYCHERLEY	Joan Benham
MR WYCHERLEY	John Harvey
AMANDA	Jane Bond
LEARY	Donald Sumpter
MR HUGGLE	Clifford Cox
VERONICA	Meg Ritchie
MCGONNIGAL	David Engers
Director	James McTaggart
Designer	John Clements
Producer	Kenith Trodd

EXT. HOUSE

Shots of house in various stages of being for sale and then sold.
Credits.

INT. THE BEDROOM

WENDY, *fully dressed, goes to the chest of drawers, opens one drawer.*
It is piled strikingly high with underwear. She shuts the drawer, opens
the one underneath it. It is piled high with gloves. Takes out a pair,
goes towards the door, stops, goes back to the chest of drawers, puts
first pair back in, takes out another pair, goes out, down the stairs to
the living room. Picks up a letter from the desk, on down the stairs.
The kitchen door is open, get a glimpse into it. She hesitates for a
moment, then goes to the door facing it. Opens it. In contrast to the rest
of the house, it is just as it was when it was being inspected. She
hesitates a second before Grieg's door, then knocks, calls out:
WENDY: Hello, Mr Grieg?
>   (*The door opens.* GRIEG *is standing in vest and jeans, a mug of*
>   *tea in his hand. He nods, holds the door wider, for* WENDY *to*
>   *pass.*)
>   Um, we phoned the builders yesterday, it seems that they
>   can come back next week to (*glances around*) put the finishing
>   touches . . .
GRIEG: (*Nods, holds up his mug*) Would you like some tea?
WENDY: Um, no thank you. Really. (*Smiles.*) So we were just
>   wondering what your plans were? (*Puts her hand on the table.*)
GRIEG: (*Blandly*) Thank you.
WENDY: Um, I mean, you said something about leaving?
GRIEG: Yes?
WENDY: Do you know when exactly? Because then we could tell
>   the men when they could come in, precisely.
GRIEG: Soon. (*Takes a gulp of tea.*)
WENDY: But you don't know more definitely than that? (*More*

*sharply, lifts her hand up, blinks, looks quickly down at her
glove, which is covered with a stain.*)

GRIEG: No. I haven't finished here yet.

WENDY: Finished what?

(GRIEG *shrugs.*)

(*After a pause*) Only you *did* say that you'd be gone (*laughs
pointedly*) and we were rather banking (*stops, looks at him*).
But it will be soon?

(GRIEG *smiles, little pause, then turns, goes into the kitchen.
WENDY watches in confusion. He comes out holding a pair of
secateurs and a cloth, puts the mug down and begins to wipe at
the secateurs.*)

It will be soon?

GRIEG: Soon, yes.

WENDY: Well thank you Mr Grieg. (*Turns, goes out.*)

(GRIEG *stands by the door, staring after her. Sound of WENDY
on the stairs, then a stumbling noise, a sudden exclamation.*)

GRIEG: (*Blandly*) All right?

WENDY: It's so – (*extremely irritated*) dark out here.

GRIEG: Oh, it is.

WENDY: Yes it is.

(GRIEG *smiles. Sounds of WENDY going up the stairs, and cut
to:*)

EXT.

*Front door opens, WENDY steps out, clearly still irritated. Slams the
door, then looks down at her glove, then at her stocking, and cut to:*

INT.

GRIEG *at the basement window, lifting back a soiled lace curtain and
seeing WENDY, with her ankle raised, and then as WENDY goes down
the path, out on his face, and cut to:*

EXT. A STREET IN HAMPSTEAD

WENDY *passes a shop window, display of lingerie, etc. She hesitates, makes to go by, then turns, goes in, looking at her watch as she does so. See* WENDY *through the window, buying. She comes out of the shop carrying her purchases in chic bags.*

INT. PUB

The pub is fairly crowded, and cut to the packages, on a chair, and STEPHEN *and* WENDY *at a table. Drinks in front of them.*

WENDY: I don't believe he's got the slightest intention of going.

STEPHEN: (*Vaguely, he is glancing around the pub*) I suppose we'll have to do something.

WENDY: He's utterly filthy. He contaminates the whole house.

STEPHEN: No, he's not very wholesome – which reminds me, it's going to be Amanda after all. Amanda and the up-and-come-and-shove-your-face-in-it Leary. (*Looking around again*) They're meant to be meeting me here, all of them. What intrigues me is I'm sure I heard something recently about the two of them, Amanda and Leary. The question is whether it's something useful, oh, here he is. (*In a low voice. Louder*) There you are.

WENDY *looks at him confused, then looks around. A man, young, bearded and scruffy, is standing in front of them, holding a script.*)

LEARY: (*North Country accent. Looks at* WENDY) Hello.

STEPHEN: Um, darling. This is Leo Leary. Wendy, my wife.

LEARY: I thought it must be, you look so alike.

STEPHEN: Is Amanda with you?

LEARY: Not quite. She's showing herself off by the door. (*Looks over towards the door.*)

(*Cut to* AMANDA *who detaches herself from someone not clearly seen, drifts over to the table. She is also carrying a script.*)

AMANDA: Hello. (*Smiles and nods at* WENDY.)

STEPHEN: Darling, Amanda Gracely. What do you think of it?

(AMANDA *rolls her eyes, pinches her nostrils.*)

LEARY: (*In a flat, expressionless voice reading from script*) My dear lady, we ought to have exchanged teething rings in the registry office, or perhaps one of those ebony do-dahs in the shape of our respective throats, because that's what we spend our time sinking our respective bridge-work into. Oh Christ. A kind of Glaswegian Noël Coward.

AMANDA: Oh Christ, especially as I've just left him. So he might be in hearing-range.

STEPHEN: Oh Christ, has he turned up. I'd better go and have a word. (*Gets up, goes over to the corner.*)

LEARY: (*To* WENDY) What do *you* do?

WENDY: (*Shrugs, smiles*) Exist.

LEARY: If you ask the house-fly the meaning of its existence, it would soon cease to exist.

AMANDA: (*To* LEARY) What's the meaning of your existence? (*Little pause, smiles.*) Now how long do I have to wait? (*To* WENDY) We're all thanking God Stephen's on this.

LEARY: (*Neutrally, looking at* WENDY) Yes, he seems to have got it all.

WENDY: He thinks you're both going to be marvellous. Actually, um (*gets up, picks up her bags*), I've got to go. (*Little pause.*) Goodbye.

(*Shot of her crossing the room, with her bags, towards* STEPHEN. *Seen from* LEARY's *point of view.* STEPHEN *is talking to a small man, carrying a briefcase. Then cut to the man –* MCGONNIGAL, *the author, talking.*)

MCGONNIGAL: No, I've seen him once or twice in those North Country things, where he falls down drunk or gets into punch-ups, but I'm just wondering if he's going to catch the style. I mean, he looks a bit short on that.

STEPHEN: Oh, he's thoroughly grotty, but it doesn't matter because (*smiles*) *I've* got the style. And it's covered far worse than him. But you don't have to torment yourself by turning up at readings, rehearsals, etc. if you don't want – oh, hello darling. You off? (*As* WENDY *nods.*) I'm just having a word with our author, the one man we can't do without.

(WENDY *nods, smiles.* STEPHEN *bends forward, slightly self-consciously, they kiss. Cut to* LEARY *watching as* WENDY *goes to the door, and then to* STEPHEN *looking at* LEARY *with a knowing little smile, and:*)

INT.

A small, cramped office. Three desks. Telephone on one of the desks. Behind this desk a middle-aged man is sitting. He is plump and bearded. Come in on his face.

MR HUGGLE: (*Tugs at his beard*) Um . . . have you done anything like it before?

WENDY: (*Voice over, not yet seen, slight rustlings*) Well, you know, just standing on street corners – and shaking my tin. (*Laughs awkwardly.*) And then once at Oxford I was driven out in a, well, sort of bikini thing. (*Long pause as* MR HUGGLE *nods, waits.*) Well, you know, standing on a taxi and saluting and (*laughs*) caught coins. (*Another pause.*) But still, (*voice earnest*) it was *for* something, I suppose . . .

MR HUGGLE: Well, we're for something. I expect Gwen's told you. (*Solicitously.*) Do you mind muck?

WENDY: (*Cut to her face for the first time. She is sitting opposite the desk, her legs close together, the chic bags, from which the rustlings on her lap, and her hand pressed down on top of the bags*). No really. (*Leans forward, more rustlings.*) I'd love to try it. (*Very intensely.*) I really want to, I mean, there are so many people who need, well, help.

MR HUGGLE: (*Worried*) Yes, yes, there are.
(*Cut to:*)

INT. KITCHEN

Carry WENDY's *face over immediately from the last scene, but bent, absorbed. Then down on various articles from the carrier bags spread out. Picks up a pair of knickers, the bra, her expression odd, the*

*telephone rings. She gives a start, as if coming out of a trance, picks
the telephone up. It is fastened to the wall.*)
WENDY: Hello. (*Little pause.*) Sorry, who? Oh – (*Carefully*) Hello.
    Yes, of course I do, we met at lunch-time, you're in
    Stephen's play. Stephen's not back yet. I'm afraid, the last
    time I saw him was with you and Amanda, shall I get him to
    – (*Pause.*) No, I'm afraid that's um, I can't. (*Little pause.*)
    No, I'm sorry, I don't think it would be a good idea.
    Goodbye.
    (*Puts the telephone down, looks at the underwear, picks up the
    bra and pants, suddenly turns her head sharply. GRIEG's face at
    the door, as he passes. He smiles, goes on down the corridor.
    WENDY shoves the underwear into the carrier bag and turns
    determinedly to the stove, and stirs something in a saucepan.*)

DINING-ROOM ADJOINING THE KITCHEN

*The table with the wine bottle on it, remains of a consumed meal also
on it. WENDY's father is at the head of the table. WENDY beside him.
WENDY's mother sits opposite, but in fact closer to STEPHEN at the
other end. There is a slight gap, in other words, between the two
couples. STEPHEN is smoking a cheroot. MR WYCHERLEY has in his
mouth a large, unlighted cigar. But come in first on STEPHEN
speaking.*

STEPHEN: The trick is to keep them on the boil for as long as I
    need them, for instance, I was telling Wendy, Leary had or
    might still be failing to have or would like to get out of
    something or other with Amanda and it's part of my job to
    find out exactly what and use it in the performances. The
    author on the other hand just haunts around hoping to be
    noticed, which he politely isn't, which is also part of my job,
    in other words it's a matter of oiling here and jarring there
    and hoping it'll turn into a – (*gestures*) – something chemical.
MRS WYCHERLEY: Darling Stephen (*include in this exchange MR
    WYCHERLEY's handsome and cynical face*), you're terribly
    good at that, it must be nice to do it to such glam people.

STEPHEN: They're the most boring people in the world, simply the most boring. Absolutely unreal.

MRS WYCHERLEY: (*As* WENDY *and* STEPHEN *exchange little private smiles*) Oh, don't say that, just like everybody else you mean?

STEPHEN: Oh worse, much worse, aren't they darling?

WENDY: Are they, darling? (*Innocently.*)

STEPHEN: Yes, they really are.

MRS WYCHERLEY: (*With an air of triumph*) But I thought they were all meant to be so camp. (*Daringly.*)

WENDY: (*Lights her father's cigar during this*) All right then? (*In a low voice.*)

MR WYCHERLEY: (*Pulling on cigar*) All right then. (*In a low voice.*)

STEPHEN: Oh some of them are. Camply boring. Which is worse than butchly boring.

MRS WYCHERLEY: (*Her eyes go to* WENDY *and* MR WYCHERLEY, *away again.*) The only thing is Stephen, I do hope it's not going to be one of those grubby pieces about illigits, and disinfectants and hospitals and coloured what-nots, don't you, darling?

MR WYCHERLEY: (*To* WENDY) I pass.

WENDY: I should think you do.

STEPHEN: Oh no, it's going to be terribly stylish. I've promised.

MR WYCHERLEY: (*Abruptly*) How's your sitting tenant?

STEPHEN: What? (*Glances at* WENDY.) Grieg? Yes, well actually he's still sitting. (*Little pause.*) Really, he's quite a character, in his way.

WENDY: He's an extremely filthy character, and so is his way.

MRS WYCHERLEY: There you are, just like one of your plays.

MR WYCHERLEY: (*With quiet authority*) I'd get rid of him, if I were you. You could always buy him out.

STEPHEN: Yes. (*Nods, glances at* WENDY.) Anyway, we'll think of something.

(*There is a pause.*)

MRS WYCHERLEY: What is exactly butch, darling?

(*Cut very directly to:* STEPHEN *full shot, in an apron, wiping a*

dish, and beside him MRS WYCHERLEY *washing up, and then,*
through the open door, from STEPHEN's *point of view, shot of*
WENDY *and* MR WYCHERLEY, WENDY's *hand over*
MR WYCHERLEY's, *her voice very low and intimate.*)

WENDY: (*Just heard*) You're looking very well.

MR WYCHERLEY: Am I?

(*Come in on:*)

WENDY: Pleasingly prosperous.

MR WYCHERLEY: But I expect I'm due to lose a little weight.
How much?

WENDY: Terribly little, daddy. Three hundred pounds? For the
decorators and other thieves.

MR WYCHERLEY: I'll make it four, on condition that this isn't the
last time. It'll be in the post tomorrow. (*Stares at* WENDY,
smiles.) All right, then.

WENDY: All right then. (*Smiles.*) Butch.

STEPHEN: (*Puts his head through the door*) Darling, is there
another drying-up cloth?

INT. THE BEDROOM

WENDY *comes into the bedroom, picks up the carrier bag, as from*
below sounds of Vivaldi. She opens the bag, peers in. Takes out a
couple of garments, looks at herself in the mirror over the bed.
Suddenly the Vivaldi stops, sounds of a door opening, closing,
WENDY *thrusts the stuff back into the bag, puts it down by the bed,*
begins to unbutton her blouse as STEPHEN *comes in. He looks at her.*

STEPHEN: I didn't hear you come up. (*He is carrying his briefcase.*
He opens it, looks in. Little pause.) You haven't told me.

WENDY: What?

STEPHEN: What he said.

WENDY: About what?

STEPHEN: About the – you know – loan? (*Turns around.*)

WENDY: Oh. (*Little pause.*) There'll be a cheque in the post
tomorrow.

STEPHEN: Oh? How much.

WENDY: Three hundred.

STEPHEN: (*Clearly slightly disappointed*) Great. (*Shuts the briefcase.*) He's sending it to you?

WENDY: I'll make another one out to you. Now, if you want.

STEPHEN: OK. (*Stares at her, smiles, comes over, sits down at her feet.*) Are you all right, then?

WENDY: Perfectly.

STEPHEN: (*Smiling knowingly up at her*) And what about Hump-them-as-soon-as-look-at-them Leary?

WENDY: (*Slight pause*) Leary?

STEPHEN: He didn't phone?

WENDY: Why should he?

STEPHEN: It's his method – or so I gather, from bits of gossip and pieces of rumours.

WENDY: Perhaps he doesn't fancy me.

STEPHEN: Oh, he fancies you all right. The real problem, though, is does he still or did he ever fancy Amanda.

WENDY: Wouldn't it be worse if the problem was me? (*As STEPHEN puts his hand on her knee, then slides it up under her skirt.*)

STEPHEN: Oh, I can handle you. At least, I'd know what was going on. (WENDY *gets up, goes across the room.*) Where are you going? (*Smiling.*)

WENDY: To have a bath, of course.

STEPHEN: Oh. (*Pulls out the bag, against which he has been pressing.*) What is in here? (*Fishes in, pulls out a pair of knickers.*) Mmmmmm.

WENDY: (*Turns, looks at them, him*) Be careful. (*Sharply*) I don't want them crumpled.

THE CHARITY OFFICE

GWEN, *tall and dark, handsome, Australian accent, and* VERONICA, *small girl, strained manner.* WENDY *at the end of the desk, writing down items in a book.* MR HUGGLE *at the other desk, is on the telephone. But come in on* (*having cut directly from* WENDY'*s*

knickers) an undefinable but filthy garment, being held by GWEN.
Then cut to VERONICA, *and then to* WENDY. *She looks at the
garment, then looks quickly away.*

VERONICA: (*Matter of factly*) Men's knickers.

GWEN: (*Drops them on top of clothes pile at* WENDY's *foot, which she
    moves.*) Men's knickers. C column darling, I think. (*As*
    WENDY *writes*) We ought to send them back.

VERONICA: (*Digging in again*) Who to? You don't think they own
    up, do you?

GWEN: (*As another object comes out*) It *can't* be!

VERONICA: Oh, we used to get masses of those, in Kilburn.

WENDY: (*Looking up*) What?

GWEN: A nappy, my dear, straight, by the smell of it, from baby's
    bum. There isn't a column for this one – put it down under
    miscellaneous.
    (*Cut to:*)

MR HUGGLE: (*His voice rising to audibility*) No, no I do see that
    and we *are* grateful for any interest, Mrs Jellybein, but I
    think that a local jumble sale is the best place – a church fête
    – (*Little pause.*) a synagogue fête then? (*Laughs.*) Oh, I'm
    sorry, I didn't mean – I'll certainly try and think of
    somewhere to place it. Goodbye.

VERONICA: What was it?

MR HUGGLE: A bone-china tea-set. In shards, I suspect. (*Watches
    as* VERONICA *pulls out another garment.*)

VERONICA: Vest.

GWEN: (*To* WENDY) You'll have gathered by now that we're the
    most chi-chi tip in town. (*Takes the garment from* VERONICA,
    drops it in one of the piles at WENDY's *foot.*)

VERONICA: They mean well.

GWEN: (*Take in* MR HUGGLE, *sitting with his hand to his forehead.*)
    What would we get if they meant badly then?

MR HUGGLE: (*Stands up, clears his throat*) I've got to go and chat
    up a lady who's talking cash, um, Veronica, would you mind
    coming along?
    (VERONICA *gets up, slightly self-consciously, goes out, followed
    by* MR HUGGLE, *who turns, nods at the other two, closes the*

door. *There is a silence.* GWEN *picks up another piece of clothing,
throws it onto one of the piles.*)
GWEN: He's married, the poor sweeties.
WENDY: Oh.
GWEN: They probably have to make do with the back of his van.

INT. THE FIRST-FLOOR ROOMS

*Furnished, decorated very elegantly. The hi-fi set is on, a Barcelona
chair, on which* STEPHEN *is sitting, smoking a cheroot. He is wearing
his dark glasses, perched on the end of his nose. He has his briefcase on
his lap, and is doing some blocking on a square of paper. He puts the
briefcase down, gets up, nodding his head slightly in time to the music.
The camera follows him, across the hall, up a few stairs, goes into a
door, glimpse of an extremely elegant little lavatory with a rug on the
floor, little stick of deodorant, a stool beside the lavatory with a book
on it. Shuts the door, little pause to music, luxurious flushing sound,
comes out, nodding his head to the music, waits as it comes to climax,
conducts the last few bars, brings arms down in a majestic sweep as the
music stops, then turns the handle of the bathroom door. Pushes. The
door doesn't open.*
STEPHEN: Darling? (*Waits. No reply.*) Darling?
(*Puts his ear to the keyhole, tries the door again, faint gurgling-
water sounds from within. From below the music starts again. He
turns around, goes down, enters the living-room.* WENDY *is
turning away from the hi-fi.*)
Oh there you are. (*Slightly apprehensive, goes to his armchair,
sits down, picks up his briefcase and blocking paper.*) Where've
you been?
WENDY: (*Sardonically*) Washing up.
STEPHEN: Oh. (*Little pause.*) Sorry, I'm just working out my
campaign to keep Amanda's tits, Leary's profile and
McGonnigal's camera instructions off screen.
(*Bends over the paper, and shot of him from* WENDY'S *point of
view. She gives a little smile at him. Goes over to the bookcase.*
STEPHEN *looks up towards her. Licks his lips slightly. She takes*

a book down, goes towards the door, followed by STEPHEN.)
(*Slightly*) Where are you going?
WENDY: To have a bath. (*They look at each other.*) You get on with
your campaign in peace. (*Calmly. Goes out.*)
(STEPHEN *stares at the door, then looks down at his paper,
slowly begins to move his head to the music, and cut to:*)

INT. THE BATHROOM DOOR

GRIEG *comes out, fully dressed, his hair slicked back, looking
unnaturally groomed. Hears a sound above, looks up.* WENDY, *in her
pants and bra, comes down the stairs, as* GRIEG *steps back into the
bathroom. She goes past the door, into the living-room.*

INT. LIVING-ROOM

STEPHEN *looks up as* WENDY *comes in, smiles at her, pretends to look
down at his paper again, then looks up covertly as* WENDY *goes to the
bookcase, puts book back, runs her hand along the shelf. He stares at
her, and cut to* GRIEG, *at the door, staring impassively at* WENDY.
WENDY *moves along, looking at book titles.*
STEPHEN: What are you looking for?
WENDY: Nothing really.
   (*This seen from* GRIEG'S *point of view, then cut to* WENDY *as she
   takes down a book, looks at* STEPHEN, *who stares back at her,
   transfixed. She turns, goes to the door,* STEPHEN *watches her,
   then frowns, runs the dark glasses up and down his nose, bends
   over the paper. Cut to* WENDY *going up stairs, from* GRIEG'S
   point of view a few steps down the next flight.)
   (*Voice over from above*) Stephen! (*More shrilly.*) Stephen!
STEPHEN: (*Comes running out of the living-room*) What? (*In a
   panic.*) What? (*Runs up to the bathroom.*)
WENDY: Look at it. Just look at it!
STEPHEN: (*Also voice over*) Christ!
   (*Cut to:*)

WENDY: (*Coming out of the bathroom, her face set, goes back upstairs to the bedroom, comes out again almost at once.*) Go down and have it out with him. The pig.

STEPHEN: (*Comes out of the bathroom, hesitates*) He's gone out.

WENDY: How do you know?

STEPHEN: I heard him.

(WENDY *turns, goes back to the bedroom.* STEPHEN *goes into the bathroom. She comes out again almost at once.*)

WENDY: That's the limit, when he starts leaving his scum in our bath for me to sit in.

(STEPHEN, *unseen, mutters something.*)

What? (*Shrilly.*)

(STEPHEN *comes to the door, holding package of Vim.* WENDY *turns, stubs her toe.*)

Ooooh! Christ! (*Limps into the bedroom, muttering viciously.*)

STEPHEN: You all right, darling? (*Stands for a moment, then goes back into the bathroom.*)

(*Cut to* GRIEG. *He turns, goes down the stairs. Then cut to* WENDY, *she is sitting on the edge of the bed, her hands clasped between her knees.* STEPHEN *comes into the room. She looks up at him blankly.*)

I've got it all off.

WENDY: I spend the day among filthy garments worn by filthy people, and I come back home to find I'm expected to sit in a filthy bath.

STEPHEN: Darling, don't be depressed. (*Goes over to her, kneels down in front of her.*)

WENDY: Why not?

STEPHEN: (*Shrugs, smiles*) It makes *me* depressed when you're depressed.

WENDY: Does it?

STEPHEN: Yes, it does.

WENDY: (*Smiles, a ghastly radiant smile*) Does it make you radiant, when I'm radiant?

STEPHEN: (*Stares up at her, gets up*) Thank you. (*Coldly.*)

WENDY: That's all right. (*Little pause.*) Daddy warned us.

STEPHEN: (*After a little pause*) That's true. And very constructive.

He didn't actually tell us how to go about it, though, did he?
Except to buy him off with money we haven't got.

WENDY: We could always borrow it from him couldn't we?
(*Sarcastically.*)

STEPHEN: What the hell's the matter with you? (*Slight shrill.*)

WENDY: (*Looks at him*) Is it really so hard for you to understand?
I just don't like the way that pig is turning our house into his
personal trough. He makes me feel sick. Can't you
understand that? Can't you really? Can't you really
understand that? (*Glares at* STEPHEN.) Also you didn't hear
him go out. You were just fobbing me off because you're too
nice or something to go down and do anything about it.

STEPHEN: I *did* hear him go out, excuse me.

WENDY: (*Suddenly calm, shakes her head*) You did not.

STEPHEN: (*Slaps his arm against his side, shakes his head*) I *did* hear
him go out.
(WENDY *stares at him, smiles, shrugs.* STEPHEN *turns, goes to
the door, flings it open. Follow him down the stairs, running.
Come to the bottom hall as* GRIEG *advances up it, dressed to go
out.* STEPHEN *does a sort of jig backwards and to the side, to let*
GRIEG *pass.* GRIEG *waits calmly.*)
Ooooops, sorry. (*Gives a little laugh.*)

GRIEG: That's all right. (*Goes on down the hall.*)
(STEPHEN *goes into the kitchen,* GRIEG *goes out,* STEPHEN
reappears, goes up the stairs and cut to WENDY *sitting on the edge
of the bed.* STEPHEN *stands at the bedroom door, then comes in.*)

STEPHEN: (*Triumphantly*) I told you. He's gone out.

INT. MORNING

WENDY *comes down the stairs, into the hall, dressed to go out. She
stands before* GRIEG'S *door, hesitates, then opens the door, looks down
the stairs, shuts the door, turns.* GRIEG *is just coming through the front
door. She glances at him quickly, then goes into the kitchen, as if she
hadn't seen him. Goes to the sink. Stiffens slightly, turns around.*
GRIEG *is standing at the kitchen door.*

GRIEG: Looking for me?

WENDY: (*Slight hesitation*) Um, oh, Mr Grieg, good morning, yes, I was just wondering, did my husband speak to you before he went this morning? (GRIEG *shakes his head.*) Oh. (*Little pause.*) I know he wanted to. (*Little pause.*) About the bath, actually. (GRIEG *tilts his head enquiringly.*) Yes, my husband and I (*stops in recognition*) we just feel that the bath isn't in your part of the house, frankly.

GRIEG: (*Nods*) You feel that?

WENDY: (*Very sharply*) So *if* you don't mind, could you *not* use it in future without at least asking us first and would you also do us the favour of cleaning it out afterwards *if* it *is* all right for you to use it, please. (*Long pause.*) Is that understood?

GRIEG: (*Nods*) Yes, I understand that.

WENDY: Good. Thank you.

(*Turns to the sink, turns on the tap, come in on her face, the tap running. She picks up a cup and saucer, holds them under the tap, on her face an expression of tension. She turns the tap off, as she does so she gives a jump, her eyes widen. Continues to stare ahead as sound of footsteps crossing the floor.*)

INT. THE REHEARSAL ROOM

Come in immediately on STEPHEN, *observed from the door, back to camera. He is making gestures with his arms and hips, very effeminate.* LEARY *and* AMANDA *are in front of him, making them back to him. Various people scattered about, drinking coffee, reading.* MCGONNIGAL *is seated at a large table by the wall, writing into an exercise book. Then* WENDY *moves forward into camera, uncertainly. Steps sideways, sits down some distance from* MCGONNIGAL. *He looks at her, nods and smiles in recognition. She nods back, watches intensely.* STEPHEN *has taken* AMANDA *by her shoulders and is doing his effeminate dance with her.* LEARY *comes over to* WENDY, *sits down beside her.*

LEARY: (*In a low voice*) I suppose Stephen asked you if I'd phoned?

185

WENDY: (*Staring straight ahead*) Yes.

LEARY: And did you tell him? (*In a low voice. Pause.* WENDY *remains staring ahead.*) Don't you think I've got enough style for you? (*Little pause.*) Well, Stephen's going to give me some of his.

(WENDY *turns, looks at* STEPHEN, *cut to him. He circles effeminately around* AMANDA, *sees her, stops, says something to* AMANDA, *comes over.*)

STEPHEN: Darling, what are you doing here?

WENDY: Can I speak to you for a minute, please?

AMANDA: (*Coming behind* STEPHEN) Now we can get the real story about Mr Grieg's bath.

(WENDY *looks at* STEPHEN, *who smiles fleetingly, embarrassed.*)

LEARY: Apparently you think some people don't rate baths.

WENDY: What? (*Looks at* STEPHEN *again.*)

AMANDA: The talcum powder bit's gorgeous.

WENDY: Talcum powder?

AMANDA: (*To* STEPHEN) I knew you were lying. *His* version is that your Grieg or whatever was poncing about the house in your talc and a finger-tip or two of your best scent behind the ears.

STEPHEN: (*Smiles falsely*) What I *actually* said was . . .

AMANDA: And Leary's furious because Yorkshire coal-miners don't get talc and scents on the National Health, or their sons don't. Or he doesn't. Or someone doesn't; anyway he's furious about it. It seems they're betraying the working classes again, and RADA boys with surly faces (*leans over* LEARY, *puts her arm around his neck*), doesn't it, darling? (LEARY *straightens, tries to look up into her face, says something that makes* AMANDA *tighten her expression and then, smiling, her grip around his throat.* LEARY *attempts to break free with his shoulders. After a second* AMANDA *steps away.*)

WENDY: (*Gets up,* STEPHEN *walks beside her towards the door*) Why did you tell them about the bath?

STEPHEN: What? No reason. It was just coffee and camping-up time before we started, one invents these things, you know.

(*Little pause.*) What's the matter? I mean, why aren't you at
    work?

WENDY: (*After a pause, shrugs*) I just wanted to see you.

STEPHEN: (*Blankly*) Oh. Great. You all right?

WENDY: Perfectly.

STEPHEN: Actually there's so much strange sex in the atmosphere
    here, I'd better not walk you to the tube. I'm beginning to
    think the key to a sane life is to go in for charity work. Oh
    Christ. (*Looking past her to* MCGONNIGAL, *who is approaching
    rapidly.*) Our bloody author, he's never been to bed with –
    (*Points a finger.*) Tim. Hello.

MCGONNIGAL: Could you spare me a moment, Stephen. There
    are a few notes I've jotted down.
    (*Cut to:*)

EXT. SHOP

WENDY *in lingerie shop.*

INT. THE HALL

WENDY *comes through the front door, packages clasped tight to her
chest as she struggles to get the key back into her handbag. Suddenly
stares ahead.* GRIEG *is bearing down on her. She strives to move out of
the way, packages slip, a few pieces of underwear (white) scatter to the
floor. She tries to crouch to pick them up.* GRIEG *watches, looking
down at her, and cut to her face, frantic, embarrassed, as she
scrambles the pieces together, stands up.* GRIEG *steps past her, smiles
into her face, goes out.* WENDY *stands for a moment, then hurries
blindly along to the kitchen, drops the packages on the table, still
clinging unconsciously to a pair of white knickers. Stands for a
moment, then goes to the telephone, dials. A little pause. The knickers
still in her hand.*

WENDY: Daddy?

EXT. GARDEN

Shot of GRIEG *working in the garden, taken from the living-room.
The hi-fi set is playing.* WENDY *at the window (*GRIEG *from her
point of view, in fact). Suddenly she looks to her left,* MR
WYCHERLEY *saunters easily into the garden, a cigar in his mouth.*
STEPHEN *and* MRS WYCHERLEY *follow,* MRS WYCHERLEY *with
a hand across her nose. They stand for a moment, talking, then*
STEPHEN *gestures to the tree at the end of the garden.* MRS
WYCHERLEY *looks towards* GRIEG, *who is still crouching, then goes
towards the tree,* STEPHEN *in attendance.* MR WYCHERLEY *stands
smoking his cigar, then glances up at* WENDY, *smiles, saunters easily
over to* GRIEG, *his hands in his pockets, stands above him.* WENDY
gives a little smile, and cut to:

MR WYCHERLEY: (*After a moment, takes cigar out of his mouth*)
    You're Grieg? (*Smoothly.*)
    (GRIEG *looks up, nods, goes on with his trowelling.*)
    And you're what is known as the sitting tenant. (GRIEG
    pays no attention. MR WYCHERLEY *smiles calmly.*) You're a
    good gardener, aren't you?

GRIEG: That's right.

MR WYCHERLEY: To tell you the truth, I didn't expect to find
    you here. There seemed to be a general impression that you
    were leaving.

GRIEG: (*Looks up at him*) And is there a general impression that
    I'm still here?

MR WYCHERLEY: (*Smiles suavely*) You taking the micky?
    (GRIEG *goes back to his trowelling.* MR WYCHERLEY *glances
    up at* WENDY, *still at the window. The music should, of course,
    sound in the garden throughout this.*)
    Or possibly conducting a piece of business. Shrewdly, eh?
    (*Little pause.*) For example, being unprepared to settle for
    less than a hundred and fifty pounds.

GRIEG: (*Looks up at him*) What'd I want a hundred and fifty
    pounds for? (*In genuine disbelief.*)

MR WYCHERLEY: (*Pulls on his cigar*) What *do* you want?

GRIEG: I can get anything I need.

MR WYCHERLEY: Very well. Two –

MRS WYCHERLEY: (*Coming up with* STEPHEN) What have *you* found?

MR WYCHERLEY: Um, I've found Mr Grieg, digging – what the dickens is that you're digging up?

(*Squats down,* MRS WYCHERLEY *and* STEPHEN *now standing around the two of them. Cut to* WENDY *still watching from the window as* STEPHEN *also crouches, and then* MRS WYCHERLEY *crouches, then, as the music achieves a superbly royal flourish* GRIEG *rises, and from* WENDY'S *point of view, looks up at* WENDY *as her family remains squatting in various accidentally worshipping postures, around him.*)

INT. THE BEDROOM

STEPHEN, *in his pyjamas, is going through the contents of his briefcase. Takes out his dark glasses, puts them on the dresser.*

STEPHEN: Um, it was all right, was it?

WENDY: (*Voice over*) What?

STEPHEN: Letting the three hundred run over a bit?

WENDY: (*Voice over*) Don't worry, no money's going to change hands.

STEPHEN: That's very decent. (*Shuts the briefcase, turns, looks for his dark glasses, puts them on, takes them off.*)

WENDY: (*Voice over*) You're a very pretty man, very very pretty. Gwen says you're the prettiest man she ever met. Do you know you're pretty Stephen?

STEPHEN: (*After a pause, staring at her – straight into the camera, in fact*) Yes.

WENDY: (*Voice still over*) Are you pleased you're so pretty?

STEPHEN: (*After another pause*) Yes. (*Little pause, goes over to the bed.* WENDY *is sitting on the edge of the bed, in pale pyjamas. He sits down beside her.*) Are you?

WENDY: Mostly.

STEPHEN: (*Puts the dark glasses down on the bedside table*) But you're prettier. (*Little pause, then thickly.*) You know I love

189

you. (*Pushes her tentatively down on the bed.*) I do. (*Smiles pleadingly into her eyes.*)

(WENDY *looks up at him, then slowly shakes her head.*) Please, darling. (*In a whisper.*) Please.

(WENDY *shakes her head again, fade out, and in on* WENDY *face up on the pillow, naked, pyjamas lying across the bed.*)

(*Voice off*) A sort of therapy party. For the whole cast-cum-ladies and gentlemen, my idea being to get all the noise and nastiness in one place for an evening, you know? Turn it into a collective experience – a purification rite or a ritual murder for mainly, frankly, Amanda and Leary. I shall be the observer of all observed, if Leary makes a lunge at you I'll have to rethink my strategy, but if he chases Amanda all evening I'll know I've got them taped until the taping. (*Little chuckle.*)

WENDY: Why do men do that?

STEPHEN: What? (*Complacently, voice over.*)

WENDY: Come wheedling for a bit of love or body or whatever it is they think they need and have a right to and when they've had it they lie there like – I don't know – men.

STEPHEN: (*After a pause*) What do you mean?

WENDY: What I've said.

STEPHEN: (*Rolls over, looks at her*) Oh darling, come on.

WENDY: (*In camera, staring up*) Come on where, darling?

STEPHEN: (*Stares at her, aghast, then rolls back again, stares up, tight-lipped*) Thank you very much. (*Tautly.*)

WENDY: You're welcome.

STEPHEN: (*After a little pause*) I thought you loved me.

WENDY: I do. (*Turns her head, looks at him, then with her finger traces the line of his nose, smiles, says flatly.*) Because you're so pretty.

INT. THE LIVING-ROOM

Party in progress. About forty guests. The hi-fi set playing some cool modern stuff, very low, and over it the row of voices. Visible among the guests several members of STEPHEN's *production group, take them in generally, then transfer to a man talking to* WENDY. GWEN *talking to*

STEPHEN, AMANDA *standing aloof, with* MCGONNIGAL *unhappily beside her. She is watching* LEARY. *Then cut briefly and tantalizingly to a shaggy head and back, to give just an impression of* GRIEG *in a corner. Come back to* WENDY *and her man.*

STEPHEN: (*Laughing boyishly, sweeping his hair out of his eyes. There should be a little play from* GWEN, *intensification of expression*) Well, actually I don't think he intends to join us this evening.

GWEN: You should have asked him up. Then we could have occupied his basement, which would have been much nicer.

LEARY: How's Stephen?

WENDY: Don't you know?

LEARY: Well, I don't suppose he handles you like the ladies and gentlemen of the cast, does he? Wouldn't the strain show in a bit of wife-beating, or sommat?

WENDY: (*Licks her lips, then with a tight smile*) Wrong class, I think.

LEARY: Is it husband-beating down in the stylish South?

WENDY: Or sommat. (*Nods.*)

(WENDY *looks from* AMANDA, *who is smiling pleasantly, to* LEARY, *whose face is suddenly set, then looks vaguely around, sees* STEPHEN, *back with* GWEN *but smiling knowingly towards her, then on past more guests, standing with a drink, looking around, puzzled, then on, sees* GRIEG *by the door, his back to her and stooping slightly.*)

WENDY: Excuse me, there's somebody there I have to, um . . . (*Walks towards* GRIEG, *determined.*)

AMANDA: (*To* LEARY, *who is watching her go*) Well, what is it with Mrs Cool-Knickers, class or sex? Or both?

LEARY: (*Savagely*) It's what you haven't got. What is it? (*Savagely.*)

(*And cut to:* WENDY *a few feet away from* GRIEG's *back.* VERONICA *suddenly brushes around from in front, her face tremulous, looks past* WENDY *blankly, sees* MR HUGGLE, *goes over to him. He looks at her in concern.* WENDY *stares after them, then looks at* GRIEG, *who, turning, smiles at her. She glares at him, goes over to* VERONICA)

VERONICA: It doesn't matter. (*To an inaudible enquiry from* MR
HUGGLE.)
WENDY: Did he – do something?
(VERONICA *glances at* WENDY, *tears in her eyes, shakes her
head, looks away.*)
He said something, then?
(VERONICA *shakes her head.* WENDY *turns, looks towards the
door. It is open.* GRIEG *has gone. She walks to the door
purposefully, and out, closing it behind her. Cut back to the
party,* GWEN *at the hi-fi set,* STEPHEN *standing beside her,
watching, slight smile on his face, and cut to his view of* LEARY
talking savagely into AMANDA'S *face,* AMANDA *smiling
contemptuously,* MCGONNIGAL *just behind them, and cut back
to:*)

INT. THE STAIRS

WENDY *goes down them to the ground floor hall. Turns on the light,
goes to the door that leads to the basement, opens it, as from above
thumps of dancing feet and loud music come. Goes down to* GRIEG'S
door, her face set, flings it open. Keep on her face, don't show
GRIEG.
WENDY: (*Controlled, smiling with the effort*) You crashed our
party. (*Little pause.*) You helped yourself piggishly to our
drink, which you gulped down piggishly, you insulted one
of my friends, a girl who's incapable of being unkind to
anyone, even a pig like you, and then you run off, like the
cowardly pig you are. You'd bloody well better go straight
upstairs and apologise to my friend before I get my husband
and some of his friends to throw you out, sitting tenant or
no sitting tenant. (*Cut to* GRIEG, *facing her, watching her
impassively.*) Do-you-hear-me?
(GRIEG, *after a long pause, walks towards her.* WENDY *steps
aside to let him pass. He grabs her hand, jerks her inside, slams
the door.* WENDY *stumbles, nearly falls. Steadies herself against
the table, stares at him.*)

GRIEG: (*After a long pause*) Enjoying your party?
> (*He comes over, stands close to her.* WENDY *stares at him. He puts out his hands, one on each side of her face.* WENDY *spits into his face.* GRIEG *smiles.*)

WENDY: Let go of me!
> (GRIEG *stares into her face, his face very close. She stares back, increasingly as if mesmerized. Then he takes her hand, pulls her out of the basement door, tugs her up the stairs, very fast. She is trying to grab at something to pull herself back, he pulls her up the next flight, to the door of the party, puts his hand at the back of her neck.*)

GRIEG: Now who'll you send down for your apology?
> (*Cut to:*)

INT. LIVING-ROOM

Party in progress, dancing, etc. STEPHEN *is hopping about with* GWEN, AMANDA *is leaning forward, talking into* LEARY's *face.* MR HUGGLE *and* VERONICA *are talking intensely. The door opens,* WENDY *comes in with a little stumble, straightens herself, whirls around, nobody notices.* GRIEG *is standing at the door, staring at her. There is a long pause, then he smiles, leans forward, closes the door.* WENDY *remains looking at it. Suddenly there is a slapping sound behind, a little scream,* WENDY *turns around, as if dazed.* LEARY *is holding his cheek,* AMANDA *is walking away from him. A slight hush, then* LEARY *strokes his cheek, laughter starts, slightly self-consciously,* LEARY *walks after* AMANDA. *Cut to* STEPHEN, *from* WENDY's *point of view. He looks towards her, makes a small amused face, then hops with* AMANDA *out of the picture. Someone comes up beside* WENDY, *at first not seen properly.* WENDY *looks up at* MCGONNIGAL, *his face, anxious, slightly pleading and cut to:*

INT. BEDROOM

WENDY is lying on the bed, staring up at the ceiling in her pyjamas. Her arms are wrapped around her chest. Shouts from below, crashes, laughter, then the front door slamming. Pause. Then the sound of feet, slow, heavy, on the stairs. The door opens, slowly, STEPHEN comes in. He walks to the chair, sits down. Brushes hair away from his eyes, smiles at WENDY.

STEPHEN: Well? (*WENDY looks at him.*) Make what you can of this. (*Speaks very carefully, smiling.*) They arrived together, they had their spicy little slap-up, they left together. He came back alone, she came back alone. He was ogling around for something, like possibly my wife, she stood watching him from a dark corner. He drank. She got his coat. They left together. (*Smiles.*) What do you make of this?

(*WENDY stares at him.*)

(*His smile slightly unfocused*) Meanwhile back in the kitchen Aussie and Gwen were running amok all over my twelve year old PA, and your charity fiend with the beard was cuddling a lady that definitely was not the bearer of his kiddies except possibly currently, actually and frankly. He fancies you, Leo Leary does. So observed the observer of all observed. (*Makes a little laughing sound, stops, gets up, smiling vaguely.*) Just a minute darling. (*Goes to the door, opens it, turns, smiles, close-up on his face, damp and his smile is sickly.*) Won't be a minute darling.

(*Cut to WENDY's face as sound of his feet running down the stairs, then as the door is flung open below, out on WENDY's face.*)

INT. CHARITY OFFICE

In on VERONICA, sitting at the desk, going through a ledger, her hand over her eyes. Cut to GWEN and WENDY, seated at opposite ends of the desk, unwrapping packages.

GWEN: (*Voice over before she is seen*) Well, everyone I saw was

pissed to the newts, which is the only sign, and there was
that lovely Leary being slapped around.
(WENDY *glances towards* VERONICA, *who stands up suddenly,
and with jerky movements picks up her handbag, goes out.*)
(*Raises her eye-brows, shrugs*) One of her really bad days.
(*Takes out of her paper a pair of baggy trousers, puts them on the
desk, as* WENDY *takes out of her paper a pair of plus-fours, puts
them on the desk.*)
They were having a terrible time –
(*Stops as the side door opens,* MR HUGGLE *comes in. Looks
towards* VERONICA's *desk.*)

MR HUGGLE: Um, Veronica popped out, has she?

GWEN: Yes.

MR HUGGLE: Well, perhaps I'll just, um. (*Goes to the main door,
and out. Closing it after him.*)

GWEN: Oh Christ! What you could call a –
(*Main door opens,* MR HUGGLE *comes back in. He is
accompanied by a small man in a black suit.*)

MR HUGGLE: (*Going to the other door*) If Veronica – when she
comes back, could you say the, um, accountant's dropped
in? (*Shuts the door.*)
(*There is a pause.* GWEN *draws another package to her, shakes
out another pair of voluminous and grubby trousers.*)

GWEN: Now we're being rejected by one of those underdeveloped
countries.

WENDY: (*Stands up abruptly*) Look, do you mind, I've got to get
back, um, do you mind?

EXT. THE HOUSE

WENDY *coming along the pavement, footsteps falter, then she goes
quickly up the path, unlocks the door, goes in. Goes straight up the
stairs to the living-room.*

PIG IN A POKE

INT. LIVING-ROOM

It's in a filthy state; glasses, bottles, ashtrays everywhere. She looks around, trance-like, steps over bits and pieces, takes off her coat, puts it on a chair, it slips to the ground. She makes a weary gesture, puts it over the chair again, looks around her. Picks up a glass, shakes her head, puts it down again. Touches her forehead, then goes to the hi-fi, puts on some Mozart. Goes to the garden window, looks out. Shot of GRIEG *in the garden, sitting on a kitchen chair, reading a newspaper.* WENDY *licks her lips nervously, opens the window, steps away.*

EXT. GARDEN

GRIEG *in the garden from behind, still reading the newspaper, strains of Mozart coming down. He lowers the newspaper, looks up. Shot of* WENDY's *face, jerking away. He goes on staring. Pause.* WENDY's *face reappears, she stares straight ahead, then looks down.* GRIEG *stares up,* WENDY *withdraws her head.* GRIEG *gets up slowly, stands in the centre of the garden, music still continuing. Then shot from the window, the music very loud, looking down at* GRIEG, *looking up, then turning his head right. Keep shot from the window, looking down as* WENDY *comes into the garden, looks at him, walks towards him, stops a few feet away. This, if possible, as the first movement comes to an end.*
WENDY: (*Her voice heard faintly*) Pig!
    (GRIEG *walks towards* WENDY. *She holds her ground for a moment, then turns, walks quickly away.* GRIEG *follows.* WENDY *begins to run,* GRIEG's *pace quickens, the garden from above now seen as empty. There is a sound from below, like a cry, then the slam of the door, then cries from within, then hold shot of the empty garden, music again in full flow, and fade out. In on:*)

INT. HALL

STEPHEN *comes into the hall, carrying his briefcase. He looks tired. Goes into the kitchen. Comes out again. Starts up the stairs.*

STEPHEN: Darling!

(*Gets to the living-room door, is about to open it, then looks up the next flight, and cut to* WENDY *standing half-way up the stairs, coming down, fully dressed in a white frock, her hair done up behind her. She is wearing* STEPHEN's *dark glasses.*) Hello.

WENDY: (*Tentatively*) Hello.

STEPHEN: Still hung over?

(WENDY *walks down the stairs towards him, slowly and carefully.* STEPHEN *stands watching, smiling but slightly puzzled. When she is a stair above, thus making their heads on a level, he bends forward, kisses her on the forehead. Puts his hands on her cheeks. She winces, just slightly. He takes the glasses off, smiling.*)

Christ! (*One of her eyes is bruised.*)

WENDY: I walked into the door. In the bedroom. (*Bravely smiling.*)

STEPHEN: Poor darling. Will it be all right? It looks ghastly.

WENDY: Yes.

(STEPHEN *kisses the air close to her eye. They gaze at each other for a moment, he puts the spectacles back on her nose, turns, stops.*)

STEPHEN: What door in the bedroom?

WENDY: The cupboard door. In the landing.

STEPHEN: (*Enters the living-room, in its state of chaos*) God, what a tip!

WENDY: (*Follows, walking stiffly*) I'll do it tomorrow, I can't go anywhere looking like this anyway.

STEPHEN: OK. (*Sinks down into a chair.*) God.

(*Shakes his head, then reaches out, turns on the hi-fi.* WENDY *stands beside him, then walks to chair opposite, sits in it, facing him.*)

WENDY: How's Leary?

STEPHEN: What? Oh, hung-over and strangely absent when we needed him.

(*Smiles, touches his head, winces slightly, long pause, and on the two of them facing each other amidst the debris, fade.*)

INT. THE LIVING-ROOM, THE FOLLOWING MORNING

WENDY *is in a sort of smock, a turban round her head, dark glasses on.
She is plugging in the hoover. She goes to the hi-fi, looks around her,
looks towards the window. Licks her lips, looks quickly away. Picks up
a few glasses with great efficiency, then puts them down again. Walks to
the window as if in spite of herself, taking off her dark glasses as she does
so and putting them in the smock pocket. Opens the window, looks out.
Then withdraws her head, turns with a look that could be
disappointment on her face, jumps. Cut to* GRIEG, *standing inside the
room.*)

WENDY: (*Very controlled, touching her glasses*) Please go.

GRIEG: (*Walks towards her, then past her, to the window. Looks out.*)
Nice view.
(*Cut to the garden, stay on the garden, and* GRIEG *looking down at
it, as:*)

WENDY: I don't care what you think of me, (*still very controlled*)
because frankly and honestly what someone like you thinks
isn't very important anyway, and I'm perfectly prepared to
concede (GRIEG *steps away from window, out of camera which
stays on the garden*) that perhaps to some extent –
(*Little silence followed by squeals, sound of tussling,* WENDY's
*squeals getting louder, glasses smashing, then sound of door
shutting. Hold shot on garden, and:*)

INT. THE BASEMENT

Track over WENDY's *clothes, scattered everywhere in the semi-
darkness, then to her lying on the bed in the plastic overall, her hair
loose. She is staring up blankly. The kitchen door opens, right.* GRIEG
*comes in, buttoning up his shirt. Picks up the secateurs, goes back
towards the door.*

GRIEG. The kettle's on, I'll have mine outside. *I've* got work to do.
(*This with the very faintest touch of self-righteousness.*)
(WENDY *lies still for a moment, then fumbles in her overall pocket,
produces the dark glasses, puts them on, stares up, and cut to:*)

INT. THE HALL

GRIEG's *basement-landing door, and the front door open simultaneously.* GRIEG *and* STEPHEN *advance towards each other,* STEPHEN *does his skip and shuffle out of* GRIEG's *way, nodding, smiling at him.* GRIEG *nods impassively back, goes out.* STEPHEN *looks after him, then goes up the stairs.*

INT. THE LIVING-ROOM

STEPHEN *opens the door, looks in. A shot of it in chaos. He closes the door, goes to the bedroom.* WENDY *is sitting before the mirror, dressed and with her hair pulled back, the dark glasses on. She looks at* STEPHEN, *at the door.*

WENDY: Hello.

STEPHEN: How are you?

WENDY: (*Shrugs*) All right.

STEPHEN: And the eye?

WENDY: Blacker.

STEPHEN: (*After a pause*) What have you been doing?

WENDY: Having a bath.

STEPHEN: You went to the office today, then?

WENDY: No. (*Turns lifts up the glasses to inspect her eye.*) You know I didn't. I was going to clear up the living-room, remember.

STEPHEN: Yes.

(WENDY *goes on inspecting her eye.* STEPHEN *laughs. Little pause.*)

Well . . .?

(WENDY *turns, looks at him impassively.* STEPHEN *shrugs.*)

It hasn't been done.

WENDY: (*Frowns*) No. We'll have to do it tonight. (*Shakes her head at herself in the mirror.*)

STEPHEN: (*Stares towards her*) We're in the studio tomorrow. So. (*Smiles slightly, a martyred smile.*) I'm getting stomach tension or something or other, inevitably.

WENDY: Are you? (*Vaguely.*) Where?
STEPHEN: In the stomach. (*Looks at her reflection in the mirror.*)

INT. THE LIVING-ROOM

The glasses gone. Order restored. But come in first on WENDY's *overall, and the part of the Hoover from hands down to knee level. Then the Hoover stops, and cut to* WENDY, *in a chair, legs hanging over the side. She is watching* STEPHEN *doing the Hoovering.*
STEPHEN: (*Still in the overall crosses to the hi-fi, as he does so, sniffs*) Must say, a funny smell these things have got. (*Clutching at the overall.*) I don't know how you could bear to wear it.
WENDY: It's only for when I've got something dirty to do.
     (*Out, and in on:*)

INT. THE LIVING-ROOM

In on WENDY. *The hi-fi going. Bach. Then cut to* STEPHEN *in the armchair, sitting with his feet up, his collar undone. His face has a set thoughtful expression, he is nodding his head very slightly to the music.*
STEPHEN: You know (*still jogging his head slightly*) I've been thinking. The time's come to do something final about our friend downstairs.
WENDY: Oh?
STEPHEN: I don't know, I mean I met him in the hall this evening, and it suddenly got to me. Why *should* we put up with him? It's the way he somehow gets into everything.
WENDY: I know.
STEPHEN: And how do we know what he's up to, anyway. As far as we're concerned he could be up and down, in and out, all day long. (*Little pause, jounces his head in a lively fashion to a lively piece of music.*) Know what I mean?
WENDY: Yes, I do. (*Also jouncing her head slightly, both of them doing it.* STEPHEN *extravagantly,* WENDY *demurely, as the record ends.*)

STEPHEN: Isn't that smashing! (*Little pause.*) I don't know, frankly and actually – (*Stops.*) God knows what Leary's up to, he's off somewhere or other every ten minute break. Amanda just grins Cheshire – Something very funny's going –

(*Stops as music starts again. He sits listening to it, looks at* WENDY, *frowns. She reaches up slowly, takes off her dark glasses, there is a pause, her face very serious, then it breaks into a sudden, frank inviting smile. Stay on this as she licks her lips, and cut to:*)

INT. THE HALL

WENDY *goes down the hall, dressed to go out, very determined, wearing the dark glasses. Hold on the door, it opens,* WENDY *comes in. Back down the hall. Opens the door to the basement. Goes down.*

INT. THE BASEMENT

WENDY *goes to the bed, sits down, takes the dark glasses off, puts them down. Folds her hands into her lap, her expression is very patient. Fade out, then in on her sitting there as sound of door from the garden opening, and closing, footsteps.* WENDY *licks her lips, stares with her hands folded at the door, as it opens. Cut on her almost school-girl face, in on her face, hair hanging dishevelled, then she raises a mug to her mouth, sips from it. Lowers the mug, and cut to* GRIEG, *standing in the kitchen door, also sipping a mug.*

WENDY: (*With casual malice*) Your days are numbered. My husband's decided to get rid of you. (GRIEG *pays no attention.*) He'll knock you about and throw you into the street bodily. (*Little pause.*) He'll think of something. He's good with people. Jarring and oiling them. (*Pause.*) He's only started noticing you now that you're not around so much. What are you around so much for?

GRIEG: What's there to be around for?

WENDY: (*After a moment, nods*) Thank you.
    (*The telephone rings distantly.* WENDY *stares up at the ceiling.*)
WENDY: That's probably him now.
GRIEG: It sounds like him.
    (*They listen to the telephone. It rings a few more times, stops.*)
WENDY: (*After a pause*) I'm going upstairs. (*Standing up, see her
    from the back, her dress is open, she is carrying a bundle of her
    underwear under her arm, stockings trailing down.*) God, why
    are you so dirty. (*Picks up one of the magazines from a pile,
    looks at it, shot of its cover, drops it back on the chair.*) Such a
    pig.
GRIEG: Watch it. (*Slightly menacing.*)
WENDY: (*Stops, turns, looks at him. Come in on her face. Licks her
    lips. Upstairs, the telephone starts again. She stares at* GRIEG,
    who stares back at her. Then, in a whisper, excited and fearful.)
    Pig. Pig.

INT. THE LIVING-ROOM

STEPHEN *and* WENDY *as the night before, only come in on* WENDY *in
dark glasses, from* STEPHEN's *point of view.*
STEPHEN: Do you still need those things? (*Voice over.*)
    (WENDY *nods.*)
    I tried to get you this morning. Here and at the office.
    Nobody knew where you were.
WENDY: I had an accident.
STEPHEN: What? (*Cut to his face.*)
WENDY: I tripped down the stairs. (*Little pause, then looking at
    him very solemnly, lifts up her skirt, shows him a bruise on her
    thigh.*)
    (STEPHEN *stares at it.*)
    So actually and everything I couldn't face the thought of all
    the grot of the office. I took the day off. (*Little pause.*) I was
    being naughty.
STEPHEN: (*Stares at her, licks his lips*) Um, Leary, um, (*Stops.*)
    Want some music?

(WENDY *shakes her head. Smiles at him.*)
(*Gets to his feet, looks vaguely around.*) Did we do the dishes?
(WENDY *still smiling.* STEPHEN *staring at her as if mesmerized.*)
I'd better go over my shooting script, um . . .

WENDY: (*Tilts her head to one side, smiles lasciviously*) Come over
here. (*He goes over.*)
(*Reaches up, touches his nose, presses it.*) You haven't told me
yet *who* is doing what to *whom.* (*Draws his hand to her and cut
to:*)
(WENDY *and* STEPHEN *on the living-room carpet. Clothes
around them, his folded into a neat pile, hers scattered
indifferently. Cut to their faces,* WENDY *is staring up, smiling.
Bruise showing.* STEPHEN's *is turned into the camera, it has a
slightly doped look, eyelids heavy. Then* WENDY's *face moves off
camera, stay on* STEPHEN's *as Bach begins. His eyelids open.*)

STEPHEN: He's got something going all right. And it's not with
Amanda. (*Eyelids begin to close again, and cut to:*)

INT.

Come in on WENDY's *face, she is seated on* GRIEG's *bed, hands folded
in her lap. Suddenly she gets up, walks across the room, opens the
door, and out. As the kitchen door opens,* GRIEG *comes in, stands, as
sound above of front door closing.* GRIEG *tilts his head to one side.*

INT.

Before the charity office door. WENDY *takes a breath, adjusts her
glasses, opens the door.*

INT. THE OFFICE

WENDY *at the door, not seen, the office from her point of view.*
VERONICA *most prominent, staring towards her; a handkerchief to her*

*mouth. Behind her, two men, tough and impassive, and the
accountant from the earlier scene.* MR HUGGLE, *plucking at his beard.*

GWEN: (*Comes up beside her, from around the other corner*) Oh, I
shouldn't bother, darling, we're closing up while Mr Huggle
and his Veronica accompany these gentlemen to the station,
to answer some questions about the books.

INT.

STEPHEN's *figure, advancing up a long corridor with* AMANDA *just
behind him, on one side.* LEARY, *on the other, and another girl behind
him. PAs, ladies and gentlemen of the staff, clustered behind him.
They advance into the camera, and as they pass,* MCGONNIGAL
*brings up the rear, carrying his briefcase. Cut to a shot of them from
behind,* MCGONNIGAL *making a little run to keep up.* STEPHEN *and*
MCGONNIGAL *are in ordinary clothes, also PAs, of course. But ladies
and gentlemen are in evening clothes, as is* AMANDA. *Watch the group
from the back, they stop suddenly, then stand before a doorway,*
STEPHEN *sitting on the desk, holding the telephone. Ringing sound,
unanswered. Puts the telephone down, as* MCGONNIGAL's *face
appears at the door.*

MCGONNIGAL: Um, Stephen . . .

 (STEPHEN *looks at him blankly, then walks past him back into
 the corridor.*)

 Could I just . . .

 (*And cut to the procession, from long shot, walking down the
 corridor. It stops again.*)

STEPHEN: Where's Leary? (*Gazes at the throng,* LEARY *not
 amongst them.*)

AMANDA: Darling, don't *you* know?

STEPHEN: (*Smiles at her, a feeble smile*) Look, I'll join you later,
 I've just remembered.

 (*He goes off down one of the corridors, left. As he does so,*
 LEARY, *unseen by him, wanders back to the group, out of one of
 the offices, as* MCGONNIGAL *suddenly hurries after* STEPHEN.
 Shot of STEPHEN *walking down the corridor,* MCGONNIGAL

hurrying after him, catching him in long shot. Then in on
MCGONNIGAL'S *face.*)

MCGONNIGAL: (*As if with an effort*) I want to know why you
haven't been passing on my notes to the actors? (STEPHEN
staring at him blankly.) I must have made fifty notes, I've
even tried to talk to Leary alone, but what with him nipping
away all the time, and you getting between us, I haven't had
a chance. In fact, (*working himself up*) I haven't had a chance
since I arrived on the scene of my own play, which also
doesn't have a chance, Stephen, and it doesn't have a chance
because nobody, yourself included, and especially yourself,
gives one goddamn about the style or the text, and now, with
three hours before recording I can't get so much as a word
with you. (*Stares boldly and slightly fearfully up at him.*)

STEPHEN: That's a very good point, Tim, don't you worry about
it, leave it to me.

(*His gaze is abstracted. He puts a comforting hand on*
MCGONNIGAL'S *shoulder, and hurries off down the next*
corridor.)

INT.

The front door step. STEPHEN *going furtively through the front door,*
then running on his toes up the stairs, flings open the bedroom door.
The bedroom is littered with clothes, bed unmade. He stands staring,
then goes downstairs to the living-room, opens the door, goes in. Stares
around, wanders across to the window, looks out. GRIEG *is in the*
garden, doing up his belt. He raises his eyes, looks towards the
window, sees STEPHEN. *They stare at each other, then* STEPHEN
turns away, goes downstairs. Opens the kitchen door. Plates, cups,
etc. everywhere. He comes out, is about to go on down the hall, then
stops. Turns around. Looks at the basement door. Walks
apprehensively towards it. Down into the basement, stops before
GRIEG'S *door, then after a second, bends, looks through the keyhole.*
As seen through keyhole. WENDY, *seen from in front, sitting on the*
bed, facing the door. She is tousled, dress partly opened, her legs

spread carelessly. A mug of tea in her hand, her head over it. She raises her head, seems to be staring straight at him. Cut to:

INT. BASEMENT

Door, seen from WENDY's *point of view. The doorknob turns, then slips back. Sound of feet running up the stairs, the front door slamming shut.* WENDY *continues to stare, then fiddles her hand across the bed, puts dark glasses on. Fade out. In on:*

INT. THE BEDROOM

Darkness. The door opens, in. A small light goes on, illuminating WENDY's *face, sleeping. Sound of footsteps moving towards her. Her eyes open blearily, cut to* STEPHEN *standing over her, his briefcase in his hand, then cut back to* WENDY's *face, her mouth spreading in a semi-conscious, sexual grin, and cut to* STEPHEN's *face, as he turns away, and cut to:*

INT. THE LIVING-ROOM

WENDY *sitting in an armchair, looking towards the window, and cut to* STEPHEN, *standing at the window, looking down. He turns suddenly, his face twisted with pain, then walks quickly out of the room.* WENDY *gets up, goes over to the window, raises it, looks out.*

EXT. GARDEN

Shot of GRIEG, *from her point of view, bending over a patch of bush, small shears in his hand. He looks up at her, looks down again. Puts the shears down. Then cut to* STEPHEN, *walking quickly across the garden, approaches* GRIEG, *stands beside the shears. Cut back to* WENDY, *close-up, her lips open in excitement, then back to the garden from her point of view as* GRIEG, *still bending,* STEPHEN *bending beside him, picks up the shears.* STEPHEN *staring down at the back of* GRIEG's *neck as* GRIEG *still bending, holds out his hand. Cut back to* WENDY's *face, close-up, she closes her eyes in horror or in ecstasy, opens them, stares down.* GRIEG *is snipping away with the shears.* STEPHEN *is walking away. Sounds of door slamming.*

INT.

STEPHEN's *footsteps. He comes into the room, brushes his hair away from his eyes, then goes across and sits down by the hi-fi set. Turns it on. Sits for a second,* WENDY *watching him from another chair. He sits facing ahead, then begins to nod, almost imperceptibly, his head to the music.* WENDY *adjusts her dark glasses. Fade out on this, and up on the two of them in the same position.* STEPHEN *staring at the television set,* WENDY *watching it indolently, the dark glasses pushed up to her forehead. On the screen:* LEARY's *face, in his evening suit.* AMANDA *in profile.*

LEARY: (*Speaking in faked-up Coward voice*) My dear lady, we ought to have exchanged teething rings in the registry office, or perhaps one of those ebony do-dahs in the shape of our respective throats, because that's what we spend our time sinking our respective bridge-work into.
(*As he concludes this,* STEPHEN *leans across, turns the set off. Sits staring ahead, then looks at* WENDY, *with her glasses up. She pokes them down with her finger, stares impassively back at him.* STEPHEN *gets up, walks across the room, to the door, goes out.* WENDY *watches. Gets up. The door opens again almost immediately,* STEPHEN *comes running across the room, his eyes and face mad, stands in front of* WENDY, *who remains sitting staring up at him. He begins to slap at her, crazy swattings. She makes a few weak defensive gestures, gets backed into a chair, her glasses knocked off.* STEPHEN *stands breathing heavily, making little crying noises.*)

WENDY: Oh Stephen (*calmly and after a long pause*) he does *much* worse.

INT.

Shot of bedroom, in disarray, clothes scattered everywhere. From below sounds of Bach, very low. Camera tracks around the room, takes in a heap of Wendy's knickers, then pans out, and down the stairs, and in on:

INT. THE LIVING-ROOM

The hi-fi on. WENDY *and* MR WYCHERLEY *over by the window.* STEPHEN *pouring a drink.* MRS WYCHERLEY *seated in one of the Barcelona chairs.*

MR WYCHERLEY: Still cultivating *your* garden, I see.

WENDY: Yes.

MR WYCHERLEY: (*Glances towards her. She remains staring down*) I take it he's settled down, then. (*Drily.*) For good. Eh, Stephen?

STEPHEN: I don't know. Do *you* think he has, darling?

WENDY: (*Smiles*) It looks like it.

(*And cut to:*)

MRS WYCHERLEY: (*Looking at* WENDY *and* MR WYCHERLEY, *their backs to her, still at the window, then looks at* STEPHEN, *who is now lolling in a chair, smoking a cheroot and playing with something out of sight*) I've been meaning to ask, what's the new play like, is it as stylish as the last?

STEPHEN: Not yet. But it will be. (*Slips the glasses on over his nose.*)

MRS WYCHERLEY: (*Again glances towards the window, where* MR WYCHERLEY *has just put his hand on* WENDY'S *arm*) Just as long as you don't get yourself censored by that ghastly woman, the one that makes all the noise, you know what *my* feelings are about coloured and illegits, but she talks as (*cutting to* MR WYCHERLEY, *his hand on* WENDY'S *arm*, MRS WYCHERLEY'S *voice over*) if the whole country was an absolute marsh of vice and licence and what have you . . . (*cut back to* MRS WYCHERLEY, *staring towards* MR WYCHERLEY)

which I must say I take great personal exception to, *and* I like the right (*Turning to* STEPHEN) not to look at what's there to be seen, after all if people don't like it they can always switch off, can't they?
(*And cut back to:*)

MR WYCHERLEY: (*Smiles at* WENDY, *who turns towards him. His hand still on her shoulder*) All right then?

WENDY: (*Vaguely*) Fine thanks. (*Moves away from him, he lets his arm drop.*)
(*Cut to* STEPHEN, *who is watching* MR WYCHERLEY *with a little smile.* MR WYCHERLEY *looks towards him, meets his eyes,* STEPHEN's *smile remains, small but triumphant.* MR WYCHERLEY *turns back to the window, and* WENDY *crosses to* STEPHEN, *as:*)

MRS WYCHERLEY: Which I must say, I quite frequently find myself having to do. Switch off, I mean.
(STEPHEN *smiling at* WENDY. WENDY *smiling back at him, nicely and yet almost impersonally, and from her to* MR WYCHERLEY, *turning away to stare coldly out of the window down on the garden, and finally to:*)

EXT. GARDEN

GRIEG *standing in the centre of the garden, his hands on his hips, staring up, seen from* MR WYCHERLEY's *point of view, and seeming to make, to the rising sound of Bach, a slow, obscene gesture.*

Man in a Side-Car

Man in a Side-Car was first broadcast by the BBC as Play for Today on 27 May 1971. The cast was as follows:

EDITH	Gemma Jones
GERALD	James Laurenson
TOMMY	David Collings
MRS MERCHANT	Sheila Beckett
DAVID	Geoffrey Matthews
HELEN	Yvonne Gilan
DR SLOCUM	Walter Horsburgh
GILES	Jonathan Lawson
WAITRESS	Tessa Lander
MEN IN COFFEE BAR	Roger Minnis, Steve King, Colin Richmond, Paul Barton
GIRLS IN COFFEE BAR	Monica Wilding, Rosemary Turner
THREE MEN IN HOSPITAL	Len Sanders, Bert Simms, Ernest Jennings
TWO NURSES	Constance Reason, Iris Fry
WARD ORDERLY	Leonard Kingston

Director	James MacTaggart
Producer	Graeme McDonald
Script Editor	Ann Scott
Designer	Stuart Walker

It is a sparsely furnished room, with one picture, mediaeval and devotional, on the wall. There is a desk beside a window. The window looks out onto a path which is, in fact, a narrow drive. The drive curves around a bend and then onto a country road. The desk is an old-fashioned school desk, with a sunken ink-well and a ridge for a pen. EDITH *is writing into an exercise book at the desk. She uses a fountain pen that she dips into the ink-well. To her left is a pile of five exercise-books, filled. Beside her, and behind her, past the window, is a bookshelf on which are arranged exercise-books and novels. She is dressed in a long (as opposed to fashionably maxi) skirt, has hair swept down the side of her face, and in her cell-like room gives off a distinctly nun-like effect. She is in her early thirties. She is writing quickly and neatly onto the page, and at regular intervals is dipping her pen into the ink-well.*

EDITH: (*Voice over, as she writes*) Mathilda began to discover that she had many things against Simon, and consequently and quite consciously began to develop a proportional esteem for herself. For example, Simon had begun to take instruction with a view to conversion. He approached his studies – for that was what he had made of the matter – with an academic devotion that was as inelegant as it was thorough, and spoke of the impending moment at church as if he were about to be awarded a prize for an achievement, an advanced degree for example. Mathilda, who had gone over to Rome at the age of thirteen because she was in love with a girl, half Italian, half Irish, wholly beautiful and almost twelve, at her second boarding school, took her own Catholicism so much for granted that she could afford to be witty at its expense. Poor Simon was frequently shocked by her little jokes, and the resulting strain between them – a strain that confirmed Mathilda in her growing sense of independence – led to some strange failures in bed. These failures were, of course, entirely Simon's. Mathilda, secretly enjoying them, marked them up as victories. Simon might well entitle himself to an adjoining pew, but his head would soon rest uneasily on the adjoining pillow.

(EDITH *smiles as she writes the last few sentences. Cut to her face, then as the smile stiffens, cut to the window beside her.* GERALD, *in goggles, a flowing scarf, gauntlets, and a very distinctive and expensive-looking leather coat with enormous buttons, is staring in at her. He turns, walks away.* EDITH *turns slowly, as if sensing him there, a second after he has disappeared, frowns slightly, then goes back to her writing.*)

It turned out, in fact, that Simon, who in the early days of their relationship, had so amused himself by making fun of her own small aspirations, was unable to see the comedy of his own larger ones. She came to the conclusion and not at all reluctantly that her husband was a fraud. She saw, with only enough pain to spicen the recognition into anticipation, that there was little prospect of their marriage lasting the course. She was too clever by half. Indeed, she was too happy by –

(*Her voice is interrupted by the explosive sound of the motor-bicycle starting.* EDITH's *shoulders jump, her pen waits above the paper as the motorbike roars off.*)

(*Her voice over, writing*) – by more than half.

EXT. THE PATH FROM THE COTTAGE. DAY

GERALD *on his motor-bicycle, which has an old-fashioned side-car. It roars around the bend, and out of sight, and as it does so* MRS MERCHANT *wheeling a pram, comes into shot. She is staring after the motorbike.*

INT. EDITH'S STUDY. DAY

EDITH *is now nearly at the bottom of the page. She writes:*
EDITH: (*Voice over*) She knew the day would come when she would say to her child-bridegroom – 'If you were half a man,

you would go.' And she equally knew that, being half a man, he would. So many divisions could be made to make a very simple sum.

(*She turns the page, shot of the blank page, her pen hovers, then writes:*)

But Simon, if he was not capable of success, was finding the consolations of malice. He –

(EDITH *smiles, screws the top back on her pen, puts it in the ledge, closes the ink-well, blots the page, closes the exercise-book, then goes out of the study. Follow her as she enters:*)

INT. GERALD'S STUDY. DAY

EDITH *enters* GERALD's *study. There is a desk, a typewriter, a camp-bed, unmade, books, papers, etc., scattered everywhere. There is an ashtray full of cigarette ends, a pair of spectacles, a pipe half-smoked, an open box of cheroots, and beside the typewriter various sheets of papers, some with fragments of typing on them. There is a sheet in the typewriter.* EDITH *makes a face, goes to the window, opens it, then goes out. Comes back in, looks down at the page, reads a few lines, goes out again, and follow her to the kitchen.*

INT. THE KITCHEN. DAY

First come in on MRS MERCHANT's *face, smiling, then cut back to* EDITH, *smiling, and she blocks the view for a second, then turns around, having lifted* GILES *out of his highchair, and is now cuddling him.* GILES, *who is about nine months old, not seen until that instant.*

EXT. A RAILWAY STATION

The motorbike. GERALD *appears with* TOMMY. TOMMY *is wearing a slightly ludicrous, very long, tatty overcoat. He is carrying an equally tatty overnight bag. They come to the motorbike;* GERALD *fishes into the side-car, hands* TOMMY *a pair of goggles and crash helmet, they get in and on respectively.*

EXT. COUNTRY ROADS

GERALD *is driving as: Credits. Follow them through country roads, and on them in different shots, some of* GERALD *in close-up. Some of* TOMMY, *some from in front, some from behind, fading on the two of them in shot advancing as credits fade.*

INT. THE KITCHEN. DAY

EDITH *is holding the bottle for* GILES, *while also drinking a cup of tea.* MRS MERCHANT *is eating a proper lunch, as the noise of the motorbike outside.* EDITH *glances up, then goes on feeding* GILES. *Sound of voices and* TOMMY's *laughter outside the back door, then* GERALD *and* TOMMY *enter, still in goggles and helmets.*

TOMMY: Well, hello then.

> (*He comes around, gives* EDITH *a kiss, bends down, clucks at* GILES. GERALD, *meanwhile is taking off his gear, smiling at* EDITH. GILES *begins to cry.*)

EDITH: Your goggles.

TOMMY: Oh.

> (*He takes his goggles off.*)

GERALD: No, it's because you've taken the bottle away.

> (EDITH *glances at him, puts the bottle down on the table.*)

TOMMY: (*To* GILES, *who is still crying*) What is it, Giles, what's the matter, don't you recognize me then, you only saw me yesterday.

EDITH: Yes, but he cried then, too.

> (*She picks* GILES *up, looks at* MRS MERCHANT, *who gets up; they go out together.*)

TOMMY: It was wind yesterday.

GERALD: Don't worry, I don't believe they *know*.

> (TOMMY *sits down, cutting himself some bread.*)

TOMMY: He never cries at me, normally. (*He shakes his head, worried.*)

GERALD: For Christ's sake – he's not going to throw you out. Well?

TOMMY: What? Oh, well like I said, they're interested Gerald, certainly, the only thing that's holding them back, likely, is they're waiting to see the second act complete.(*He eats ravenously.*) That's all.

GERALD: Did they have any constructive suggestions?

(EDITH *comes back into the room.*)

TOMMY: I hope you don't mind, Edie – (*Holding up the bread.*)

EDITH: Please. (*Neutrally, she begins to clear up. To* GERALD) Do you want anything?

GERALD: Just some sense.

TOMMY: Well – well, no, well he liked it, Gerrie. (*To* EDITH) That's Humphrey Jones, Edie, I worked with in Cardiff I mentioned to you who's got hold of that new theatre club in Chiswick, he's a smart bastard – no, all he said (*back to* GERALD) was he liked its *tone* and that when we got it worked through to the curtain to let him be the first to refuse. (GERALD *laughs.*)

You know what I mean, first *refusal* he wants, it's the next thing to an option. Edie, could I have one of those yoghurts if you've got one?

(*He turns around in a practised way, opening the fridge, takes out a yoghurt.*)

EDITH: But he's not taking an option?

TOMMY: Well I couldn't insist on it could I as – I'm a friend, see.

EDITH: (*Ironically*) Well, that's all right then.

GERALD: What does that mean?

(TOMMY *is spooning down the yoghurt at great speed.*)

EDITH: The director of a new theatre's likely to find himself with a lot of new friends as well. Or would he make it a principle to buy options on the work of strangers only?

GERALD: Where's Giles?

EDITH: Having his nappy changed.

GERALD: Mrs Merchant doing it?

EDITH: (*Pretends to think*) Unless he's doing it himself.

TOMMY: But what really matters is that I could see he was excited
by it, he wouldn't pretend over that, you know –
(*He is watching* GERALD, *who gets up, picks up the overnight
bag, and goes out.*)
(*To* EDITH) He's not a complete bastard.

EDITH: Merely a clever one.
(*She looks at* TOMMY *who is smiling slightly shiftily. There is a
pause.*)

TOMMY: Um, I was wondering, could you spare –?

EDITH: Please.
(TOMMY *turns around, opens the fridge, takes out another
yoghurt.*)
What is it about?

TOMMY: What? Our play? Hasn't Gerrie told you?

EDITH: No. Nor have you.

TOMMY: Well, you never asked before. (*Laughs.*) I mean, I
assumed . . .
(*He opens the yoghurt, begins eating.*)

EDITH: Well?

TOMMY: Well. (*Laughs.*) It sounds very modish in outline, you
know. (*Pause.*) Well . . . (*He laughs again.*)

EDITH: I like quite a few of the current modes.

TOMMY: Well, in fact it's about these four queers who ran a
butcher's shop. Two of them draggy queens, see, and two of
them butch –

EDITH: (*Poker-faced*) Butch Butchers.

TOMMY: (*Laughs desperately*) That's one we did cut out, no, you
see, it's the sort of sexual and emotional permutations and
combinations – well, it's all in the dialogue and the tone, see,
there's no plot as such, but if it's played in the right style it
could be something special. (*Little pause.*) A cross between
Racine and Orton. (*Little pause.*) Not just another
commercial camp-up, Edie.

EDITH: Ah. An uncommercial camp-up?

TOMMY: Oh, Edie! (*Little pause.*) Why are you being so
depressing then?

EDITH: Self-protection.

TOMMY: For Gerald you mean?

EDITH: Actually, I meant for myself.

TOMMY: I'm sure it'll come off.

EDITH: Yes. Almost at once. If it gets on.

TOMMY: Well, I'm very hopeful.

EDITH: (*Stares at him unwinkingly*) Good.

TOMMY: (*Finishes his yoghurt*) I must say, it's nice to be back. I've missed you all.

EDITH: You've only been away for the night.

TOMMY: Yes, well, it feels like a couple of weeks.

EDITH: Perhaps that's because it was going to be. A couple of weeks. We all adjusted to that prospect.

TOMMY: Oh? You didn't expect me back today then?

EDITH: No. Not actually.

TOMMY: But Gerald phoned last night – he left a message with Stewart to come back as soon as they'd read it at the theatre.

EDITH: Ah. In that case it must have been an emergency. (*She gets up.*)

TOMMY: Well, how's the novel going?

EDITH: I've done two days' work, since you last asked.

TOMMY: Oh, good.

(*As* EDITH *goes out*) Humphrey Jones said he loved your last, to tell you especially.

EDITH: (*Reappears, smiles*) Oh, good. (*She waits.*)

TOMMY: Yes, he loved it. (*Rather feebly.*)

EDITH: Good.

(*She goes out, and as she does so* TOMMY *wheels round to the fridge.*)

INT. GERALD'S STUDY. DAY

He is sitting before the typewriter, spectacles on, staring down at the manuscript. The overnight bag is at his feet. EDITH *stands at the door.* GERALD, *pointedly, doesn't look up.*

EDITH: Can I speak?

GERALD: (*Still looking down*) You can.

EDITH: You summoned him back, then?

GERALD: (*Still looking down*) Yes.

EDITH: Why?

GERALD: I was getting bored.

EDITH: We did agree that we might try two weeks without him.

GERALD: Not quite. *You* said *you* could do without him. You asked me whether I could understand your feelings. I said I did. There was thus agreement about your feelings. None at all about policy.

EDITH: David and Helen are coming to dinner tonight. Or had you forgotten?

GERALD: On the contrary. I specifically mentioned it to Tommy, by way of an inducement.

(*As* TOMMY *appears behind* EDITH) Edith was wondering whether you could really face David and Helen tonight. I've been reassuring her.

TOMMY: No, I'm looking forward to it, who are they exactly?

GERALD: Her publishers. Manic depressers. But never mind – you'll have lots to eat. Edie'll make sure of that. And lots to drink. I'll make sure of that.

TOMMY: (*Grins*) Ahh, just what I need.

(*Close-up of* TOMMY's *face, beaming, seen from* EDITH's *point of view, then she goes out.*)

INT. EDITH'S STUDY. DAY

EDITH *is at her desk, writing. See her from side, including a shot of the window.*

EXT. GARDEN

EDITH's *point of view, from her study window:* MRS MERCHANT *is sitting in a deck chair, reading.*

MAN IN A SIDE-CAR

INT. EDITH'S STUDY. DAY

Throughout this, there's also the sound of a distant typewriter.
EDITH: (*Writes, as voice over*) He was turning into a way of life
with a strong moral point of view. Mathilda would have
found this boring if she hadn't known, indeed cherished the
knowledge that this was merely a stage towards something
even less consequential. During his time with her he had
abandoned everything in turn. He had abandoned his art, for
which he had no talent; and then his religion, for which he
had had no feeling, and then his love-making, for which he
had had no desire. Shortly he would abandon failure, for
which he had no stoicism, in favour of a more sensational
posture.
(*There is the sound, dim, of* GILES, *crying.* EDITH *frowns,
makes to write another sentence, then turns to the window, raps
on it, points.*

EXT. GARDEN

MRS MERCHANT, EDITH's *point of view, gets up, goes off screen.*

INT. EDITH'S STUDY. DAY

EDITH *turns back to her writing. Fade out. In on* EDITH *writing
again.*

EXT. GARDEN

MRS MERCHANT, EDITH's *point of view, playing with* GILES, *in his
pram.*

INT. EDITH'S STUDY. DAY

EDITH: (*Voice over*) Mathilda felt that although . . .
    (*The typewriter stops*)
    . . . she had little time for Simon at the moment, she would
    manage to find some for his next phase. He promised, for a
    change, to be interesting. Also it would enable her to practise
    her newly acquired mercilessness, as well as to test her . . .
    (*All this over, as sudden shouts of laughter from* TOMMY *and*
    GERALD. *She frowns, goes on writing, as the shouts continue* . . .)

INT. GERALD'S STUDY. DAY

GERALD *and* TOMMY *are crouched on the floor playing tiddly-winks,*
with pennies and sixpences. Beside each is a pile of half-crowns.
TOMMY *is playing. Come on them both from the door, then cut to*
TOMMY'*s face. Frowning in concentration as he is about to wink a*
tiddly into the pot. He does so, and then another one, very practised,
extracts two half-crowns from GERALD'*s pile, then moves back to do*
one a long way away, then shakes his head, moves forward to one closer
in.
GERALD: You're gutless, Tommy.
    (TOMMY *pays no attention as he takes aim, very serious.*)
    For a quid?
TOMMY: (*Looks up*) Let's see it.
    (GERALD *reaches into his pocket, takes out a pound, puts it*
    between TOMMY *and the cup.*)
    And if I miss?
GERALD: Oh, I never take anything from you, do I?
TOMMY: Done and done, boyo.
    (*He crouches down, concentrating very hard. There is a sudden*
    stillness, then he winks the tiddly in. He lets out a shout, reaches for
    the pound note. GERALD *puts his foot down on the pound. See*
    GERALD'*s face smiling from* TOMMY'*s point of view.* TOMMY
    crouching, GERALD *standing above him.*)
    Oh, come on, Gerrie, it's mine, I won it.

GERALD: Not yet.

> (GERALD *bends down, extracts the pound from under his shoe, holds it up, and as* TOMMY *reaches for it, flicks it away from his fingers. He keeps this up for some time,* TOMMY *clutching,* GERALD *whipping away, until* TOMMY *suddenly closes on* GERALD; *they begin to wrestle, crashing about, clutching at each other half-laughing, half-gasping, until they roll to the floor.* TOMMY *has* GERALD *pinioned and is reaching for the pound, when:*)

EDITH: (*Voice over: Focus on* TOMMY *and the pound*) I hate to disturb you, but could you make less noise please.

> (*There is silence, then* TOMMY *gets up grinning sheepishly. He puts the pound note in his pocket.* GERALD, *still on the floor, turns his head, grinning, towards* EDITH.)

TOMMY: Um. Oh I'm sorry, Edie, it was my fault entirely, we had this idea about a wrestling scene, see, you know male wrestling is all the vogue now, on stage and screen, of course, we'll have it done in the nude, but we wanted to get . . . wanted to get . . . (*He begins to laugh, helpless.*)

> (GERALD *still lies smiling, staring up at* EDITH.)

(*Helplessly*) Get – get I'm sorry, Edie. Sorry.

> (EDITH *looks at them both, turns, goes out. On* TOMMY *and* GERALD. TOMMY *is still laughing, his laughter dying down.* GERALD *gets up, smiling. There is a pause, heavy, empty, then* GERALD *turns, goes to the desk, sits down.* TOMMY *goes to the camp-bed.* GERALD *sits staring at the typewriter.*)

GERALD: (*After a pause*) What about a drink?

TOMMY: Oooh.

INT. THE SITTING ROOM. NIGHT

A table, laid for dinner. DAVID, HELEN, TOMMY *and* GERALD *sitting or standing, holding drinks. But come in first on* TOMMY's *face, as he raises the glass to his lips. He is already slightly tight. Then take in* DAVID *and* HELEN, *sitting rather stiffly, and then* GERALD, *watching, smiling.*

223

TOMMY: No, no look (*expansively*) that the boys look like the girls and the girls look like the boys in Cannabis Street or Cannibal Street or wherever that doesn't matter, see, that just gives us twice as many to fancy, doesn't it? Eh? (*He laughs.*)

(HELEN *and* DAVID *join in.*)

But you see uni-sex has been going on for years, yes it has, in the States they've had those creature-ladies and blue-ringed hair and goggles that are male martians, I'm sure of it, and in Russia, you know, more elemental, they've gone in a straight line with pills and operations, like that, to get the best of both worlds, child-bearing muscle-men, what about, no I'm serious, all of those shot-putters or putt-shotters and javelin throwers and mile runners the authorities caught shaving in the bogs, eh? Well, that's all right, who minds a bit of cheating in the name of sport, but look, reverse it for a moment, think of it this way, supposing yes supposing our test team, our fast bowlers, were really women, eh? Supposing these South African apartheid blokes were destroyed by an opening pair of fast bowlers from Yorkshire who had little ladies' problems and had to be rested for them, eh, well, wouldn't that be lovely, we destroy the white man at cricket with our ladies like we destroyed the black man with our ladies, eh? So what happens then to white supremacy – like male supremacy, down the flush bowl with it – (*Laughing.*)

(HELEN *and* DAVID *also laugh.* HELEN *gets up.*)

Where are you going, Helen?

HELEN: I'm just going to see if Edith needs a hand.

TOMMY: Oh yes, oh that's good, what about our World Cup side, eh, did it take a sex test, hormone count or whatever . . .

INT. KITCHEN. NIGHT

EDITH *is mixing something on the stove.* HELEN *comes in.*

HELEN: Can I do anything?

EDITH: (*Suppressing slight irritation*) Oh no thanks. I'm fine.

HELEN: I must say, we're enjoying Tommy. He's terribly funny.

EDITH: (*Neutrally*) Ah – yes.

HELEN: He lives with you, does he?

EDITH: In a sense. He has done, off and on, since we were students. We take him so much for granted we scarcely know he's around.

HELEN: Gosh, I'd have thought that was quite difficult.

EDITH: Yes. It is.

HELEN: He's incredibly Welsh, isn't he?

EDITH: Sometimes. When he's had enough to drink.

HELEN: (*After a pause*) David's terribly excited about your new one. He says it's nearly finished.

EDITH: (*Brightening*) Yes. Next month if I can keep it up – God willing, etc.

HELEN: I don't know how you manage.

EDITH: (*Laughs*) By becoming extremely selfish.
(*She takes a dish out of the stove.*)

INT. LIVING-ROOM. DINNER TABLE. NIGHT

They are seated round the table, but come in first on TOMMY's *face, he is blinking slightly, and tighter. He raises the wine-glass to his mouth, as* GERALD *says:*

GERALD: Nappies.

DAVID: What?

GERALD: Didn't we decide you'd call it nappies. You said, 'Let's be brutal, that's what it's all about.'

DAVID: (*Doubtfully polite*) Nappies?

TOMMY: (*Laughing*) Brutally would be crappy nappies.

EDITH: There isn't a title.

DAVID: I must say, I'm rather relieved.

GERALD: But darling, didn't you – ah no, it was Giles that was all about nappies, brutally. I'm getting your children confused.
(*To* HELEN) Do *you* have any children? I always forget.

HELEN: Yes, two actually.

GERALD: Two *actually*! As opposed to metaphorically – like
    Edith's novels. Do you enjoy them?
HELEN: Yes, of course. They're brilliant. They're my favourites.
GERALD: It's nice to hear someone being honest about their own
    offspring.
    (HELEN *and* DAVID *laugh*.)
HELEN: I thought you were talking about Edith's novels.
GERALD: Oh, do you think of them as your children, too?
EDITH: Helen was talking about her actual children, actually. As
    I think you've grasped.
    (*There is a slight pause*.)
GERALD: Well, I certainly have now, haven't I? What do you
    enjoy about them, Helen? All they do is eat, defecate and
    sleep. Extremely enjoyable for the baby, but slightly
    disgusting for the rest of us.
DAVID: On the contrary. Babies are –
TOMMY: Why does Giles get that rash on his bum?
GERALD: It's their urine.
    (GERALD *passes* TOMMY *the wine. He fills his glass to the brim*.)
    Acid in their urine.
EDITH: Could the rest of us have some, please.
    (GERALD *looks at her, as if puzzled*.)
GERALD: Oh the *wine* – I thought for a moment you meant –
    (TOMMY *erupts with laughter, as* GERALD *pours the wine
    around. After another pause,* DAVID *says:*)
DAVID: Tell me – I've often wondered – how do people write
    plays together. Do you alternate scenes, or what?
GERALD: Or what.
DAVID: What?
GERALD: Yes.
DAVID: I'm sorry.
GERALD: That's all right.
    (DAVID *laughs, clearly getting angry*.)
DAVID: I'm afraid I don't understand –
TOMMY: What?
DAVID: I said I didn't understand.
GERALD: I'm sorry.

TOMMY: Why?

GERALD: He didn't understand.

TOMMY: What?

GERALD: How we write plays.

(*Cut to* EDITH's *face. She is watching* GERALD *and* TOMMY *through this, almost as if studying them.*)

DAVID: (*Controlling himself*) Anyway, what it amounts to is that you've given up writing novels.

HELEN: Oh, did you . . .

(*She stops.*)

GERALD: Writing novels? (*As if astonished.*) What novels?

DAVID: Oh come on, I read it.

GERALD: Ah, my *novel*. I gave up writing that some considerable time before it was published.

EDITH: It was a good novel.

TOMMY: (*Emphatically*) It was a bloody good novel.

DAVID: Yes, I liked it.

TOMMY: (*Vaguely, and with seemingly no sense of context*) Christ.

INT. LIVING-ROOM. NIGHT

They are all sitting around having coffees, and brandies, but come in on GERALD, *smiling, as* TOMMY *says:*

TOMMY: (*Voice over*) No, well you see it was like this . . .

(*Falteringly*) I was – she was a demi-vierge, can you credit of forty-three and a half, I think it was, and I was a raw boy of thirty-one precisely, well I didn't know what I was saying, excuse me a minute.

(*The sound of* TOMMY's *feet, stumbling. A door slamming. Still on* GERALD's *face as we cut to a shot of the group as a whole, evidently embarrassed, and then cut to:*)

EDITH: (*Perfectly collected*) She could have stayed up. Got a Fellowship at Newnham. It never occurred to me she had a novel in her. Is it any good?

DAVID: Well, very accomplished and acceptably derivative.

(*Dreadful sounds off of* TOMMY *being sick.*)

227

EDITH: Really? Derivative from?

HELEN: From you. I'd call it plagiarism.

    (*More sounds from* TOMMY.)

DAVID: Let's just call it flattery.

    (GERALD *appears at the door.*)

GERALD: Darling. (*Cheerfully.*) Where's the mop?

INT. THE BEDROOM. NIGHT

A double bed, with a bedside table on either side. On GERALD's *a reading lamp, a bottle of sleeping pills, and a pile of paperback books, littered. On* EDITH's, *a reading lamp, and a baby-alarm. Also one book,* Persuasion, *with a book-marker in it. But none of this seen as yet. Come directly in on* EDITH's *face, she is staring up at the ceiling. The sounds of* GILES's *breathing through the baby-alarm are audible but not yet explained. There are sudden little cries, followed by the heavy breathing.* EDITH *moves her arm, and turns down the baby-alarm. As she does so,* GERALD *enters.*

GERALD: (*Beginning to undress*) He's lying down. I thought he was heroic the way he came back in and told that story against himself, didn't you? Do you think he gave them pleasure?

EDITH: About as much as he gave me, I should think.

    (*Cut to her face, as* GERALD *goes on undressing, off-screen.*)
When did you start getting him drunk? This afternoon?
(*Little pause.*) You know, you do go very well together.
You're so predictable, like a rather silly married couple that everyone else has outgrown. How do you see yourself? As a *succès manqué*? Does he represent your last hold on your old self, attractive, dominating, etc., and so forth?
(GERALD *climbs into bed, lies down beside her.*)
The glamour is entirely in the vocabulary. A failure. An unhappy husband. A desperate man. Try – flop. Flop's the right word for you. No Graham Greene connotations, no dimmed brightness, no forlorn flickers of promise. Flop.
You're a flop and Tommy's a miserable, despairing parasite.
What the Americans call a bum.

INT. HALL OUTSIDE THE BEDROOM. NIGHT

TOMMY *is standing outside the door, listening. He is in a state close to collapse, exhausted.*

EDITH: (*Voice over*) What was interesting *and* poignant, about his performance tonight, was its desperation. Didn't you feel it? (*Sharply*) Don't do that!

GERALD: (*Voice over*) Why not? We always used to celebrate the guests' departure with a spasm of analysis and a bout of love.

EDITH: (*Voice over*) What I'm celebrating tonight has nothing to do with you. In fact, that *is* what I'm celebrating. I witnessed Tommy's desperation and your malice this evening without even embarrassment. He was sad and you were trivial, and really I quite enjoyed it. Like recognizing a perfect definition. Your behaviour was definitive. I said don't! (TOMMY *puts his hand to his forehead.*)

INT. BEDROOM. NIGHT

GERALD *is leaning over* EDITH, *grinning,* EDITH *is staring up. The sound of* GILES's *breathing is audible.*

EDITH: Would you please turn out the light. Because if you're going to go on grinning anally down at me, I'd rather not see you.
(GERALD *maintains his position.*)
You don't really think they're going to do your play, do you? Surely you know Tommy better than that. I do, anyway. He never showed it to them.
(GERALD *goes on grinning down at her.*)
What you've written is a flop. A flop's flop. And Tommy knows it.

GERALD: Do *you* know what I've got against you? Your chin. You've got the chin of a boxer. The tension of not punching it is driving me mad. I'd like to have you in the ring, belting away at your chin. Your novels stink. They make you lots of money and you sell the film rights, but they stink.

(*He rolls over, turns out the light. There is a pause.*)

EDITH: (*In the darkness*) Yes, but Tommy still didn't show your play to anyone. Not even a Welshman. He'll be leaving in the morning.

GERALD: Oh no he won't.

EDITH: Do you want a bet?

INT. GERALD'S STUDY. NIGHT

TOMMY *is sitting on the camp-bed. He begins to take off his shoes and socks. He looks forlorn, beaten. His hand moves, and he picks up a piece of bread, puts it into his mouth, chews on it desperately, and on his face:*

INT. THE KITCHEN. DAY

Come in on TOMMY's *face, munching, as if carried over from the last scene.*

EDITH: (*Voice over*) You're a pig.

(TOMMY *looks startled, then cut to* EDITH *looking down at* GILES, *to whom she is giving a bottle.*)

TOMMY: And he'll grow up to be a big strong pig, like me, see.

(EDITH *looks at him coolly, goes on feeding* GILES.)

(*Clears his throat apprehensively*) Um, while we're on the subject of pigs, Edie, in relation to myself see, I – well, I've been awake all night, worrying and guilty – I thought – (*attempts a charming smile*) – I'd outgrown that kind of thing, it must have been the train journey and being tired with it, you know.

EDITH: From here to Waterloo is thirty-five minutes.

TOMMY: (*Laughs*) Yes, that's true, well you know British Rail. (*Laughs.*) Anyway, I thought I had an apology to make. (*Pause, he looks at* EDITH, *who addresses herself to* GILES.) I did like your friends, very charming I thought they were. (*Pause.*) I hope I'm forgiven then.

230

(EDITH *looks at him, makes as if to speak as:*)

MRS MERCHANT: (*Comes through the door*) Good morning.

EDITH: Good morning. He's just finished.

(*Lifts him out of the chair, hands him to* MRS MERCHANT.)

MRS MERCHANT: (*Taking him*) And how's my ba-ba today? (*Carrying him out.*)

(EDITH *suppresses a grimace of irritation.*)

TOMMY: It's funny the way she talks to him like a sheep, eh? (*Laughs.*)

EDITH: You know I'm going to ask you to leave, don't you? (TOMMY *stares at her, licks his lips.*)

It's time, Tommy. You've been with us since we started living together – and that was a year before we got married. Four years, interrupted by short breaks of three months or so, and your six months' spell in Cardiff. Now I want you to go, and not to come back.

TOMMY: (*Staring at her helplessly*) But – Edie – because, you mean because of last night? I'll never – never – I promise –

EDITH: You see, you talk to me as if I were your older sister, or mother, someone you make promises to, that you're slightly frightened of, that will look after you and make everything all right again. (*She shakes her head.*) I don't feel protectively towards you. Not any more.

(*After a pause* TOMMY *nods his head.*)

TOMMY: Could I stay then until we've completed the play? It'll only be to impose on you another week or so? (*With dignity.*)

EDITH: Why? You know the play's no good. You didn't take it to anyone in London.

TOMMY: Do you think I'd lie about a thing like that?

EDITH: Yes. (*Smiles.*) Don't look so incredulous. You lie a great deal. About things like that, and more important things. (*She gets up, comes over, stands behind him, touches his shoulder.*)

Just go, Tommy. Like a good boy. (*Both tenderly and ironically said.*)

TOMMY: (*Turns, clutches at her hand*) But what will I do – what?

(*The door opens.* EDITH *moves away from* TOMMY *as* GERALD
comes in.)

GERALD: Good morning.

INT. EDITH'S STUDY. DAY

EDITH *is watching* MRS MERCHANT *and* GILES.

EXT. GARDEN

MRS MERCHANT *is wheeling* GILES *in the pram down the path.*

INT. EDITH'S STUDY. DAY

EDITH *turns, sits down at her desk, opens the exercise book, unscrews
the top of her pen, dips it in the ink, makes as if to write. Her pen
hovering over the page, as she reads the previous sentence:*

EDITH: . . . could not deny that the excitement the process of
cleaning up gave her (*Begins to write*) . . . was oddly pleasant, and
although cerebral in its planning was becoming – was becoming –
was becoming – (*Lifting the pen up, she gazes down at the paper*) –
cerebral in its planning was becoming – (*She dips her pen into the
ink, it hovers over the page*) – was becoming –

INT. GERALD'S STUDY. DAY

TOMMY *is sitting on the bed, hands clasped between his legs.* GERALD
is sitting at the desk-chair, doodling.

GERALD: Why?

TOMMY: Because she told me to.

GERALD: I haven't. (*Little pause.*) What will you do? Go home to
Llannelly?

TOMMY: No, I'll go to London.

GERALD: You've been to London.

TOMMY: I can always wash dishes for a bit.

GERALD: No you can't. Not any more.

TOMMY: (*After a pause*) No.

GERALD: Where will you live?

TOMMY: Well, I can – perhaps I can go and stay with someone for a time, until I've settled down.

GERALD: No you can't. They won't have you. Not any more.

TOMMY: No.

GERALD: It's all ended, all that, Tommy. They're all married, to one sex or the other, they've got houses or flats, children or positions, one or two are even dead. They'd like to see you now for ten minutes in a pub, from an accidental meeting, and even so they won't ask you your address or give you theirs. There's nothing for you in London.

TOMMY: (*After a pause*) And do you know, I can't do it any more, I can't, Gerrie. I'll tell you something: it frightens me, London. Not just people who don't want to hear my voice when I telephone them, or the pubs nobody goes to any more, no, it's the whole place, the whole feel of the place and all eleven million of them, however many it is, it makes me feel too little.

GERALD: That's because you're too old. So what will you do, Tommy?

TOMMY: I don't know. I don't know. Of course Edie's right. I can't go on like this, living off you.

GERALD: Why not?

TOMMY: Because – (*Thinks*) – she won't let me. (*Laughs.*)

GERALD: Well, there's always this, isn't there? (*He holds up the manuscript.*) Perhaps this will save you, if Humphry Jones is to be trusted.

TOMMY: But there's still the second act –

GERALD: Is Humphry Jones to be trusted? (*Little pause.*) Tommy?

TOMMY: (*Looks at* GERALD) No.

GERALD: You didn't take it to him then?

TOMMY: No, Edie's wrong about that, I took it to him, and I

233

walked about for two hours while he read it, it was very kind of him, you know, on the spot he read it, and then I went back and he told me he thought it wasn't very interesting, straightforwardly and honestly, like a good friend should. So he's a good friend, you see. I've got a friend in Humphry Jones. He'll always turn me down on the spot.

GERALD: But it doesn't matter what Humphry Jones thinks, does it? *You've* still got confidence, haven't you? *You* still like it, don't you?

TOMMY: (*After a pause*) No. I think it stinks, you know.

GERALD: So what will you do, Tommy?

(*Hold on his face, staring at* TOMMY.)

INT. EDITH'S STUDY. DAY

Come in on her pen-nib, poised above the page. Then it stabs down, begins to write.

EDITH: (*Voice over*) Positively sexual in its execution. (*Repeats.*) And although cerebral in its planning was becoming positively sexual in its execution. She had felt the same sensation when completing her General Paper for her Oxford Scholarship. She was in control, the prize was hers. In the very exactness with which she organized and made lucid her originality there was a respect for convention that could have been interpreted as contempt. So poor Simon's career as her husband was about to be brought to a neat finish, with, of course, a respect for the conventions that marked her contempt for him. Under these circumstances it would have been delightful to make love to him for a last time. She would see if it could be arranged. The method of dispatch was so orderly, surely a bravura flourish could be permitted. She –

(*She is interrupted by the roar of a motorcycle from outside. She turns to the window, looks out.*)

MAN IN A SIDE-CAR

EXT. GARDEN

EDITH's *point of view from window:* GERALD, *in his gauntlets, helmet and gloves, is starting the motorbike, while* TOMMY *in his ludicrous overcoat, is getting into the side-car. The motor-bicycle roars off, up the path.*

INT. EDITH'S STUDY. DAY

EDITH *smiles contemptuously, returns to her exercise-book, dips in her pen.*

EDITH: (*Voice over continued*) – now saw her mercilessness as a
   quality of mind –

INT. A WIMPY BAR IN A SMALL TOWN. DAY

GERALD *and* TOMMY *are seated at a table.*

GERALD: Has it occurred to you that if she hadn't met us when
   she did, she'd never have written a word. Not a word.
   Except possibly for a few academic reviews in academic
   journals. She didn't aspire to creation. She had a first from
   Oxford and a great gift for thinking dully about dull books.
   She only took up novels because I was finishing mine and
   you were in the middle of thinking about beginning yours. If
   I'd been a weightlifter, she'd have gone in for that.

TOMMY: In the end, she'd have lifted heavier weights.
   (*A* WAITRESS *puts a coffee in front of* GERALD, *a Wimpy, a
   piece of cake and a coffee in front of* TOMMY.)

GERALD: It took me two years to write my novel, Tommy. Do
   you remember?
   (TOMMY, *who is raising the hamburger to his mouth, nods.*)
   It was gestured at, at the bottom of long reviews on other
   novels.

TOMMY: I remember.

GERALD: And in three years, she's written four novels –

235

TOMMY: (*His mouth full*) Five almost.

GERALD: And she gets whole reviews to herself, with a
photograph inset that was taken when she was twelve. She
gets interviewed on average once every three months, with
sometimes a reference to myself in the text, or a picture of
me striking a husband's pose to the left of her elbow, or with
an ear and half an eye showing behind Giles' face. But that's
not it, no, that's not it. What it is, is that she sits there in her
chaste little cell over her bloody exercise-books imitating a
schoolgirl imitating a nun, and she still doesn't know how to
write a novel. She has a special little gland that other people
haven't got, that functions away glandularly, and it makes
her richer and richer and more and more famous, and that's
not it, either, no, that's not it, it's not even the sum of the
injustices of her victories and successes, it is simply that she's
killing me. Killing me, yes, that's it.

TOMMY: Killing you?

GERALD: Oh, I don't mean that she's ending our marriage. She's
doing that. You today, me tomorrow. Your departure is the
means to my end. I mean, she's making me dead.

TOMMY: You hate her then?

GERALD: I'm in love with her. You know, the way one might be
with a schoolgirl or a nun. Aren't you?

TOMMY: What? In love –?

GERALD: Oh come on, Tommy. You've *always* been in love with
her. I've only just started.

(TOMMY *shakes his head*.)

Why, you've slept with her, haven't you?

(*As* TOMMY *stares at him, transfixed*.)

That year when we were living together. All three of us.
Didn't you sleep with her?

TOMMY: Look Gerald, I don't know what you're talking about.

GERALD: Didn't you fancy her, then?

TOMMY: (*Laughs*) Well of course, that's a different question, isn't
it?

GERALD: No it isn't. Everyone was sleeping with everyone. I took
it for granted you did with her.

TOMMY: Why didn't you ask me before, then, if you've thought that?

GERALD: I wanted to preserve the proprieties. It doesn't matter any more. So you can tell me. (*Smiling*.) How often did you sleep with my wife?

TOMMY: (*Laughs*) Well you know, I can't remember. You know, Gerrie –?

GERALD: You do remember, Tommy. Was it once – (*Holds up a finger*) twice – (*Holds up two fingers*.)

(TOMMY *holds up two fingers*. GERALD *continues to hold up two fingers also. They sit staring at each other, holding up two fingers. Then* GERALD *smiles*.)

Did you enjoy it?

TOMMY: (*Shrugs*) Well no, (*lowering his fingers*) it wasn't very successful, it was you she wanted, see.

GERALD: I'm sorry to hear that.

(GERALD *begins to laugh*. TOMMY *also laughs*. GERALD *draws* TOMMY's *cake to himself, and while he is talking, covers it with various condiments, pepper, salt, mustard, tomato sauce, etc*.)

Sometimes when you're walking along a street you see a schoolgirl with her satchel, her legs they go down very vulnerable, almost pitiful, into their socks and shoes. Do you know what I mean?

(TOMMY *is staring in horror at the cake*.)

And one in a hundred has a face, exquisite, sealed off, and you put out of your mind what you know goes through theirs, and you feel it inside you, caught between cherishing and despoiling. (*Little pause*.) The desire to rape nuns is, of course, conventional fantasy. I won't bore you with it. Here – you've had my cake. Now eat yours.

(GERALD *pushes the cake at* TOMMY.)

TOMMY: Like hell I will, boyo.

GERALD: It's the price you have to pay, Tommy. If you're to inherit my mantle.

(TOMMY *shakes his head, laughing uncertainly, and then stares down at the cake, back at* GERALD, *and on his face*.)

INT. EDITH'S STUDY. DAY

Register the sound of her laughing quietly, over the last shot of
GERALD. EDITH *writing.*

EXT. GARDEN

MRS MERCHANT *and* GILES *approach up the path.*

INT. EDITH'S STUDY. DAY

EDITH *writing.*
EDITH: (*Voice over*) And so he departed, for the last time, from
    their bedroom, with his tail between and not metaphorically,
    his legs. With his clothes bundled in his arms and his face
    bulging with unconsummated aggression, he was not a
    particularly dignified spectacle. But he had pathos, of a kind
    that Mathilda knew –
    (*She turns, looks out of the window.*)

EXT. GARDEN

EDITH's *point of view,* GILES *and* MRS MERCHANT *now in the very
middle of the path.*

INT. EDITH'S STUDY. DAY

EDITH: (*Voice over*) – in the solitary (*writing quickly*) but by no
    means lonely years to come. She – she –
    (EDITH *stops, smiles at the page, then screws the top on to her
    pen, closes the ink-well, blots the page, closes the exercise-book,
    stands up, stares, smiling, out of the window.*)

238

MAN IN A SIDE-CAR

EXT. GARDEN. DAY

From EDITH's *point of view.* MRS MERCHANT *lifts* GILES *out of the pram.*

EXT. COUNTRY ROAD. DAY

The motor-bicycle is roaring at great speed along the road. Cut from GERALD's *face, impassive behind goggles, etc., to* TOMMY's *eyes staring in fright.* TOMMY *attempts to attract* GERALD's *attention, the motor-bicycle roars on, past the camera, see it from behind, suddenly slowing and then stopping.* TOMMY *scrambles out of the side-car and runs, clutching his stomach, to the bushes.*

EXT. THE GARDEN. DAY

EDITH *is pushing* GILES *in the pram slowly up the path, towards* MRS MERCHANT.

EXT. THE ROAD. DAY

The motorbike roaring along the road, cut from GERALD's *face, to* TOMMY's, *crumpled in misery.*

EXT. THE GARDEN. DAY

EDITH, MRS MERCHANT, GILES, *in the middle of the path as before. Sound over of the motorbike and as they look up, the motorbike is roaring towards them, and cut to their reactions, then to* TOMMY's *face, stiff with horror. Then* GERALD's, *indecipherable behind the goggles, etc.*

239

INT. LIVING-ROOM. DAY

Come in directly on GERALD's *face, now without goggles, helmet, etc.*
He is sitting impassively. Then take in TOMMY, *sitting on the sofa,*
clearly shaken. The door opens, MRS MERCHANT *comes out, walks*
past GERALD, *stiff-faced.* GERALD *follows her with his eyes, then*
looks towards the door, as EDITH *comes out, closing it behind her.*
Baby noise off from GILES.

EDITH: You nearly killed us all. Do you realize that?

GERALD: It *was* a close thing, wasn't it? Old Tommy would have
thrown up his gâteau vinaigrette if he hadn't already thrown
it up.

EDITH:Are you being defiant, or are you actually a little mad?

GERALD:A little mad actually. (*He gets up and goes to the door.*)
You've got a lunatic on your hands. I give you warning. (*He
smiles, goes out.*)

TOMMY: (*To* EDITH, *who is staring after* GERALD) Edie . . . um,
you know, he's, well –
(EDITH *turns, looks at him.*)
It's – it's – look Edie, he isn't well, there's something wrong
with him, I don't mean he tried to run you over or anything
like that, see, but he might do something desperate, if you
ask me.

EDITH: And if I ask you, what would you suggest?

TOMMY: You shouldn't be alone together, not just now, Edith.

EDITH: Tommy, I asked you to go. Are you going to, please.

TOMMY: He hates you, you know.

EDITH: Of course he does. Why should he make an exception of
me. He almost certainly hates you too.
(EDITH *goes out.* TOMMY *stands for a moment, on his face an*
expression of rage.)

INT. GERALD'S STUDY. DAY

GERALD *is lying on the camp-bed, smoking a cheroot.* TOMMY *comes*
in.

TOMMY: I'll stay if you tell me to . . .

GERALD: (*Looks at him*) *Tell* you to?

TOMMY: Yes.

GERALD: Well, I won't. I'd prefer you gone. I need you
somewhere else, Tommy.
(TOMMY, *after a moment, goes to his suitcase under the camp-
bed, drags it out, begins to shut it.*)
Could I have my shirts back, please.

TOMMY: I've soiled them.

GERALD: The soil may belong to you, the shirts belong to me.
(TOMMY *takes out the shirts, puts them on the bed, closes the
suitcase.*)
How romantic, to travel light. You don't mind if I don't
take you to the station after all?

TOMMY: (*Looks at him, after a pause*) Will there be a train?

GERALD: At the station? Well, if you don't find one there, you
won't find one anywhere.

TOMMY:(*Suddenly firm*) Could I have my coat, please.

GERALD: It's behind you.

TOMMY: The one I inherited.

GERALD: Inherited?

TOMMY: The one I ate that cake for.

GERALD: Oh, you misunderstood me. I was speaking poetically.

TOMMY: (*Desperately*) What is it you want me to do, then?
What?

GERALD: Go.
(TOMMY *turns, goes out of the door.*)

INT. EDITH'S STUDY. DAY

EDITH *is standing at the window looking out, and from her point of
view, through the window, sees* TOMMY *plodding up the path.*

MAN IN A SIDE-CAR

EXT. GARDEN. DAY

From EDITH'*s point of view,* TOMMY *plodding up the path. He is carrying his suitcase, and wearing his ludicrous overcoat.*

INT. EDITH'S STUDY. DAY

For a moment EDITH *looks uncertain, as if perhaps on the verge of calling out to* TOMMY.

EXT. GARDEN. DAY

There is the roar of the motorbike and GERALD *comes into view, stops beside* TOMMY, *talks to him.* TOMMY *gets into the side-car.*

INT. EDITH'S STUDY. DAY

EDITH *turns away to her desk. She sits down at it, stares ahead for a moment, then unscrews the top of her fountain pen, opens the exercise-book, then sits staring at the page. On her face.*

INT. THE BEDROOM. NIGHT

EDITH *is lying in bed reading* Persuasion. *Beside her the baby-alarm is on. The sound of* GILES'*s breathing. Hold on this, then the roar of the motorbike, and immediately, from the baby-alarm,* GILES'*s cry.* EDITH *starts, sits still, then makes as if to get up. The crying stops. She gets back into bed, sits tensely. A few snuffling noises from the box, then silence. Sound of a door opening and closing, footsteps.* GERALD *comes in, closes the door behind him. On his face is an expression so impassive that it is sinister. He begins to get undressed.*
EDITH: I think you'd better sleep in the study. As it's free now.
GERALD: No, I'll sleep with you tonight. It'll be the last time.

EDITH: Yes.

(*There is a silence as* GERALD *goes on undressing. Keep on* EDITH's *face, watching him. It is very composed, but a hint of excitement.*)

GERALD: By the way, Tommy informs me you've slept with him.

EDITH: Really?

GERALD: You did then?

EDITH: Tommy is a liar. I've never gone in for adultery.

GERALD: I wasn't asking after your religious habits. I was indirectly asking whether you and Tommy had ever copulated with each other.

EDITH: Are you hoping he did? Do you think that jealousy is less demeaning than envy?

(*As* GERALD *gets into bed*) I'd be grateful if you'd wash. You're dirty.

(GERALD *lies staring up at the ceiling.* EDITH *picks up* Persuasion.)

GERALD: There is, I suppose, the faint possibility that Giles isn't mine?

EDITH: Would it make any difference if he weren't?

GERALD: (*Reaches past her, turns off baby-alarm.*) I'd like to think he'd disgust me just as much if I were sure he were.

EDITH: You are literally hateful. Full of hate. *Did* you try to harm him this afternoon?

(GERALD *suddenly rolls over, looks down at her, then takes the book from her hand, and drops it over the edge of the bed.* EDITH *laughs.* GERALD *puts a hand on her breast.*)

EDITH: (*Ironically*) Oh dear.

(GERALD *slaps her.*)

You don't have to do that. I'm yours.

(GERALD *stares at her blankly, and* EDITH *smiles. He begins to make love to her. As he does so,* EDITH's *hand comes out, turns on the baby-alarm. Her hand withdraws but stay on the baby-alarm. A few small cries come from it, and cries from* EDITH, *then on a full cry from* EDITH, *cut to:* EDITH's *face, she is flushed and smiling. A small, triumphant smile. Then take in* GERALD *beside her. He is lying, staring up.*)

243

(*She turns towards him*) Oh dear. (*Pause.*) I'm sorry.
(GERALD *goes on staring up. Then suddenly he begins to cry.*
EDITH *stares at him, her smile becoming suddenly uncertain.*)
Gerrie – (*whispered*) Gerrie –
(*And aghast she puts her hand to his head, stares into his face. He is still crying.*)
Gerrie –
(*He stares at her pathetically. He rolls away, gets out of bed, picks up his clothes, goes to the door, turns, stares at her. On his face, an expression of dreadful malevolence. He goes out.* EDITH *stares after him, makes as if to follow him, then lies back, hold on her face, suggesting time passing. Her expression tense. Then the roar of the motorbike, the sound fading away. A pause.*)
(*Her voice slightly shaky*) That's that, then. (*Little pause.*)
Consummatum est. (*She laughs, still shakily.*)

INT. GERALD'S STUDY. DAY

Hold on the room, in its slovenliness. Then EDITH *comes on camera. Purposefully, almost violently, she rips the covers off the camp-bed. Then a series of shots, montage, of her cleaning out and cleaning up the room, with a kind of fanatical intensity, culminating with two last shots, sustained longer than the others, of her wrapping up* GERALD's *manuscripts in brown paper, tying them into a parcel, then putting the hood over the typewriter. Move back to the door, where* EDITH *stands when she has finished. Take in the room, bare and as if purged. She turns, goes out.*

INT. BATHROOM SINK. DAY

On EDITH's *hands, as they are briskly washing themselves,* EDITH's *face in the mirror as she combs her hair.*

244

MAN IN A SIDE-CAR

INT. EDITH'S STUDY. DAY

She goes to the window, stands for a second, then turns to her desk, picks up the exercise-books to the left, the ones filled, holds them almost devotionally, smiles. She puts them down, sits down, takes out her pen, opens the ink-well then turns the exercise-book open. The page is blank. She frowns, turns back a page. Also blank. She picks the exercise-book up, riffles through it, blank. In horror she picks up the filled exercise-books, riffles through them. On the last page of the last exercise-book, scrawled in large letters: 'Go back to page one.'

INT. THE KITCHEN. DAY

EDITH *is sitting at the table, staring ahead. Her face is over-composed, as if against panic. She gets up, goes to the phone, opens the address book beside it, begins to dial. Then cut to shots of her finger on different telephone numbers, dialling with the other finger, to suggest numerous phone calls being made, then cut to* EDITH *sitting at the table again. There is the sound of a motor-car outside, a honk. She gets up, picks up a coat and handbag, already arranged on a chair, goes to the back door, opens it. And finds herself facing* MRS MERCHANT, GILES *in her arms.* EDITH *blinks in a shock of recognition.*

EDITH: Um, um – I've got to go to London on – um, something urgent. Could you do Giles until, I um – if I'm late? It's terribly urgent.

MRS MERCHANT: Of course, it's nothing serious, is it?

EDITH: Yes. (*Makes to go.*)

MRS MERCHANT: I'll tell Mr Dunlop you've gone.

EDITH: Oh, he won't be – yes, if he comes, tell him he must wait for me. He must. All right?

(*She looks at* GILES, *kisses him as if remembering, goes out.*)

EXT. GARDEN. DAY

Shot of EDITH, *from* MRS MERCHANT's *point of view, getting into a taxi.*

INT. DAVID'S OFFICE. DAY

Come in on EDITH's *face, seen from* DAVID's *point of view. She looks exhausted.*

EDITH: Credit where it's due. It's effectively humiliating. I spent the morning on the telephone to people I haven't seen for months, for years. Asking them if they'd seen my husband. They hadn't, of course. But they found the question interesting. One or two hinted that I'd dropped them with my success. I longed to say that I'd been merciful. If I'd dropped them when I'd been a failure they'd have had to attribute some fault to themselves. This way I gave them the opportunity to blame me. The afternoon I spent in familiar half-forgotten pubs, not knowing whose eyes to dodge and whose to catch. None of them looked as if they could have belonged to my past, but they might all have belonged to *his*. I don't know. I can't remember. How could I? (*Little pause.*) I should have thought. I should have *thought*. But it was the one unthinkable thing. (*Little pause.*) But he thought of it. Why didn't I? I should have slept with them under my pillow, had them chained to my wrist, hidden them under the floorboards, until he'd gone. (*Little pause.*) But I've worked out this much. He wouldn't have put the black ones there if he'd decided to (*with an effort*) destroy the other ones. He'd have left torn pages, or embers, or nothing. He *must* be going to use them – as hostages, so to speak. (*She smiles.*) What shall I do? (*Lips tremble.*) David? (*She attempts a smile. On her face.*)

MAN IN A SIDE-CAR

EXT. DRIVE. DAY

Taxi coming towards the drive. But carry on shot of EDITH's *face from previous scene, and then cut to:*

INT. KITCHEN WINDOW. DAY

MRS MERCHANT's *face staring out, desperately worried.*

EXT. GARDEN

MRS MERCHANT's *point of view. A taxi draws up, beside a car.* EDITH *gets out, paying the taxi-driver hastily, looks at the car, begins to run towards the house.* MRS MERCHANT *hurries to the door, opens it, and see her face worried, from* EDITH's *point of view.*

MRS MERCHANT: I don't know what's wrong, Dr Slocum's with him now.

    (EDITH *runs past her.*)

INT. GILES'S ROOM. DAY

Terrible cries coming from GILES. DR SLOCUM *is straightening up from the cot, stethoscope dangling from his ears. He turns, stares at* EDITH, *his face severe.* EDITH *stares back at him, panic-stricken.* MRS MERCHANT *comes in behind her.*

EDITH: Oh God, what's the matter?

DR SLOCUM: I've not the slightest idea. His lungs are in excellent shape, at least.

EDITH: (*Confused, shouting*) What?

    (*She goes to the cot, looks down at* GILES. *She picks him up.* GILES *begins to calm down.*)

DR SLOCUM: But whatever it was, I can't believe it was worth calling me out for. We've got the summer flu epidemic on our hands, you know.

EDITH: Called – who called?

(*She looks accusingly at* MRS MERCHANT.)

MRS MERCHANT: (*Indignantly*) I didn't –

DR SLOCUM: The call was from your husband. (*Packing his bag.*) He said your child needed attention. (*Straightening, and on his face, cut to:*)

INT. BEDROOM. NIGHT

EDITH *is in bed, reading. The book held up to her face. She lowers the book. She is crying, silently. She wipes her eyes with the sheets, lies still for a moment. Then turns out the light, there is a pause. The light comes on again. She lies staring ahead, as if trying to remember something, then suddenly turns her head to the baby-alarm which is silent. She stares at it in panic, then grabs it, turns up the sound. Still nothing. She makes to get out of bed, suddenly remembers the on-off switch. Fumblingly she checks it, turns it to on. The sound of* GILES *breathing. She turns the light on. Picks up the book, resolutely, begins to read.*

EDITH: The sod! The hateful sod!

(*Fade into a shot of* EDITH *asleep, the light on, the book open beside her. It is still night. There is over, the distant noise of the motor-bicycle, very muted, being driven at the lowest possible throttle. Her eyes flicker open. She stares ahead, then sits up as the noise goes on, slightly louder. The noise stops. Cut to her face, listening, waiting. Sounds of a key in the lock, a door opening, closing quietly, footsteps, other doors opening and closing. Then silence.* EDITH *gets up, goes to the bedroom door, opens it. Follow her through to:*)

INT. VARIOUS ROOMS. NIGHT

GERALD'S *study. On to her own study, the door is open. She goes to it.*

INT. EDITH'S STUDY. NIGHT

What appears to be GERALD's *back – it is, in fact,* TOMMY, *in* GERALD's *coat. His head is bent low as he fumbles inside* EDITH's *desk. Cut to her face, resolute as she walks quickly and softly over, puts her hand on his arm.* TOMMY *jumps, looks up.* EDITH *stares into his face, see it full in camera, from her point of view, then back to* EDITH.

EDITH: What do you want?

TOMMY: Oh, I'm sorry Edie (*nervously*) I – I – was just – well, see the thing is Gerald asked me to get something for him.

EDITH: He's got them all. There aren't any more.

TOMMY: What? Sleeping pills? He says he hasn't, Edith, no, look. (*He holds a bottle out in the palm of his hand.*) He said you kept an extra bottle in your desk –

EDITH: You came here for that?

TOMMY: (*Shrugs*) Well, he asked me to come and get them, Edie. He said he needed them.

EDITH: (*After a pause*) What are you doing in his coat?

TOMMY: Well, he gave it to me in the end, you see. I won it in one of our bets. It was a cake I had to eat, he –

EDITH: Where is he, Tommy? Where is he?

TOMMY: Well, I promised him I wouldn't say. He said you'd ask, he made me promise, Edie.

EDITH: He's got my exercise-books, you know. My novel. I want them back.

TOMMY: Of course you do. Of course.

EDITH: He's not in London then?

TOMMY: No.

EDITH: Has it occurred to you that he's ill?

> (TOMMY *looks at her as if wavering.* EDITH *goes to him, clutches his arm.*)
>
> Tommy, take me to him. (*Little pause.*) Please.
>
> (TOMMY *looks at her. She is pleading, but there is something deliberately sexual in her appeal.*)
>
> Please? (*Wonderingly.*) Don't tell me anything. Just take me to him. You didn't promise him you wouldn't do that, did you?

TOMMY: No. (*Little pause.*) Do you mean now?

EDITH: (*Gently*) Please, Tommy.

TOMMY: (*After a pause*) But what about Giles, you couldn't leave him all by himself then, could you?

(EDITH, *as if realizing, shakes her head.*)

EDITH: I'd – I'd – (*Stops.*) Well then, ask him to give me a ring, will you please.

TOMMY: Yes. Yes, I'll do that.

(*He hesitates, then takes* EDITH *in his arms, kisses her gently on the mouth, then stands hesitant.*)

I'll tell him to give you a ring then.

(*He goes out. Keep on the door, sound of doors opening, then* EDITH *goes to the hall, and through to:*)

INT. THE KITCHEN. NIGHT

EDITH *goes to the window, looks out.*

EXT. THE GARDEN. NIGHT

There is a figure on the seat of the motor-bicycle, in crash-helmet and goggles, indistinct. She stares towards it, through the window, assuming that it is TOMMY. *The figure raises an arm, in salute, then* TOMMY *appears, in goggles and helmet, climbs into the side-car. All this from* EDITH's *point of view.*

INT. THE KITCHEN. NIGHT

EDITH *stares at the motorbike, then, realizing, runs to the kitchen door.*

EXT. THE GARDEN. NIGHT

EDITH *opens kitchen door, as* GERALD, *on the seat, kicks the motorbike into life, it cruises up the drive. Cut to* EDITH's *face, and from that cut to:*

INT. EDITH'S STUDY. MORNING

EDITH *is sitting at the desk, she stares blankly ahead, then takes a fresh exercise-book, opens it. She picks up her fountain pen, lifts the lid of the ink-well. Dips the pen in. Her pen hovers. She writes:*

EDITH: (*Voice over*) Mathilda felt that – Mathilda felt that she –
    Mathilda felt – Mathilda – Mathilda –
    (*Having stopped writing, she turns her head, looks out of the
    window, and, from her point of view, cut to:*)

EXT. THE GARDEN. DAY

Shot of MRS MERCHANT, *with* GILES *in the pram, just leaving the house.*

INT. EDITH'S STUDY. DAY

EDITH *suddenly screws the top back on her pen, snaps the ink-well shut, very quickly hurries out of the room.*

EXT. THE GARDEN. DAY

Shot of MRS MERCHANT *and* GILES *as if through the study window, as* EDITH *runs up to her, takes over the pram, begins to push it.* MRS MERCHANT *walks beside her, as, over, the sound of the telephone ringing.* EDITH *stops. Turns around, runs back to the house, all this seen as through the study window, then cut to:*

INT. THE KITCHEN. DAY

EDITH *hurrying to the telephone, picks it up a fraction after it stops ringing. The dialling tone is audible. She stands holding it, then puts it down. She stands looking at it, then goes back to the open kitchen door.*

DAY.

From EDITH's *point of view at the kitchen door,* MRS MERCHANT *and* GILES, *waiting.*
EDITH: (*Shouting*) I shan't be coming. You go on.
  (MRS MERCHANT *turns, goes down the path.* EDITH *watches, then turns, goes back in, shuts the door.*)

INT. THE KITCHEN. DAY

EDITH *goes to the stove, puts on the kettle, and cut to* EDITH *sitting at the table, drinking a cup of tea. The telephone rings. She leaps up, goes over to it, picks it up.*
EDITH: Hello. Hello.
  (*There is a click of the receiver being replaced at the other end. She puts the telephone down, goes back to the table. Sits. The telephone rings again. She leaps up, it stops ringing. She stares at it. She sits down, almost gingerly. It rings. She gets up. It stops ringing. She remains poised between sitting and standing, staring at the telephone, and cut to:*)

INT. GILES'S BEDROOM. DAY

Come in on GILES, *nappy off, then come in on* MRS MERCHANT, *dropping the dirty nappy into a bucket. She smiles down at* GILES *and cut to* EDITH *at the door, comes in, stares down at* GILES.
EDITH: Hello darling.

MRS MERCHANT: I was just going to do his rash.

EDITH: Were you? I'll do it.

> (*As* MRS MERCHANT *opens the jar of ointment,* EDITH *dips her finger into it, takes some ointment out on the end of her finger, when the telephone rings.* MRS MERCHANT *turns towards the door, as if to answer the telephone.*)

I'll get it.

> (*She pushes past* MRS MERCHANT, *handing her* GILES, *and leaves the room.* MRS MERCHANT *looks at* GILES, *then puts her finger into the jar, as the telephone stops ringing. There is a short pause.* EDITH *reappears.* MRS MERCHANT, *not seeing her, is about to apply the cream.*)

(*With a tight smile*) I said I'd do it.

> (*She is still holding her fingers ahead of her. On them, baby-cream.* MRS MERCHANT *steps aside, offended.* EDITH *advances towards* GILES, *as the telephone rings.* EDITH *stiffens, then making an immense effort, goes on dabbing the cream. The telephone goes on ringing. She goes on dabbing the cream, finishes, wipes her fingers. The telephone is still ringing. She turns to* MRS MERCHANT.)

Would you do his nappy, please.

> (*She walks out of the room, and cut to:*)

INT. THE KITCHEN. DAY

EDITH *walks steadily towards the telephone, picks it up. She waits a second, as if expecting a click. There is a pause.*

EDITH: Hello. (*There is a silence.*) Hello. Giles?

GERALD: Gerald.

EDITH: (*Smiles very slightly*) Gerald. Yes.

GERALD: You asked me to give you a ring.

EDITH: Yes. (*Ironically*) Thank you.

GERALD: I've given you several. I shan't be giving you any more.

> (*Click, as he hangs up.* EDITH *stands there, holding the receiver, then bangs it down, then picks it up and bangs it down several times, in a fury. Stops, begins to walk away. The telephone*

253

rings. EDITH *turns, stares at it, then picks it up.*)
Edith? Gerald here. Hello again! Look old girl – it occurred to
me you might want something. Is there anything?

EDITH: (*Controlling herself*) You know what I want. (*There is a
silence.*) Don't you?

GERALD: (*After a pause*) Me?

EDITH: I want my novel back. (*Long pause.*) Are you there?

GERALD: Yes – yes, I'm here. Is there anything else you want?

EDITH: I'd like to talk to you. Properly.

GERALD: Would you like to see my room? Where I'm living, and
how I've settled down?

EDITH: Yes. (*Quickly.*) Where is it?

GERALD: Oh, better to pick you up, I think. If you don't mind
riding in the old side-car, that is?

EDITH: No. That'll be all right.

GERALD: Say in an hour.

EDITH: Yes. Yes. In an hour.

GERALD: In an hour.

(*Click as he puts the telephone down.* EDITH *replaces the
telephone, turns, sees* MRS MERCHANT *standing before her,
holding* GILES. *Looks at her, looks at* GILES, *then, as if
realizing.*)

EDITH: Oh. Mrs Merchant. Um, would you mind terribly holding
the, um . . .

(*Cut to:*)

INT. THE KITCHEN. DAY

MRS MERCHANT, *her face staring out of the window.*

EXT. THE GARDEN. DAY

From MRS MERCHANT'*s point of view. At kitchen window see* EDITH
walking down the path to the motorbike. There is a man sitting on it in
GERALD'*s coat, goggles, etc.* EDITH *says something to him, cut to:*

TOMMY: All I know, Edie, is he told me to bring you. Isn't that all right?

(EDITH, *after a pause, gets into the side-car, it roars off. And cut back to:*)

INT. THE KITCHEN. DAY

MRS MERCHANT *at the window, turning away. And cut to:*

EXT. THE HOTEL. DAY

The motorbike pulling up before a large shabby house converted into a shabby private hotel. TOMMY *gets off.* EDITH *gets out,* TOMMY *takes* EDITH's *arm, they walk up the steps to the front door, and cut to:*

INT. THE HOTEL. DAY

They go up grubby stairs, passing a lounge-type room. From which comes the noise of a television set. Then up more stairs past various doors with numbers half-erased. They reach the last two doors, next to each other.

TOMMY: This is his, Edie.

EDITH: I think I'd better do this alone, if you don't mind.

TOMMY: Of course, Edie.

(*He turns, to go to the other room, stops as* EDITH *makes to knock.*)

Look, I'll be in here if you need me. See.

(EDITH *looks at him, then turns to* GERALD's *door, knocks. There is no reply.* EDITH *knocks again, then turns the handle. The door opens. She goes in. The light is on. The bed is unmade. There are clothes spilled everywhere, and a general sense of muddle and squalor. Propped against the mirror there is a note, on which is written: 'This is my room'.* EDITH *reads the note, turns, looks around. Makes as if to go out, then turns, goes to the*

255

chest of drawers, cupboard, bed, each one in turn, hunts rapidly through them, then stops, stares around, and cut to: TOMMY's *room. It is in the same condition as* GERALD's. TOMMY *is sitting in an armchair. Come in on his face, looking towards the door, then cut to:*)

EDITH: (*At the door*) He's not there. (*Little pause.*) Of course.

TOMMY: Oh.

(*He gets to his feet, as if about to go and look.*)

EDITH: He's not there. He never intended to be. Where is he?

TOMMY: I don't know. (*Little pause.*) Edie, I don't know. Look, he said I was to pick you up and take you to his room, seeing as you wanted to see it, that was all, Edie.

EDITH: (*Advances towards him*) You're lying. You're lying. (*Stands in front of him.*) All the money you've borrowed and never mentioned again – all the food you've guzzled – the drink you've got drunk on to give yourself the courage to bore and insult my friends – who do you think buys him those shirts you make dirty, his coat – that coat – *I* gave it to him, my books gave it to him, to you – you owe me, you owe me. (*Punching at his chest.*) Now you tell me, tell me, tell me! (*Her voice is rising hysterically, and cut to the hall, before the front door.* TOMMY *holds the door open for* EDITH. *She steps out, he follows, his hand on her arm. He closes the door, and from the doorstep, their point of view, cut to:*)

EXT. THE HOTEL. DAY

GERALD *in* TOMMY's *coat, on the motor-bicycle, driving away.* TOMMY *and* EDITH *stand staring after him, and cut to:*

EXT. THE DRIVE. DAY

Come in on MRS MERCHANT, *medium shot, coming up the drive. Her walk – seen from in front is jerky, odd. Hold, then cut to:*

INT. TAXI. DAY

EDITH *is sitting forward, staring towards* MRS MERCHANT, *who is walking towards them, she taps on the glass, stops the taxi. She opens the window and leans out of it. Close-up of* MRS MERCHANT's *face, seen from* EDITH's *point of view. Tears are streaming down her cheeks. She makes to open her mouth, closes it, clearly very distraught. But there is something sinister in the effect.* EDITH *gets out, starts after her, clutches her arm.* MRS MERCHANT *turns, says something,* EDITH *says something then turns, runs towards the house.* TOMMY *has got out of the taxi, and is following slowly. He stops, turns back to the taxi.*

INT. THE KITCHEN. DAY

EDITH *flings open the door shot from inside the kitchen then a brisk montage as she runs through the house, comes to Giles's room, goes in.* GILES *is asleep.* EDITH *turns, comes out, walks back to the kitchen.* TOMMY *is standing just inside the door.*

EDITH: He's here somewhere.

TOMMY: Is he?

EDITH: He must have been. He's just sacked Mrs Merchant.
   (*She goes to the door, looks out.*)

EXT. GARDEN. DAY

From EDITH's *point of view at kitchen door, see taxi still there. There is a short, intense silence, then* GERALD's *motorbike starts up (not seen) and roars around the house into sight, up the drive, past the taxi and away. There is a pause.*

INT. THE KITCHEN. DAY

EDITH *turns, looks at* TOMMY.

TOMMY: (*Licks his lips*) I haven't got any money, Edith.

EDITH: What?

TOMMY: For the taxi. To get me back to Guildford, see.

(EDITH *starts to laugh, stops, opens her handbag, fumbles in it. Then looks at* TOMMY.)

EDITH: You've got to make him come here and talk to me.

(*She takes a five-pound note out of her wallet, hands it to him.*) Will you?

(TOMMY *looks at the money, then at* EDITH.)

TOMMY: This is a fiver, did you know, Edie?

EDITH: (*After a slight pause*) I haven't got anything smaller. That's all I have.

(TOMMY *puts his hand into his pocket.*)

TOMMY: Oh, look, I've got a pound. I won't need this after all.

(*He hands it back to* EDITH.)

Thanks.

EDITH: Please, Tommy. (*Cut to her face.*) Please.

INT. EDITH'S BEDROOM. NIGHT

EDITH *is asleep*, Persuasion *lying open beside her. The lamp is on the floor, lamp-shade tilted, to soften the light. The baby-alarm is on. Gentle sounds of* GILES *breathing. Keep on* EDITH's *face. She sits up suddenly, stares around. Gets up, walks to the door. There should be something almost somnambulistic in her movements.*

INT. LIVING-ROOM. NIGHT

She goes down the hall, opens the door to the living-room. Stands blinking. Then cut to GERALD *sitting in a chair, in* TOMMY's *coat, facing her. Cut back to* EDITH.

GERALD: (*Smiling, voice gentle*) I've come, you see.

EDITH: Yes. (*Quietly*) Just a minute. I'm not properly awake. I've got to be awake to say the right words, haven't I? (*She smiles, goes out.*)

INT. BATHROOM. NIGHT

Cut to EDITH *washing her face under the cold tap.*

INT. LIVING-ROOM. NIGHT

Then cut to EDITH, *drops of water still on her face, coming back to the sitting-room. It is empty. She stares around as* GERALD *comes out of* GILES's *room, closing the door quietly.*

GERALD: It's all right, I haven't gone. (*He sits down.*)

EDITH: You've grown so expert in your games. (*Smiling, gentle.*)
    They're very literary. Literal, in fact, That's why I have to get the right words.
    (*She is walking slowly towards him, then crouches down at his feet, takes his hand.*)
    There. I've got you.
    (GERALD *puts his hand on hers.*)

GERALD: I didn't realize you wanted me.

EDITH: Please Gerrie, could I have it back? Please.
    (*She smiles up at him.*)

GERALD: (*Carefully*) Would you say you wanted it more than anything?

EDITH: Is that what you've been proving to me? I knew it already. I've known it since I started writing – since about the third paragraph of my first novel. It's the only thing nobody would ever have to prove to me. I'm not ashamed, either. I'm not ashamed.

GERALD: And what would become of me, if I gave it back? How would I sustain your interest? You've tried to catch my every move, these last few days.

EDITH: You could come here again, if you wanted. For as long as you wanted. And Tommy too.

GERALD: Would you love us?

EDITH: (*After a pause*) I would do my best.

GERALD: I could make love to you?

EDITH: (*With a slight, malicious smile*) You could do your best.

GERALD: Ah! (*He smiles. Touches the side of her cheek.*) And if it's too late? If I haven't got the exercise books any more?
(EDITH *thinks, then very carefully:*)

EDITH: I think I'd like to see you die.

GERALD: (*Nods*) Then it's too late for me. I haven't got them any more.
(EDITH *stares up at him, frozen. Then slowly gets up, walks to a chair opposite, sits down, looks at* GERALD. *She tries to smile.*)

EDITH: What did you do with them?

GERALD: (*Shakes his head*) It doesn't matter any more. Not to me.
(*He puts his hand into his pocket.*) Did you find the right words, do you think?
(EDITH's *mouth is trembling, but her voice is controlled, as if with a tremendous effort.*)

EDITH: I shall start again. And once I've started, what you've done won't mean anything.
(GERALD *is holding sleeping pills, not of course registered by* EDITH – *in his cupped hand. He begins to pop them into his mouth, as if they were Smarties.*)

GERALD: You'll be able to say of me . . . (*popping them into his mouth nonchalantly*) . . . that I was literal to the end.

EDITH: Perhaps doing it again is only right. It'll be different, there will be things to add – but above all – you won't be here. What you've done *will* mean something. But to me. Not to you. You're so much waste, got rid of. And there's nothing more you can do to hurt me, you see.

GERALD: I know. That's the appalling thing about you.

EDITH: (*Smiles*) Would you go now, please. (*Getting up.*)

GERALD: Oh. Aren't you going to stay. I thought you wanted to see me – um, die. (*Modestly.*)
(EDITH *stares at him, aghast.* GERALD *throws the last few sleeping pills into his mouth, swallows them down with a gulp. Then shows her the bottle.*)
Isn't that what you wanted?

EDITH: (*After a pause*) How many have you taken?

GERALD: Twenty-two.

EDITH: You're a child. A nasty child.

(*Long pause, she stares at him.* GERALD *is staring up at her.*)

GERALD: And my games are so literal. But the words *were* yours. Weren't they the right ones, after all?

EDITH: (*After a pause*) Do you want me to telephone for a doctor then? If you do, say so.

GERALD: Oh, that's *your* business.

EDITH: I'll do what *you* tell me to do.

GERALD: Then – do whatever you think is best. You have your church, your art, and your education. If the maxims you derive from each should conflict, you will have to choose.

EDITH: (*After a pause*) How do you feel?

GERALD: A trifle nervous. But physically tip-top. The system needs about twenty minutes to absorb them. After that it's down-hill all the way. But I believe the decline can be arrested until I go into a coma.

EDITH: In other words, you can reach the telephone unaided.
(*She turns, goes out. Cut to* GERALD's *face, he smiles, uncertainly. There is a pause.* EDITH *returns, walks past him, into* GILES's *room. There is the sound of a protest from* GILES, *sleepy. She comes out, carrying him. Walks past* GERALD, *and out of the room. Cut to* GERALD's *face. He sits resolutely. Crosses his hands in his lap. Licks his lip. His face twitches slightly. He raises a hand, scratches at his cheek as if he had an itch there. Then lowers his hand, raises it, scratches again, blinks.*)

INT. BEDROOM. NIGHT

EDITH *is sitting up in bed, staring ahead.* GILES *is lying beside her, asleep. She picks her watch up from the table, looks at it, puts it down. She turns, looks down at* GILES *and, cut to his face asleep.* EDITH's *hand, shaking, goes to his hair, touches it and cut from this to:*

MAN IN A SIDE-CAR

INT. LIVING-ROOM. NIGHT

GERALD's *face, eyes closed, mouth open in a yawn. His hand is resting against his cheek. His eyes blink open. He stares blearily around, heaves himself up, gropes forward, stands swaying, and cut to:*

INT. BEDROOM. NIGHT

EDITH *is sitting up, staring ahead with great intensity. She closes her eyes, opens them. Suddenly there is a crash, eerily distanced. Her head jerks in alarm as the room fills with heavy breathing. She looks towards the baby-alarm. The breathing is coming from it. She jerks her head away, stares ahead. Then reaches out a hand trembling slightly, to the alarm, turns it off. Then she sits with her head sunk on her chest, eyes closed. Fade out on this, and fade up on* EDITH *lying, her face sideways on the pillow, her thumb in her mouth, staring into* GILES's *face, also sideways on the pillow, thumb in his mouth, asleep. She straightens slowly, turns to the baby-alarm, still sucking on her thumb. She reaches out a hand. Turns on the knob. The breathing is now stertorous, rasping. She turns the knob off quickly, blinks and as if coming to herself, swings her legs out of bed. She hurries out of the bedroom and cut to:*

INT. HALL. NIGHT

EDITH *is in the hall, and from her point of view. Cut to the door to* GERALD's *study. It opens.* EDITH *is staring at it, making incomprehensible noises of fear.* TOMMY *is standing there, in* GERALD's *coat, goggles pushed up on his forehead, helmet and gauntlets under his arm.*

TOMMY: I'm cold. (*Slightly whining.*) He told me to wait outside, with the bike, where is he then?

    (EDITH's *lips move for a second. She gives a ghastly grin.*)

EDITH: Asleep.

    (*Cut to:*)

INT. GILES'S BEDROOM. NIGHT

Come straight in on GERALD, *lying on the floor, snoring heavily. The baby-alarm microphone close to his face. Then cut to* TOMMY's *face, shocked and bewildered, staring at* GERALD.

TOMMY: Ohh – Ohh – look now – look – Edie we've got to – look.
(*Little pause.*) What are we going to do, then? What are we going to do?
(*Cut to* EDITH's *face. She is staring at* TOMMY. *Cut to:*)

EXT. THE DRIVE. DAWN

In on GERALD's *face, in close-up, in goggles and crash helmet. Then draw back, to see him in the side-car, with his head back and his mouth open, breathing deeply. Then his face is drawn slowly out of camera and cut to* TOMMY *and* GERALD, *on the motor-bicycle and side-car respectively, pulling quietly down the drive, from* EDITH's *point of view watching from the window, then cut to her face at the window, staring out.*

EXT. FIELD. DAY

A path across a field. The motorbike travelling slowly and eerily across it, and from a distance, see the motor-bicycle stopping. TOMMY *pulls* GERALD *out of the side-car, lowers him to the ground, then* TOMMY *walks away, running, walking, running, and cut to:*

EXT. MRS MERCHANT'S HOUSE. DAY

The gate to the front door, MRS MERCHANT *standing before it, arms akimbo.* EDITH, *with the pram.*

MRS MERCHANT: I've never been spoken to like that before. Never in my life.

EDITH: He'll never speak to you like that again. I promise. (*Little pause*.) He left me – just after he – he'd spoken to you. He said he wouldn't come back. (*Little pause*.) We've always had such a good relationship, Mrs Merchant. (*Little pause*.) Please. We need you, Giles and I. We do need you.

INT. THE KITCHEN. DAY

Come in on TOMMY'*s hand, raising a cup to his lips, then to his face. He looks desperately tired.* EDITH *sits opposite, watching him.*

TOMMY: Could it be murder, Edie?

EDITH: It was suicide.

TOMMY: But legally? I mean, if the police –?

EDITH: He wanted to kill himself. He wanted to do it in the way that would hurt me most. He was determined to be hateful to the end. (*Little pause*.) He had the right to kill himself. I had the right to defend myself from the consequences of his doing it here.

TOMMY: You said yourself he was ill. He needed help –

(EDITH *looks at him very coldly*.)

EDITH: Well, you didn't give it to him, did you?

TOMMY: No. I gave it to you instead.

EDITH: Why?

TOMMY: You know why, now. Don't you?

EDITH: Are you in love with me?

TOMMY: I've always been, Edie. Always. (*Little pause*.) And did Gerrie ask you about it? About whether we'd ever slept together?

EDITH: (*After a pause*) No. Anyway, it was a long time ago.

TOMMY: Still, he asked *me*. I was just wondering –

EDITH: What did you tell him? (*Little pause*.) *Did* you tell him?

TOMMY: Certainly not. No. I told him it was ridiculous.

EDITH: And so it was. It always is. Quite ridiculous. Everything is ridiculous. Gerald's death.

(*The telephone rings.* EDITH *and* TOMMY *stare at each other. She gets up, lifts the telephone from the receiver, staring at* TOMMY, *then turns away, puts it to her ear.*)

Hello. (*Little pause*.) Yes, it is. (*Brightly smiling*.)

INT. HOSPITAL WARD. DAY

EDITH *and* TOMMY *walking along it, past various beds, to a bed near the end, screened off. There is a* NURSE *with them. The* NURSE *pulls back the screen and cut from* TOMMY'S *face and* EDITH'S *face to a* MAN, *sitting up, grinning, his arm in a sling, having his pyjamas changed, and cut to* TOMMY *and* EDITH *walking on to the next bed, screened. The nurse opens the screen for them, and cut to* GERALD'S *face on the pillow, eyes open, breath very faint, then* EDITH *is sitting in a chair beside him.* TOMMY *standing beside her. He looks down at* GERALD'S *face, he makes a sound, turns his face away, clutches at* EDITH'S *hand, and on the tableau:*

INT. THE KITCHEN. DAY

TOMMY *and* EDITH *sitting at the table, a cup being raised to* TOMMY'S *lips.*

EDITH: (*Almost desultory*) That's your fifth cup. You'll be ill.

TOMMY: (*After a pause*) Four, I've only had four cups.

EDITH: That's still too many.

(*Little silence, as* MRS MERCHANT *comes into the kitchen, walking on tip-toe. She stops by* EDITH, *looks down at her compassionately.*)

(*Wanly smiling*) I'll be all right. Really. Tommy's going to look after me, for a little.

(MRS MERCHANT *gingerly touches* EDITH'S *arm, she goes out. There is a silence.*)

You had two cups in that ghastly room, and two in the hospital canteen. It's your fifth.

TOMMY: (*Thinks, nods*) Fifth. (*Little silence.*) I won't have any more.

EDITH: What are you going to do now? Are you going to stay here?

(*After a pause,* TOMMY *nods.*)

I won't want you here.

TOMMY: I know.

EDITH: But you'll stay anyway?

TOMMY: Yes I will, Edie. I don't mind being inferior, see. I don't mind.

(EDITH *looks at him, with a weary smile.*)

EDITH: I shall despise you.

TOMMY: Sometimes. Other times you won't notice me, even. And I'll be nice to Giles. (*Little pause.*) I have no shame.

EDITH: No. That's your strength, isn't it?

TOMMY: Of course people will despise you for living with me.

EDITH: I'm quite strong too. (*She gets up, goes out of the kitchen.*)

INT. EDITH'S STUDY. DAY

She enters, turns on the light, goes to the window, looks out. Suddenly she crosses herself, closing her eyes and lowering her head. She smiles ironically, turns to the desk. On the desk are the exercise-books, neatly piled, and as the camera comes in on them sounds of great chords of religious music, organ, which goes on as EDITH *approaches the desk slowly, as if in a trance, picks them up as if holding something sacred, turns around, her eyes aglow. The music still going on, solemn and magnificent, and:*

TOMMY: (*At the door*) So he put them back then?

(*The music stops. There is a silence.*)

EDITH: You see. You see. I was bound to get them back. I'm a novelist. (*In a whisper.*) That's all I am. That's all I want to be. I shall go on writing novels until I die. If God is good to me, I shall die as I finish a sentence. His Will Be Done.

(*Cut to* TOMMY's *face, staring at her, stay on his face as organ music, over, starts again, gently, mixing into* EDITH *at her desk.*)

EXT. GARDEN. DAY

The organ music going on, as through the window to her side we see MRS MERCHANT *in a deckchair, holding* GILES *in her arms, in an accidentally religious posture, and kneeling beside her,* TOMMY, *beside whom is a small jug of soapy water. He has his hands to his face, as if in prayer, blowing a mighty bubble. This shot freezes into a still, as the organ music continues, and: Titles superimposed. Fade out.*

Plaintiffs and Defendants

To Alan
for Ben, Simon, Peter and Charles

Plaintiffs and Defendants was first presented by BBC Television on 14 October 1975. The cast was as follows:

PETER	Alan Bates
HILARY	Rosemary McHale
CHARLES	Dinsdale Landen
JEREMY	Daniel St George
JOANNA	Georgina Hale
SALLUST	Simon Cadell
JOSH	Benjamin Whitrow
MRS SAWSBURY	Rosemary Martin
MR ROSE	Victor Langley
MAN I	David Rose
DOCTOR	Tom Kempinski
Director	Michael Lindsay-Hogg
Designer	Richard Henry
Producer	Kenith Trodd

INT. JOANNA'S BED-SITTER

PETER *is lying in bed, staring blankly into camera.*

JOANNA: (*Voice over*) . . . the thing about Josh, you see – well, he
   didn't discover about himself until he was nearly thirty, it
   must have been awful for him.

PETER: (*Politely*) Must have been.

JOANNA: (*Voice over*) He's still the only person in the world I can
   talk to. Except you. I can talk to you, right?

PETER: Right.

JOANNA: You and Josh. You're incredibly different, though. He's
   a great talker and you're a great listener.
   (*Cut to* JOANNA, *sitting in the corner of the bed, one shoulder
   hunched, smoking.*)
   (*After a pause*) I'm being boring, aren't I, sorry. (*Sounds of*
   PETER *moving.*) Is it time, then?

PETER: (*Beginning to get dressed*) Well – nearly, I'm afraid, Jo.

JOANNA: (*Sits watching him*) It's funny how I always want to say
   something and then stop myself, all except this time. I'm
   sorry.

PETER: (*Dressing*) Say what?

JOANNA: Something to stop you going.

PETER: What have you said?

JOANNA: Nothing.

PETER: Oh, I see.

JOANNA: Do you want to go, is that it?

PETER: Of course not.

JOANNA: We've never spent a night together. Never.

PETER: No. I'm very bad-tempered in the morning.

JOANNA: Are you?

PETER: Yes.

JOANNA: I can't imagine you bad-tempered. Or anything but
   polite. No other moods except polite and randy. You are still
   randy for me, aren't you?
   (PETER *laughs, slightly embarrassed.* JOANNA *laughs.*)

273

You're the only man I've ever wanted, in this way. Ever.

PETER: What are you going to do this evening?

JOANNA: Oh, see Josh, I don't know. Do something to keep my mind off.

PETER: But that cover you're designing –

JOANNA: I'll start on that after midnight. I like to work after midnight.

PETER: (*Straightening from doing up his shoes*) You don't think that being freelance cuts you off a bit? I know working in an office has its hazards but –

JOANNA: I wouldn't get much of a lunchtime, though, would I? And I need long lunch hours, right? (*Smiling.*) When you have them?

(PETER *smiles.*)

I like them better even than evenings like this. The afternoons afterwards are like dreams, but the nights go on a bit. Go on then, make a run for it before I begin –

(PETER *comes over, bends to kiss her.* JOANNA's *arms go around his neck, clasp him. Cut to* PETER's *face, in* JOANNA's *clasp, slightly desperate.*)

No claims, right?

PETER: I'll see you soon.

JOANNA: (*Letting him go*) Do you know when exactly?

PETER: Not exactly.

JOANNA: But soon?

PETER: Of course. It's going to be a hell of a week or two –

(JOANNA *smiles, pained. Nods.* PETER *raises his hand in salute, goes to the door, opens it. All this from* JOANNA's *point of view.* PETER *closes the door. When it's almost closed, see* JOANNA *from his point of view. She is sitting hunched, lighting another cigarette. She turns her face, looks towards him. The door obliterates her as it closes, and on the closed door, titles begin.*)

EXT. TURKISH BATHS

Titles continue. PETER *enters.*

PLAINTIFFS AND DEFENDANTS

INT. TURKISH BATHS

Titles. PETER *washing himself vigorously.*

EXT. TURKISH BATHS

PETER *emerging, and*

INT. HALL. PETER'S HOUSE

He enters, puts down briefcase, touches his hair, glances at watch.
Then goes down hall, opens door to kitchen. Cut to:

HILARY

In her late thirties, is bent over a pile of papers marking them. Her
briefcase is on the kitchen table. She looks up, smiles.

HILARY: Hello.

PETER: Hi. (*Smiles back.*)

HILARY: Won't be a minute. (*Goes on marking.*)
   (PETER *picks up a mug from a kitchen shelf, sits down at the*
   table with it, pours himself some coffee.)
   You eaten?

PETER: Yes, I had a bite.

HILARY: Good. (*Scribbles something on the bottom of the essay.*) You
   know that staff meeting last week – where I made a few brief
   points about marking adults as if they were children, and the
   resistance from almost everyone?

PETER: But you carried the meeting.

HILARY: Until this evening. When a deputation of students
   demanded to know why we'd stopped grading their essays –
   they said it wasn't fair, as it meant they didn't know where
   they stood.

PETER: God!

HILARY: Well, this one knows where *she* stands all right. (*Pushing the essay away.*) C? plus.

PETER: She'll want to know more about that question-mark.

HILARY: How did the case go?

PETER: (*Thinks*) Oh, we lost. And the lecture?

HILARY: All right after ten minutes. I slid from *Little Dorrit* to *Bleak House* and got pretty knowing about the law. You look very dapper.

PETER: Do I?

HILARY: Oh, of course the party – how was it?

PETER: I didn't go.

HILARY: Why not?

PETER: Didn't feel in the mood.

HILARY: (*Has got up, comes around behind him, puts her hands on his shoulder, kisses him*) Your hair's wet.

PETER: Is it? (*Feels it.*) I had a shower.

HILARY: A *shower*, where?

PETER: I had a game of squash with Sallust. My pupil. It seemed a better idea than the party.

HILARY: And who won?

PETER: He did. Quite convincingly, actually.

HILARY: Darling, do you think you *ought* to play with him? He must be much younger than you and in top-notch condition – ?

PETER: Oh, I gave him a run, you know. (*Yawns.*)

HILARY: How's he getting on?

PETER: Oh, all right – gets on my tits now and then – passes me notes on points that help the Judges while away another fifteen minutes of my life – ambitious little sod – he's all right.

(*Door opens. JEREMY enters, he is about sixteen.*)
Hello.

JEREMY: Hi. Is there an apple?

HILARY: In the bowl on top of the fridge.

(*JEREMY goes over, takes an apple.*)

PETER: Did you go to the flicks?

JEREMY: What?

PETER: Cinema? (*Little pause.*) Moving pictures. Movies. You said at breakfast you were going to the movies.

JEREMY: Oh. Yeah. (*Bites into his apple.*)

PETER: What did you see?

JEREMY: Oh, that famous Renoir thing.

HILARY: *La Grande Illusion?*

(JEREMY *thinks, shakes his head.*)

PETER: *La Règle du Jeu.*

JEREMY: Yeah.

PETER: I wish I'd known it was on, I could have just done with that this evening. That marvellous little Jewish Count – the rabbit shoot – every time I think of his face it makes me want to cry.

JEREMY: What, the rabbit's?

HILARY: Didn't you like it, darling?

JEREMY: Yeah, I did. Quite.

PETER: Oh come on, Jeremy!

HILARY: Darling, if he didn't like it, he didn't like it. They've got to discover their own classics –

PETER: Well, what are they?

HILARY: Darling, what's your idea of a classic?

JEREMY: Classic? (*Thinks.*) I never think about whether it's a *classic* or not. Just about whether I liked it.

PETER: And you didn't like *Règle du Jeu?*

JEREMY: (*Who has been moving towards the door*) I said I quite liked it.

HILARY: That's true, darling. He did say he quite liked it.

(JEREMY *goes out.*)

PETER: (*After a pause*) He didn't like it.

HILARY: Perhaps he tried, though.

PETER: Is that what the question-mark's for? In C question-mark plus.

HILARY: You didn't give him much chance.

PETER: A chance? With Renoir? He claims to be what they call a film buff, which I thought might mean that he could end up editing or directing or even reviewing the bloody things but he talks as if he already distributes them.

(*Cut to:*)

INT. THE BEDROOM

HILARY *in bed, reading, spectacles on, seen from* PETER's *point of view, as he hangs his trousers on the chair. She looks up.*

HILARY: I don't remember getting you yellow knickers.

PETER: No, I picked up a fresh pair, for the game, I'd forgotten – (*Coughs.*)

HILARY: That cough. You've got to stop. (*Goes back to her book.*)
(PETER *climbs into bed, lies staring ahead, and cut to a blown-up picture of a Junior Colts cricket eleven, seen from* PETER's *point of view. First, the picture as a whole, then various faces, ending with possibly the young* PETER's. *Cut back to his face, smiling slightly, then frowns as a very light snoring noise impinges. He turns, looks down at* HILARY, *who has fallen asleep.* PETER *gently takes the book from her hands, puts it on her side of the bed, then the spectacles, lays them on top of the book, looks down at her face, cut to* HILARY's *face, in sleep.* PETER *kisses her forehead, and cut to:*)

INT. PETER'S ROOM IN CHAMBERS

SALLUST *sitting in a corner.* PETER *gesturing a woman in her middle thirties into a seat. With her,* ROSE, *a middle-aged solicitor, who also sits down.*

MRS SAWSBURY: (*After a pause*) I didn't realize there'd be two of you –

PETER: Mr Sallust is my pupil. It's customary for him to sit in, I hope you don't mind. He'll be helping me with your case. Mr Rose, I've had a look at the statement Mrs Sawsbury gave you – there are just a few things I'd like to clear up. Did you explain to Mrs Sawsbury?

ROSE: She knows you're to be her Counsel.

PETER: Good. Mrs Sawsbury, I'll have to ask you some fairly brutal questions, but they're questions the other side are bound to put to you, so we must be quite clear on your responses, all right?

MRS SAWSBURY: Yes.

PETER: Now – (*looking at the statement*) now your present income comes entirely from the alimony settled on you by your husband, that's right, isn't it?

ROSE: Yes.

MRS SAWSBURY: No, I've got a job now.

PETER: (*Glances at* ROSE *very briefly, then away again*) What job?

MRS SAWSBURY: Usherette, in a cinema.

PETER: West End cinema?

MRS SAWSBURY: Yes.

PETER: And what does that bring you?

MRS SAWSBURY: Twenty pounds a week.

ROSE: You didn't mention this to me, Mrs Sawsbury.

MRS SAWSBURY: I only started last week. But I've been looking for work for a long time – we can't live on the alimony, not these days.

PETER: No, of course not. And you haven't asked for more from your ex-husband?

MRS SAWSBURY: No, I never wanted his money anyway, I'd rather do without his help. I thought (*looks at* ROSE) it would make a difference if I could bring them up without his help.

PETER: What hours do you work?

MRS SAWSBURY: Three afternoons and three evenings.

PETER: Sounds rather nice. And who looks after the children?

MRS SAWSBURY: I've got them into one of the Council nursery schools.

PETER: But your oldest child – the boy – Kevin – is old enough to go to school, isn't he?

MRS SAWSBURY: I've got the choice until next year. They can stay at the nursery until half-past five.

PETER: Oh yes. Very practical. (*Little pause.*) And in the evening? On the three evenings – ?

MRS SAWSBURY: I have a friend who looks after them.

PETER: Gives them their tea and puts them to bed?

MRS SAWSBURY: And stays in with them.

PETER: You don't pay your friend?

MRS SAWSBURY: No, I don't.

PETER: A real friend, then. (*Smiles, little pause.*) Now what do *you* estimate your husband's income at?

MRS SAWSBURY: Well, it varies – I know it's got more since he left – but it goes from year to year.

ROSE: In his statement he puts it between four and five thousand a year. Three and a half would be more accurate.

MRS SAWSBURY: Anyway, I don't see what that's got to do with it, besides, he's got another child now. That's what's so unfair.

PETER: It's part of their case that he can give your children certain advantages, you see.

MRS SAWSBURY: He can't give them my love.

PETER: What about your ex-husband's new wife?

MRS SAWSBURY: They don't *know* her – except as somebody who stuffs them with chocolates and takes them to the pictures. And their coloured TV, of course, but they're not advantages, are they?

PETER: (*Smiles*) Only if you like Westerns.

MRS SAWSBURY: Lucille hates them.

PETER: But you'd agree that they get on reasonably well with her? Your children do –

MRS SAWSBURY: They don't mind going.

PETER: Do they look forward to it?

MRS SAWSBURY: Only for the treats. But they wouldn't miss them if they weren't promised by their father.

PETER: (*Looks quickly at* ROSE, *who acknowledges the look, then down at the statement.*) Mrs Sawsbury, I said some of my questions would be brutal. Well, here's one. Are you ready? (MRS SAWSBURY *nods.*)
Are you living with anyone?

MRS SAWSBURY: It's my flat, I've the lease.

PETER: Well then, is anybody living with you?

MRS SAWSBURY: No.

PETER: It's very important, Mrs Sawsbury. The other side claims that there is a man – they have evidence –

MRS SAWSBURY: No.

PETER: The friend who looks after the children. Is it a man or a woman?

MRS SAWSBURY: (*After a pause*) A man.

PETER: And does he ever spend the night in your flat?
(*The telephone rings.*)
Sorry. (*Picks it up quickly.*) Hello. (*Little pause.*) Look, I'm
sorry, but I can't talk, I'm in the middle of a conference.
(*Little pause.*) I can't say at the moment. Sorry. Goodbye.
(*Puts the telephone down.*) Sorry. (*Looks momentarily
distracted.*) Um, yes, does he, Mrs Sawsbury?

MRS SAWSBURY: Well only sometimes, when he's late back.

PETER: And does he spend those nights in your bed? I'm sorry,
Mrs Sawsbury.

MRS SAWSBURY: (*After a pause*) Yes.

PETER: And do you have any plans to marry?

MRS SAWSBURY: He's a Catholic, and so's his wife. (*Pause.*)
Well, why not, we're both lonely, his wife hates him, she
doesn't mind, his daughter's grown-up, *she*'s married now,
nobody cares – and *he*'s got somebody in *his* bed, hasn't he,
and if he can do it, why shouldn't I?

PETER: I'm not judging you, Mrs Sawsbury, but I must know,
for your sake, what we're to expect in court.

MRS SAWSBURY: Well, what *am* I to expect? I mean, he can't just
come after two years without doing anything except send his
cheques in, and take my children away because he's got more
money than me because he can work and I can't and because
he's married again. He can't do that – that's not justice, is it?

PETER: Why do *you* think he wants them back?

MRS SAWSBURY: To spite me.

PETER: He says he loves them.

MRS SAWSBURY: Then why did he leave them in the first place?
If you love people you stay for them, don't you? I didn't take
them away from him, he took himself away because he said
he couldn't stand it any more, and now he's trying to take
them away. Everything's always come so easily to him, but
they're not going to. I won't let them. (*Pause.*) I won't, you
know.
(*Cut to:*)

INT. PETER'S ROOM IN CHAMBERS

MRS SAWSBURY *and* ROSE *gone*. PETER *sitting back, smoking,*
SALLUST *watching him.*

PETER: Well, Tommy, what do you think?

SALLUST: She's very unengaging.

PETER: Well, not to her elderly Catholic lover. Nor, perhaps, to
her children. So possibly not to the judge – at least, if he's
elderly, Catholic and childish. Some of them are.

SALLUST: I hope she doesn't get on to her ex-husband when she
gives evidence. It'll seem as if she's only hanging on to them to
spite him.

PETER: He's a swine. No, he probably isn't.
(*The telephone rings.*)
(*Hesitates, fractionally, picks it up*) Yes. Oh, well put her
through, please, I'm free now. (*Listens.*) Yes, yes, that'll be all
right. Goodbye. (*Puts the telephone down.*)

INT. JOANNA'S BED-SITTER

PETER *and* JOANNA *are standing in the middle of the room.*

JOANNA: I've got a lot of ham and assorted crudities.

PETER: I'm not hungry, thanks.

JOANNA: There's some Scotch.

PETER: God no. I've got some briefs to look at this afteroon. Well,
how are you, then? Been, um, doing anything interesting?

JOANNA: Oh, a few covers from those people where we met.

PETER: Good.

JOANNA: A few ups and downs with Josh, right?

PETER: Josh?

JOANNA: That friend of mine I told you about. His affair with that
actor came to a sticky end, I'm sure I told you. (*Pause.*)
Anyway, he's been in one of his depressions, losing hair and
fattening, so I've been on call as his favourite mother. It's too
ridiculous.

PETER: Poor Jo. (*Little pause.*) Poor Josh, come to think of it.

(JOANNA *laughs and cut to* PETER *suppressing wince*.)

JOANNA: Sorry about phoning. But your coming around at lunchtime was such a habit and then you stopped – I worried whether you were all right, right?

PETER: No, I'm sorry I had to be so circumspect, there was somebody with me. (*Pause.*) Sorry, by the way, I haven't been able to get around, it's been very difficult, what with one case and another . . . haven't had a moment . . . how'd you get hold of my work number, by the way?

JOANNA: I looked it up.

PETER: That was very clever of you.

JOANNA: (*Laughs*) Matter of fact, I did manage to get a glimpse of you.

PETER: Where?

JOANNA: On the tube, actually. I was in the next carriage and saw you through the windows, it was weird.

PETER: Weird, really, what was I doing?

JOANNA: Well, do you really want to know? (*Laughs.*) Well, you were smoking and you had some work in your lap, and you were looking at a girl who was sitting a bit down from you. She was very young and she was reading an enormous book. I made one of those calculations only unlib. spinsters are supposed to make, you know, that she could just about have been your daughter.

PETER: (*Lighting a cigarette*) How long did you watch me for?

JOANNA: Oh, a few stops. Any of your cases been interesting?

PETER: Only if you're interested in mess. And defeat.

JOANNA: Well, one side usually wins, you told me, right?

PETER: At the moment, I appear to be representing the other side. Why didn't you join me at one of the stops?

JOANNA: I wasn't sure you wanted to see me. To tell you the truth I was following you.

PETER: (*After a pause*) Really? How far?

JOANNA: Well, to your front door. And then Jeremy came up on his moped – it was Jeremy, right? He went in.

PETER: On a moped and through the front door, yes, that was probably my son.

283

JOANNA: (*Laughs. There is a pause*) I shouldn't have told you, right? I swore to God I wouldn't.

PETER: It doesn't matter.

JOANNA: It matters to me, as I'm trying to cut down on humiliations.

PETER: That's because you know you're (*hesitates*) worth more than a lunchtime doss-down with a married man.

JOANNA: That's all it's been, then?

PETER: Well, it's not been much else for you, I shouldn't think. Jo, I'm sorry, it was all my fault, I know that.

JOANNA: (*Smiles in pain*) Well, I thought *you*'d give me my cards with some style. I mean, be original . . .

PETER: I'm sorry.

JOANNA: For the past two weeks, since you stopped coming, I've been waiting by the phone. I didn't dare go out, even if it meant missing a chance of a commission. I even thought you might be ill. (*Laughs.*) I worried for you, or an accident or (*shrugs*) – is it because of following you?

PETER: You did know I was married, I told you at once. I have a life – (*pause*) – also I meant it when I said you were worth more – I mean – (*smiles*) – there are lots of males between homos like Josh and husbands like me, it's sad that you should waste yourself –

JOANNA: Couldn't you say outright that you've stopped fancying me and I've become a nuisance?

PETER: I've stopped fancying you and you've become a nuisance. (*There is a pause,* JOANNA *shocked.*) Is that really any better? It's certainly not true. I still fancy . . .

JOANNA: (*Cutting in*) Yes, well, you can go now, if you want.

PETER: (*Makes to say something, checks himself, goes to the door*) I'm sorry about the clichés. My manners have been appalling, right the way through.

(JOANNA *stares blankly, smoking. Hold on her, then cut to:* PETER *beginning to close the door behind him.*

JOANNA *lets out a wail, it turns into a scream, she gets up, races crazily around the room, wailing, knocking over work-table etc.*

Cut to PETER'*s face appalled, caught at the door and on this cut to:*)

EXT. LONDON SUBURBAN GARDEN

Point of view upstairs window. ALISON, *very pregnant,* HILARY *and five children ranging from three to twelve. Their cries muffled. Cut to:*

CHARLES'S FACE

Staring out of the window.

PETER: (*Voice over*) If I hadn't gone back I'd have spent the next three months waiting to hear of her suicide – or worse.

CHARLES: (*Waving, smiling down*) Would she really go that far?
(*Cut to* PETER *on a polystyrene bag, in an ascetic male preserve, do-it-yourself bookcases, school textbooks, unmarked and marked school essays on the desk. Around the walls there are pictures of school groups. One of these is the same as the one in Peter's and Hilary's bedroom.*)

PETER: The point is, one doesn't know. At least, I don't. But once I *had* gone back in, it was bound to move in a fairly predictable sequence, a slap on the chops to stop her hysterics, a cup of tea to soothe her, a cuddle to stop her trembling, a fuck to – (*Gestures.*)

CHARLES: (*Sits in the opposite polystyrene*) Do you think that's ended it?

PETER: I don't know. There's no way of glossing a fuck, is there? I tried to make it forlorn and farewell.

CHARLES: Couldn't you have said something?

PETER: What? If I said anything ambiguous, she would have ignored the other and real meaning. If anything explicit –

CHARLES: You'd have been picking up the furniture again. I thought you'd decided to give up that sort of thing anyway.

PETER: This sort of thing I never tried to take up.

CHARLES: Well, casual affairs.

PETER: Yes. Although there's nothing casual about this one now. Yes, I had given it up. But there was a party and I – I had some fantasy that I might be lucky with some pertly careless little creature – dreams, dreams. Because there was old reality standing by herself in a corner and myself gravitating ineluctably towards her as usual. I can't explain it. (*Little pause*.) She's ghastly! Look, old cheese, you did mutter something about a –

CHARLES: (*Gets up, goes to Scotch, syphon and two glasses on the desk*) But in bed, surely?

PETER: Yes, but so ravenous. Making love to somebody you can't stand but who's infatuated with you makes you believe you have a soul. Otherwise why do you feel so rotten? And afterwards the mandatory post-coital cigarette, she smokes with a shoulder hunched (*imitates* JOANNA *smoking*) and if I attempt a joke, her *laugh*. (*Imitates* JOANNA *laughing*.) (CHARLES *laughs*. PETER *laughs slightly*, *offers* CHARLES *a cigarette*. CHARLES *with a slight smile shakes his head*.) And then the endless squalid complications of turning up at home smelling just right – not freshly showered but not, of course – oh God! (*Sits depressed for a moment*.) You've given up smoking.

CHARLES: Apparently I'm lucky in my metabolism. I scarcely suffered. I had to take over the soccer one afternoon, and I couldn't keep up with the under-14s. And I suppose I believe schoolteachers ought to set an example – and as a father, come to that.

PETER: I set just the right example for Jeremy. He models himself on everything I'm not. My vices have moulded an ascetic – have you given up alcohol too?

CHARLES: Well – yes, really.

PETER: Christ, Charlie!

CHARLES: You don't think – (*Going to the window, looking down. Cut to:*)

EXT.

From CHARLES's *point of view.* ALISON *and* HILARY *talking, children playing.*

CHARLES: (*Voice over*) You don't think you should tell Hilary?

PETER: (*Voice over*) Good God, why?

(*Cut to:*)

INT. CHARLES

CHARLES: Well, if this girl's as unstable as you say, she might – you know. And it would be better if it came from you first.

PETER: I'd rather take the risk. She's finding her new lectureship exhausting enough – I don't want to create any unnecessary – (*Gestures.*)

CHARLES: Yes, but if the girl does – it would be much worse. Besides, she'd understand, surely?

PETER: Understand what? That I'd been unfaithful to her for ten years, on and off. You don't think she'd settle for one infidelity, do you – we'd be working back through our married life together – (*Shudders.*) The habits of confession and recrimination root very quickly, you know. I hear enough of them at work, I don't want to go through them at home. (*Gets up, goes to the window, looks out.*) When's it due?

CHARLES: Next week some time.

PETER: Alison looks amazingly sprightly.

CHARLES: Oh, she scarcely notices any more. Except when she's not.

PETER: Will this be your last?

CHARLES: Only if it's a boy. She'll go on until she produces one –

EXT. GARDEN

From PETER's *point of view.* ALISON, HILARY *and the children. Joined by a nubile girl of about fifteen.*

PETER: (*Voice over*) How old *is* Caroline?

CHARLES: (*Voice over*) Fifteen.

PETER: (*Voice over, keeping* CAROLINE *in perspective as she bends over one of the other children*) Mm.

CHARLES: (*Voice over*) Something I better warn you about, Pete.

INT. THE STUDY

PETER *turns, faces* CHARLES.

CHARLES: We've gone vegetarian, I'm afraid.
(*Cut to:*)

INT. PETER'S AND HILARY'S KITCHEN

PETER *is washing up a few dishes. He is in his pyjamas.* JEREMY *enters, goes to fridge, takes out a bottle of milk, pours some into a glass.*

PETER: Is that all you want?

JEREMY: Yeah.

PETER: Have a good day?

JEREMY: It was all right.

PETER: Get a lot done?

JEREMY: Mmm?

PETER: Work. You were going to spend the day on your work, weren't you. Your A levels?

JEREMY: I've just come in.

PETER: I know you've just come in. But before you went out –

JEREMY: I did some.

PETER: (*After a pause*) Good.

JEREMY: (*Goes towards the kitchen door, stops*) The telephone kept going.

PETER: Oh. Who was it?

JEREMY: I don't know. When I answered they hung up. From a call-box.

PETER: Probably for you then?

JEREMY: No.

PETER: How do you know?

JEREMY: Because they wouldn't have hung up when I answered.

PETER: But the call-boxes these days – (*Turning away.*) The vandals have scarcely left one intact. (*Turns back.*) Tell me – (JEREMY *is exiting from the kitchen.* PETER *turns back to the sink. Above, the sound of the telephone ringing. Cut to:*)

INT. THE BEDROOM

HILARY *is lying in bed, spectacles on, reading. One hand extended casually over the telephone. Sound of a cough, door opening, closing.*

HILARY: God, that cough of yours.

PETER: Wasn't that the phone?

HILARY: Yes.

> (*The telephone rings.*)
> (HILARY *picks it up, gaze still on the book, waits.*) 348 0720. Hello. (*Puts the telephone down.*)

PETER: Who is it?

HILARY: Don't know. The pips are doing their endless pipping –

PETER: Probably somebody for Jeremy.

HILARY: Shouldn't think so.

PETER: Why not? (*Getting undressed.*)

HILARY: He's very considerate.

PETER: (*Looks at her in astonishment*) Even if he were, he'd hardly be phoning us up, as he's already in the house. One of his friends –

HILARY: Not at this hour.

> (PETER *gets into bed, lies back, looks across at the Junior Colts picture.*)

I wish Jeremy had come today. Caroline's really very nice –

PETER: A little young, surely.

HILARY: What did you and Charlie talk about upstairs, or were you just hiding?

PETER: Oh, about all the things he's given up. Which is really the last twenty years, when you think about it. What did you and Alison talk about?

HILARY: Her womb. She was admiring it for its fertility – rather as one admires Dickens for his.

PETER: (*Laughs*) Macrobiotic. Onion and parsnip stew, Russian salad, fruit salad, no alcohol, Christ! (*Coughs slightly.*)

HILARY: It's economics, of course. They can't have children *and* all the other vices. They do look extremely healthy on it, though. (*Pause.*) Well, they're our best friends. You and Charlie had a grubby public school dorm affair when you were passing through adolescence together, and you did your national service at the same barracks. So now they're our best friends at thirty-eight.

PETER: I neither had a dorm affair nor did my national service with Alison.

HILARY: And I suppose they'll be best friends to the end, won't they? They'll go on and on, Sunday lunches and monthly dinners until something happens to change them, a death possibly. (*Shudders.*) Why did I say that? (*Laughs.*) Anyway, I suppose we love them, don't we?

PETER: I don't know. Old friends are like old habits. Once you've got them it's too late to wonder whether you actually want them. (*Coughs.*)

HILARY: If Charles can do something about his smoking, can't you?

PETER: Mmmm.

HILARY: (*Turns her head, looks at him*) Don't you care that I care?
(PETER *turns his head, looks at her, puts his hand out, touches her on the cheek, then suddenly leans over, kisses her.*)
Please make an effort.
(PETER *kisses her more passionately, then more passionately again.*)
(*Pushes him away*) That's not the issue. Besides, I've got a hard day tomorrow. I'm giving a lunchtime lecture as well as the evening seminars. And a Board of Studies meeting –
(PETER *looks at her, falls back on the pillow.*)
Oh, don't take offence. (*Pause.*) All right, do. (*Turns out her light, turns her back on* PETER.)
(PETER – *his light still on, lies staring across the room, and cut to*

*the photograph of the Junior Colts. See it in close-up, then
moving from face to face, pausing on a face that could be*
PETER's.)
(*Voice over*) Look, it's not bloody fair, I must get some sleep
if I'm to cope tomorrow!
(PETER *blinks, turns.* HILARY *is sitting up in bed, glaring at
him.*)
Please turn out your light! (*Leans across him, turns it out.*)
(*There is a silence. A very slight cough from* PETER.)
Give us a cuddle then.
(*Another silence, then the sound of* PETER *getting out of bed.*)
(*After a pause*) Pete?
(*The sound of the door closing.*)
Silly bugger! (*To herself.*)

INT. THE KITCHEN

PETER *is sitting at the table, smoking.*
HILARY: (*At the door*) Do you prefer this to sleeping with me?
PETER: It's more stimulating.
(HILARY *stares at him, then goes out, closing the door,
emphatically.* PETER *sits for a moment, then stubs out his
cigarette, gets up, hesitates, goes out.*)

INT. THE BEDROOM

HILARY *is in bed, her light on.* PETER *gets in beside her, puts his light
off.*
HILARY: Well, what *is* the matter with you?
PETER: Nothing.
HILARY: Then that's all right then, isn't it? (*Turns her light off.*)
(*There is a pause.* HILARY *turns her light on, looks down at*
PETER, *lying with his hands folded under his head.*)
You're being exceptionally childish.
PETER: What?

(HILARY *turns her light off.*)

PETER: (*Turns his light on*) What do you mean – childish?

   (HILARY *turns away from him.*)

PETER: Christ! (*Turns his light off.*)

   (*There is a pause.* HILARY *turns her light on. Looks at* PETER *again, gets out of bed.* PETER *sits up, stares after her, as* HILARY *goes out of room.*)

   Oh Christ! (*Gets out of bed, follows* HILARY *out, slamming the door behind him.*)

INT. KITCHEN

HILARY *and* PETER *sitting opposite each other, smoking.*

HILARY: (*Talking in a whisper*) – no use your blaming me, I'm upset by it too but I can't help it. But you know I'm not off you, and you know I love you, it's just that – it's a strain, at the moment, I keep revolving the next day's lectures or what's worse, last week's, I really wonder whether I should have undertaken them, I don't seem to have the stomach for addressing large groups on – and I keep wondering whether I'm boring them or stupefying them and what the difference is. (*Pause.*) Am I in danger then?

PETER: (*Also whispering*) What? What of?

HILARY: Of your looking elsewhere. I don't think I could bear that.

PETER: Don't be silly.

HILARY: I do worry about it, you know. And the unfairness of it.

PETER: It's not at all unfair. I *was* being childish –

HILARY: No, I meant the unfairness to me. Or us. Women. How when I'm in my forties, which is tomorrow almost, you'll still be very attractive –

PETER: So will you.

HILARY: And then when I'm in my fifties – or when you're in your sixties even, going by current trends – I'll just be a woman in my sixties as far as you're concerned –

PETER: You don't believe that.

HILARY: I'm talking about my worries, not my beliefs. I can
perfectly well imagine myself struggling not to check your
pockets or your underwear drawer before doing both
probably – it's very humiliating. (*Pause.*) You know damn
well I'm not frigid –

PETER: (*Emotionally*) Darling! (*Takes her hand.*) Look, let me tell
you –
(*Door opens.* JEREMY *enters. There is a pause.*)

JEREMY: Anyone want a cup of tea?

HILARY: Darling, shouldn't you be in bed?

JEREMY: I've got a free class tomorrow. (*Putting the kettle on.*)
Don't have to be in until ten. (*Sits down.*)
(HILARY *and* PETER *exchange glances. There is a silence.*)

HILARY: What have you been doing?

JEREMY: Oh nothing really.
(*Hold on the three of them for a moment.*)

PETER: (*After a long pause*) So much for Pascal.

JEREMY: What?

PETER: Wasn't it Pascal who said that all human evil came from
our not being able to sit alone in a room, doing nothing?

HILARY: If we *could* all do that, there wouldn't be any humans
left to do it. (*Brightly.*)
(*Cut to:*)

INT. BEDROOM

Lights out.

HILARY: (*Voice over*) I know he does.

PETER: So do I. In that it would be most unnatural if he didn't.
But that would only account for the odd half hour of his day,
surely. What does he do for the rest of the time?

HILARY: Recuperates.
(PETER *laughs, so does* HILARY *and cut to:*)

INT. PETER'S ROOM IN CHAMBERS

ROSE, MRS SAWSBURY, SALLUST *and* PETER. PETER *clearing his throat, waits.*

MRS SAWSBURY: But it was only the once. It only happened the once. He doesn't drink heavily as a rule, but he was feeling very low, his daughter's husband had been very rude to him, and he went to the pub. He's not a drinking man. I don't know where they got hold of this – this sort of lie.

PETER: The trouble is, it's not exactly a lie. He did hit them, unfortunately.

MRS SAWSBURY: Only the boy.

PETER: And pushed the girl.

MRS SAWSBURY: He didn't hurt them.

PETER: Probably not – as they made so much noise. They wouldn't if they had been really frightened.

MRS SAWSBURY: He's very fond of them, and they know it. He was ashamed afterwards, he cried.
(*There is a pause. The telephone rings on the desk.*)

PETER: Excuse me. Who? Look, I can't take any calls, I'm – what? Who? I haven't got an appointment – (*Listens.*) Well, he can try then. (*Puts the telephone down, slightly abstracted.*) Sorry. (*There is a pause.*)

MRS SAWSBURY: It's not fair if something like that counts against us. Will it?

PETER: (*Pulling himself together*) One can never be quite sure what does count. We'll do our best to make the Judge understand.

INT. PETER AND SALLUST

PETER: They've got a private detective, of course.

SALLUST: Shouldn't we get one?

PETER: It's too late. They'll be living their lives as if we already have.

SALLUST: Of all the times to get drunk and clout the kids! Do you think we've got a chance?

PETER: Of what?

SALLUST: Of winning.

PETER: Oh yes. So has opposing counsel. I shouldn't think
anybody else has, though.

(*The telephone rings.*)

PETER: (*Answers it*) Still there? (*Looks at his watch.*) All right. (*Puts
the telephone down.*) Don't feel up to anybody else's misery just
at the moment.

(*Door opens.*)

Mr James, isn't it?

JOSH: Yes.

(JOSH *enters. He is in his mid-thirties, with a strained, unhappy-
looking face.*)

PETER: This is my pupil, Mr Sallust. You haven't come to us
through a solicitor, have you, Mr James?

JOSH: No.

PETER: I should warn you that really you should see a solicitor –

JOSH: It's a private matter, you see. (*Pause.*) About a friend of
mine. Miss um, Pelley.

PETER: (*Puzzled for a second, then controlling himself*) Oh. Then
perhaps, Tommy – ?

SALLUST: Of course. (*Goes out.*)

(*There is a pause.*)

JOSH: I don't know if she's mentioned me to you – Josh.

PETER: Yes, I believe she did, once or twice. (*Lights a cigarette.*)

JOSH: I'm sorry to come in on you like this – I didn't know what
else to do.

(PETER *waits.*)

I'm frightened.

PETER: What of?

JOSH: Her. *For* her, that is. You see, I went around last night, she
wasn't normal. Well – even for her. She was talking rather
wildly –

PETER: What about?

JOSH: You. She hasn't stopped that, but there's a kind of despair,
you know, beyond her usual – desperation – (*Looks at* PETER)
You see, you're the third man in a row to go wrong on her.

295

PETER: I see. (*His hand is trembling slightly.*) I was under the impression that you and she –

JOSH: Oh no. I'm homosexual. I slept with her once or twice, when she needed comforting. I expect she makes more out of it to other people – at the moment I'm no use to her. I would be if I could.

PETER: I don't know what I can do.

JOSH: If you could just bring yourself to talk to her – she wouldn't let me in this morning, but I could hear her through the door, whimpering – I know how awful this must be for you, I'm sorry to ask.

(PETER *sits smoking, trying to control himself.*)

I expect all you wanted was a quick lay. It's not fair, is it?

PETER: (*Smiles shakily*) Thank you.

(*Cut to:*)

INT. JOANNA'S BED-SITTER

JOANNA *is in bed, in pyjamas.* PETER *is sitting in the chair beside the bed.*

PETER: But surely you must see a doctor.

JOANNA: (*Smiling bravely*) No, it's only flu, I tell you. (*Laughs.*) You would come around suddenly after all this time and catch me in this state. (*Lights a cigarette.*)

PETER: Should you?

JOANNA: Won't hurt me. Anyway, the number *you* smoke – (*Affectionately.*)

PETER: Yes.

JOANNA: I couldn't actually make out from our last time whether you were going to come back.

PETER: Well, now you know. (*Smiling.*)

JOANNA: Yes. I feel better – you've got a medicinal smile.

PETER: That must mean it's hard to swallow.

JOANNA: What? (*Laughs.*)

PETER: Can I make you some tea – or – ?

JOANNA: (*Shakes her head*) You've been very busy then?

PETER: Yes.

JOANNA: I haven't followed you again.

PETER: What about phoning?

JOANNA: (*Looks at him*) Mm?

PETER: Have you tried phoning me?

JOANNA: I won't do it again. I just wanted to hear your voice . . .

PETER: Instead you heard my wife's and my son's.

> (JOANNA *lies down, turns her face away, begins to cry.* PETER *looks at her with a kind of desperate irritation, then moves over to the bed, takes the cigarette away from her fingers, puts it into the ashtray.*)

JOANNA: (*Puts one hand into his lap*) You want to go, don't you?

PETER: No – it's just that I've got to be back in chambers –

JOANNA: You can go now, if you like.

PETER: No, no, I can stay on a bit.

JOANNA: (*Cries out*) I love you.

> (PETER *closes his eyes in horror.*)

> I won't do anything to make you unhappy, I swear. If I can just see you –

> (PETER *fumbles with his free hand for a cigarette. Cut to:*)

INT. HILARY'S AND PETER'S BEDROOM

HILARY *is lying in bed, staring up at the ceiling. Her face is tight with anger. There is the sound of coughing,* PETER *enters, naked. He is carrying his clothes. He dumps shoes on the floor, goes to a drawer, chucks pants and socks on to the chair.*

HILARY: How's Jeremy?

PETER: He's in his room.

HILARY: But how is he?

PETER: I don't know. He's in his room and I'm here.

HILARY: I thought you might have looked in on him, to say good-night.

PETER: I said it from my usual place, a tentative foot or two on the other side of his door.

HILARY: Yes, but I thought you might have looked in on him tonight.

PETER: Really? Why?

HILARY: To apologize.

PETER: For what?

HILARY: For being so offensive.

PETER: Offensive? I thought we were having a high-powered discussion as to the relative merits of Laurel and Hardy –

HILARY: *You* were having the discussion.

PETER: I allowed him to display the full range of his critical vocabulary. I counted five 'whats', and seven 'yeahs', and six 'all rights'.

HILARY: We know you did. You counted them out loud, if you remember. He merely said that he *quite enjoyed* Laurel and Hardy.

PETER: No, he didn't. He said they were all right. And that's all he said.

HILARY: Why should he say more – especially under an assault like that.

PETER: I've heard you talk about students in your seminars with *their* 'all rights', and 'quite liked its' –

HILARY: Jeremy is not a student in my seminar. He's our sixteen-year-old son. Whose behaviour, I might say, was remarkably adult under the circumstances.

PETER: And who provides the circumstances? Not every youth these days is lucky enough to have a father who conforms to the propaganda, crop-headed, authoritarian, grammatical –

HILARY: His sole offence this evening was to be younger and nicer than you.

PETER: That makes two offences, both serious. (*Gets into bed, coughs slightly.*) Anyway, *he* didn't seem to mind.

HILARY: If you really think that, then you're being stupid. (*Switches off her light.*)

(PETER *lies staring angrily ahead. Cut to Junior Colts picture.*) You've been ghastly all evening. The one evening I have off during the week and when Jeremy's home – all of us having a proper family dinner together, which I spent the afternoon thinking about and getting ready – and you come home scarcely able to look at anyone, you drank too much before the meal, and then ruined the meal with your egoistical – it was unforgivable.

PETER: You think that unforgivable? You should come to court one day and find out the sort of thing *my* sort of people don't forgive each other.

HILARY: Would you like Jeremy – and myself – to be that sort of people?

PETER: At least I'd know where I was. A son who scarcely addresses a remark to me, a wife who moralizes and blackmails.

(HILARY *hits him. They sit glaring at each other, then* HILARY *collapses back on the bed.* PETER *remains sitting upright, staring at the Junior Colts picture. Cut to it, then back to* PETER, *as sound of muffled sobs over. He sits staring impassively, then turns, looks down at* HILARY. HILARY *is lying, her shoulders shaking.* PETER *looks down at her, his expression quite detached, but sad. He leans over, then puts his arms around her, lifts her up against himself.*) I'm sorry. I didn't mean that.

(HILARY *struggles against him, almost frantically.*)

(*Clutches her to him*) Don't, don't, don't, don't. (*Soothingly.*)

(HILARY *subsides. Occasional deep sobs.*)

You know I love you. (*Strokes her hair. Coughs very slightly.*) You know that.

HILARY: And who else do you love?

PETER: Jeremy.

HILARY: And no one else? No girl or woman that –

PETER: No one else. Nothing else either. Perhaps that's my trouble.

HILARY: You used to love your work.

PETER: It's not very lovable at the moment.

(PETER *strokes her hair, then kisses her on the mouth. Kisses her again, more passionately. Begins to caress her.* HILARY *at first resists, then acquiesces, then begins to respond with passion. Cut to* PETER *lying back, coughing.*)

HILARY: (*Leaning over him, concerned*) That was a race against time. Or death, it felt like. You certainly don't love yourself, do you?

(*The telephone rings.* HILARY *and* PETER *look at each other.*)

HILARY: 348 0720. (*Listens.*) Pips. (*Looks at* PETER, *puts the telephone down thoughtfully.*)

PETER: (*Urgently*) Take if off the hook. (*Reaches across.*) (*The telephone rings.*)

HILARY: (*Picks it up*) 348 0720. (*Waits. Pause.*) Which hospital? (*Little pause.*) Yes, we'll take the call. Here – *you*'d better – (*Hands the telephone to* PETER.) It's a hospital – they've reversed charges.

PETER: (*Clutching the telephone, waits, then*) Hello – I can't hear – which hospital. (*Listens.*) Who?
(HILARY *watching intently.*)
Yes, it is. (*Pause.*) Charlie, hello! What – oh Charlie, wonderful – it's Charlie – a son!

HILARY: (*Smiling*) Thank God!
(*Cut to:*)

INT. JOANNA'S BED-SITTER

JOANNA, *fully dressed, is sitting in a corner of the bed, smoking.*
PETER *is standing.*

JOANNA: I thought this was one of your late nights. When you're not expected home –

PETER: Yes, it is.

JOANNA: And so you've just looked in to say you could only look in, right?

PETER: Well, to see how you were. I've got a long-standing engagement with my pupil.

JOANNA: What's the point of your coming around then?

PETER: I thought you liked me to.

JOANNA: Not like this. There's no point to it.

PETER: What will you do this evening?

JOANNA: Don't worry.

PETER: Well, you'll be all right?

JOANNA: Yes, thanks.

PETER: O K. Well – see you next week perhaps. Right?

(*Goes to door, opens it; as he closes it, cut to shot of* JOANNA, *from his point of view sitting as if indifferent on the bed. The door closes on her and cut to:*)

INT. HALL

PETER, *on the other side of Joanna's door, apprehensively listening. Then turns, walks away, swinging squash bag and briefcase, with an air of release.*

INT. SQUASH COURT

PETER *and* SALLUST *playing,* PETER *running rather flounderingly, his face working, breathing hard, loses the point and rests collapsed against a corner, coughing.*

INT. THE CHANGING-ROOM

SALLUST *under a shower,* PETER *sitting on a bench, shaking. Towel around his middle. He has a cigarette, unlit, in his mouth.* SALLUST *emerges.*

PETER: Was that a cold shower?

SALLUST: Mmm.

PETER: Christ!

SALLUST: Well, I go on sweating for hours if I have a hot one. And as I'm taking my girlfriend to the opera –

PETER: Didn't know you liked opera? (*Little pause.*) Didn't know you had a girlfriend, either. Well, I must have assumed you had –

SALLUST: I won't have her for long if I have to keep taking her to the opera. How do you feel?

(PETER *grunts.*)

You used to be pretty good once, usedn't you? (*Towelling himself vigorously*) Very nice touch –

PETER: Not really. It's always been cricket for me. Sometimes I still remember a particular shot – I'd never done it before, it was in an under-15 match – it was a late cut. I didn't even know I was going to do it – or was doing it – (*Gets up, demonstrates*) until I'd completed it – like this – and the ball was at the boundary. The one moment in my life when I felt a touch of sublimity. (*Laughs.*) I try and recall it occasionally, before I go to sleep. (*Begins to dry himself.*)

SALLUST: You know, it just struck me the other day that I was twenty-eight and already too old to be any of the things I still dream I might be – a professional tennis player – or – (*Stands, with a wondering look.*)

PETER: What? (*Turns, looks, smiles.*) Eh?

SALLUST: Actually, a – um – (*Vaguely, collapses to the floor.*)

PETER: (*Runs to him, lifts up his head.*) Tommy, Tommy . . . God . . . Tommy.

(*Two men, carrying squash bags, appear at the end of the dressing-room, come towards* PETER, *one of them smoking. Then hurry forward, bend over to look at* SALLUST.)

FIRST MAN: Can you do that? Your mouth, kiss him? That business?

(PETER *looks at him, then bends over, begins a clumsy kiss of life on* SALLUST.)

FIRST MAN: I'll go and get . . . (*Hurries off.*)

PETER: (*With* SECOND MAN, *crouching beside him, goes on kissing, draws his mouth away*) I can feel him, he's beginning.

(PETER *puts his mouth back over* SALLUST's, *and on his life-kissing, other man beside him, a cigarette between his fingers, cut to* FIRST MAN, *standing, scratching meaninglessly at his cheek.* SECOND MAN *standing beside him, smoking another cigarette. A* THIRD MAN, *possibly a doctor, kneels by* SALLUST, *and now wearily straightening.* PETER *observed in the distance, almost obscurely, sitting on the bench, staring blankly ahead and smoking. Various other figures around, including a porter. The* THIRD MAN *gets up, goes over to* PETER, *sits down beside him.*)

THIRD MAN: OK?

PETER: I felt his breath coming. Out of his mouth.

THIRD MAN: It was probably your own breath coming back at
  you, I'm afraid.

PETER: He just keeled over. (*Gets up, walks mechanically over to*
  SALLUST's *body.*)

THIRD MAN: They'll be here in a minute. You look as if you
  could do with –
  (PETER *bends down, picks up* SALLUST's *towel, puts it carefully
  over* SALLUST's *genitals.*)

THIRD MAN: I'm sorry.

PETER: He was my pupil, you see. (*Meaninglessly.*)
  (*Stay on group as long as possible, then cut to:*)

INT. COLLEGE LECTURE ROOM

HILARY's *face, seen through the glass-and-wire panels of the door.
She is talking, spectacles on, from notes. As she talks, she lifts her
head, as if from instinct, looks towards the door, and:*

INT.

From HILARY's *point of view see* PETER, *on the other side of the
glass.*

INT. CHARLES'S STUDY

They are sitting on the polystyrene sacks, as before. But first,
CHARLES's *voice over, as image maintained from previous scene.*

CHARLES: One of our boys did that – he was fifteen.
  (*Cut to him, pouring a healthy dose of Scotch into two glasses.*)
  Perfectly fit. Suddenly collapsed on the football pitch. In the
  midst, so to speak.

PETER: (*Taking a glass*) Thanks.
  (*He is by the window, offers* CHARLES *a cigarette.* CHARLES
  takes it.)

What is it?
(*Turns, looks out of the window. Cut to:*)

EXT. GARDEN

From PETER'*s point of view.* CAROLINE *appears, walking slowly.*
HILARY *and* CAROLINE *at further end, bent over pram.*
PETER: (*Voice over*) Half-way upon this way of life I'm lost upon –
CHARLES: (*Voice over*) Having had twenty years –
　　(JEREMY *appears, walks after* CAROLINE, *catches up with her.*
　　Says something. CAROLINE *shrugs.*)
CHARLES: Having had twenty years, twenty years of *entre deux*
　　guerres, no, that's something else –
　　(*Cut back to:*)

INT.

PETER'*s face, turning impassively away from the window.*
CHARLES: (*Smoking*) The worst is to come, I suppose. The death of
　　friends, all the deaths in waiting, including our own. But it's
　　the death of children that haunts me. Sometimes in the night –
PETER: Don't!
CHARLES: (*Grunts*) What was he like?
PETER: Just a pupil. Callower than some, in fact I took less notice
　　of him than most of my recent ones until our game – we talked
　　for the first time, you know, the way people do after squash – I
　　patronized him a bit, ignored him quite often, and tried to
　　conceal my irritation when he passed me damned stupid notes
　　in the middle of a plea. He was all right. (*Little pause.*) I don't
　　know.
CHARLES: Everything else all right?
PETER: Mmm?
CHARLES: That girl?
PETER: Oh God, I don't know. I'm keeping it at bay, for the
　　moment.

CHARLES: What?

PETER: Whatever conclusion there's to be. (*Notices* CHARLES's *cigarette.*) Thought you'd given up?

CHARLES: Started again in the hospital waiting-room. (*Inhales deeply, coughs.*)

PETER: (*Coughs*) Still, that's something to celebrate.

INT. THE COURT

JUDGE *enters, everybody rises, then sits, and as* COUNSEL *for* MRS SAWSBURY *rises, the camera cuts from face to face, on* MRS SAWSBURY *sitting behind* PETER, *with* ROSE, *to* MR SAWSBURY, *to the* JUDGE, *then back to* MRS SAWSBURY, *tautly apprehensive, then to* PETER *turning, smiles encouragingly,* MRS SAWSBURY *smiles tightly back. Credits.*

Two Sundays

**To Alan
for Ben, Simon, Peter and Charles**

Two Sundays was first presented by BBC Television on 21 October 1975. The cast was as follows:

CHARLES	Alan Bates
PETER	Dinsdale Landen
ALISON	Rosemary Martin
HILARY	Georgina Hale
BOY	Steven Gover
BOWLER	Andrew Burleigh
HOUSE MASTER	Benjamin Whitrow
SCHOOL MASTER	Victor Langley
SCHOOL MASTER	Simon Cadell
CHILDREN	Paul Stencil
	Benjamin Bolger
	Daniel Bolger
	Amelia Bolger

Director	Michael Lindsay-Hogg
Designer	Richard Henry
Producer	Kenith Trodd

INT. MORNING

BOWLER, *waking in the morning. Blinks, looks about him, makes a move to get out of bed. Cut to:*

INT. PETER'S BEDROOM

PETER *getting out of bed, looks and clearly feels dreadful.*

PETER: Oh Christ!

HILARY: (*Off*) Mmmmm?

PETER: It's eight thirty.

HILARY: (*Off*) Wah – ?

PETER: Eight thirty. (*Little pause.*) Eight thirty. (*Little pause.*)

HILARY: (*Off*) Mmmmm.

PETER: Shan't tell you the time again.

HILARY: (*Off*) Won't have to. I know. It's eight thirty.

PETER: But it won't be the next time you ask.

HILARY: Good.

PETER: (*Glares at her*) We've got a long bloody drive.

HILARY: I've got a long bloody drive. (*Off.*) You've got your
  usual bloody hangover.

  (PETER *turns, goes out in his underwear and cut to:*)

EXT.

CHARLES, *running across school playing-fields, in long shot. The
sound of bells ringing, several boys walking, sitting. He comes closer
and closer, his head swaying, eyes slightly glassy, breathing heavily
until he's full in camera and then gone on past it. Hold on the school
playing-fields, and cut to:*

TWO SUNDAYS

EXT. A SCHOOL YARD

Different school, although this is not explicit. Several boys again, this time wearing school suits, in some cases gowns, white shirts. Come in on a BOY *in a gown, sitting, reading.*

BOY: Je suis le roi d'un pays pluvieux.

> (*Sound of bells. He looks up, then around, as if looking for someone. Then bends over his book. See him from a sudden point of view that turns out to be* BOWLER's. BOY *is smiling, as cut to:*)

EXT.

BOWLER, *from* BOY's *point of view, advancing towards him in grey flannels, white shirt, carrying cricket boots. Gets to him.*

BOY: Good morning then.

BOWLER: Hello.

BOY: Unusual togs for a Sunday morning.

BOWLER: They've put me down for a nine net.

BOY: I expect you'll enjoy that.

BOWLER: It's for the Junior Colts.

BOY: Gratters. (*Ironically.*) And luck.

BOWLER: We're fagging Refec at break.

BOY: To Hell with all that.

BOWLER: We'd better go.

> (BOY *gets up, they move towards a building, slowly, and cut to:*)

INT. PETER'S AND HILARY'S KITCHEN

HILARY, *dressed, is drinking a cup of coffee, reading a paper.* PETER *is leaning against the fridge door, dressed, drinking coffee, smoking. He coughs slightly.* HILARY *glances at him.*

PETER: Where's Jeremy?

HILARY: In the toilet.

PETER: The toilet!

HILARY: That's the word they use.

PETER: Who?

HILARY: Everyone in the Juniors, from the Headmistress down. They always say it.

PETER: Always? (*Going to the fridge.*) Lively conversationalists then. (*Opens the fridge door, takes out a bottle of wine.*)

HILARY: What's that?

PETER: Bottle of wine, isn't it?

HILARY: For breakfast?

PETER: For lunch. Last time they were on some herbal rubbish, I'm not risking that again. If he doesn't hurry, we won't make it for lunch. How can an illiterate spend so long on the lavatory?

HILARY: (*Calling*) Darling! Darling!

(*And cut to:*)

INT. CHARLES'S STUDY

Still in his running shorts, etc.; sweat dripping off him, is standing at his desk, one plimsolled foot on a chair, turning over the pages of a manuscript.

ALISON: (*Off*) Are you in there?

CHARLES: Yes, darling. (*Listens, hand on a page.*)

(ALISON's *footsteps off.* CHARLES *closes the manuscript, puts it unhurriedly away, as:*)

ALISON: (*At door, she is very pregnant*) They've started breakfast.

CHARLES: I'll just have a shower.

ALISON: Couldn't you after?

CHARLES: Oh, I pong fearfully.

ALISON: Well, we've got a lot to do, I haven't started the casserole . . . and I would like to tidy up . . .

CHARLES: (*Following her out*) Don't worry, darling, We'll cope.

(*Cut to:*)

BOY AND BOWLER

Walking down a passage. They stop.

BOWLER: I thought we weren't allowed in Music until after prep.

BOY: No, it's all right on a Sunday.

BOWLER: You sure?

BOY: So I'll see you there after your nets. There's something I
    particularly want you to hear . . .

MASTER: (*Off*) Hey, you two, aren't you fagging Refec?
    (*Cut to* MASTER, *at end of passage, not seen clearly, just a
    shape.*)

BOY: (*Off*) Sir.

BOWLER: (*Off*) Sir.

MASTER: Come on then.
    (*Seem to be coming in on him, instead come in on:*)

INT. CHARLES'S AND ALISON'S KITCHEN

*Three boys, aged eight, six, four, around the table. A girl, aged two,
in a high chair; all eating.*

CHARLES: Well, we've got a jolly nice day in store for you chaps,
    haven't we, Mummy?

ALISON: A jolly nice day.

CHARLES: (*Sits down*). We must all be particularly nice to Jeremy,
    until he's used to us. He'll be the odd one out.

ONE OF THE BOYS: (*Off*) Don't like Jeremy.

CHARLES: (*Cheerfully*) You've forgotten him, it's been such a long
    time.

VOICE: But I remember I don't like him.

OTHER VOICE: Nor do I.

CHARLES: Then let's begin by pretending to like him, and if we
    practise hard, we'll end up by doing it.

TWO SUNDAYS

INT. PETER AND HILARY IN A CAR

PETER *is slumped down, smoking.* HILARY *is driving.* JEREMY *is in the back, strapped in.*

PETER: How did this come about, anyway?

HILARY: It was a conspiracy. The wife of your oldest friend invited the wife of his oldest friend and her husband, the oldest friend, to lunch. We wanted to ruin your Sunday.

PETER: You didn't have to accept.

HILARY: I had no choice. That's not true, I had a choice of any one of the next eight Sundays.

PETER: Then why didn't you choose the eighth?

HILARY: To avoid having this conversation then. (*Pause.*) It'll give Jeremy someone to play with, won't it, darling?

JEREMY: (*Off after a pause*) I hate them.

PETER: Then you, at least, shouldn't be too bored.

    (*Cut to:*)

INT. CHARLES'S STUDY

He is putting the manuscript into a large brown envelope. Sound of car drawing up, opening and closing of doors, voices in greeting. Goes to the window, opens it, and as if from his point of view cut to:

EXT.

From point of view music room window, looking down over school yard. The yard is full of boys going off in different directions, walking together, separately, some standing in groups. BOWLER *comes into picture, now dressed as* BOY, *only without the gown. He looks up, and cut to:*

TWO SUNDAYS

ALISON, HILARY, JEREMY

With other children, in the garden, and PETER, *from his point of view looking up, sees* CHARLES, *who is smiling down. Cut to* PETER's *face, smiling slightly, and looking up, and cut up to:*

MUSIC ROOM WINDOW

BOY *at it, indistinct, looking down, seen from school yard,* BOWLER's *point of view. And cut to:*

INT. CHARLES'S STUDY

PETER *in it, lighting a cigarette, sighing, suddenly looks towards the door, as it begins to open. And cut to:*

INT.

Music room door opens. BOWLER *enters. He is dressed as in previous scene. He looks towards gramophone, cut to* BOY, *just putting record on. He turns.*

BOY: It's to be Berg.
BOWLER: Oh.
> (BOY *bends over gramophone.* BOWLER *sits down, adopts a listening posture.* BOY *fiddles with the gramophone, then as scraping noise of needle on the pre-music grooves, walks to sit down, and cut to:*)

INT. CHARLES'S STUDY

CHARLES *enters, carrying a quarter of a bottle of Scotch and two glasses, one of which has a long drink in it.*
CHARLES: Sorry. I got it in specially and then forgot where I put it.

316

PETER: Very sweet of you.

CHARLES: (*Puts the full glass down on the desk, opens the bottle, makes as if to pour, stops.*) You'd better look after yourself –

PETER: Thanks. (*Little pause.*) What are you drinking?

CHARLES: (*Little laugh*) Ribena, actually. I seem to have acquired an addiction to it – because of the children – well – (*Lifts his glass.*)

(PETER *has poured, lifts his glass, coughs slightly.*)

CHARLES: Well – (*As if trying to think of something to say.*) Oh, there's something I wanted you to hear. It might amuse you – one of my sixth formers did it.

(*He goes over, turns on a tape-recorder, sits down.* PETER *makes an expression of bored irritation when* CHARLES's *back is turned, sinks down, sips, smokes.* CHARLES *sits down, as tape whirrs. There is a long silence. There is a ping, followed by two more pings. Silence.* PETER *makes an expression. Sudden crashing of chords, and cut to:*)

INT. MUSIC ROOM

The climax of the Berg 78". The two boys sitting. The record stops. BOY *gets up, goes over, takes the record off, keeps his back to* BOWLER. *Bends over to put the record back in its sleeve.*

BOWLER: (*After a pause, clears his throat*) It's jolly bloody good.

BOY: (*Looks at him*) Yes?

BOWLER: Well I liked it.

BOY: But did it make you laugh?

BOWLER: Laugh.

BOY: It's very and fantastically witty.

BOWLER: *You* didn't laugh.

BOY: Oh, I know all the jokes.

BOWLER: Then what did you put it on for?

BOY: Your entertainment, of course. And I wanted to concentrate on the grief, for once.

(*He puts on another record, walks back, scratching pre-music begins, and cut to:*)

INT. CHARLES'S STUDY

PETER *sitting back, cigarette drooping from his lips, eyes half-closed as if in boredom, occasionally wincing. See his face from* CHARLES's *point of view, then his eyes taking* CHARLES *in.* CHARLES *from* PETER's *point of view, staring at him, looking away.*

Through this, over, on the tape, lavatory flushing, dogs barking, bird calls, savagely discordant violins. Then silence. Tape whirring. A sudden girl's scream, terrible, from the tape. Silence.

PETER *raises his eyebrows interrogatively.*

CHARLES: I'm not quite sure whether this is part of it. The silence I mean. It goes on for twenty minutes. (*In a low voice.*)

PETER: Oh. (*Short pause.*) May we not acknowledge it? Rather than listen to it. Or whatever it is one does to silence.

CHARLES: (*After another short pause*) Yes, yes, perhaps one had better – I just wanted you to get a sense of its effect. (*Gets up, goes over, bends for a moment.*) Once or twice I've fancied I heard something *behind* the silence. But it's never the same, so I suppose it must be imagination. (*Turns it off.*) Perhaps that's what he intends. Well – (Looks at PETER *eagerly.*)

PETER: A sixth-former, did you say?

CHARLES: Yes, but quite young. Just sixteen. A precocious lad. I have hopes he'll pull off an Oxford place, at the very least. He's utterly individual. I think I told you last time we had quite a business coming to a policy on hair styles?

PETER: (*Clearly not remembering*) Oh yes.

CHARLES: And finally decided on a completely liberal view. Well, you can imagine what we got – hair to the shoulders, Afro-styles, the lot. (*Laughs.*) Except from young Tedhurst. Young Tedhurst went bald.

PETER: Really? Disease or design?

CHARLES: Oh, design, I'm sure. And now this, for his Creative Art's Project. Most boys wrote stories, or painted, or built things, you know – but young Tedhurst – (*gestures to the tape-machine.*)

PETER: What will you say to him?

CHARLES: The truth of course. That I think it very, very interesting.

PETER: Well, that should do the trick.

CHARLES: How do you mean?

PETER: That a bald, sixteen-year-old futuristic musician is entitled to exactly the same attention as any other boy.

CHARLES: (*Puzzled*) Well, of course he *is*.

PETER: Yes. (*Pause*.) Anyway, you're obviously still enjoying school, then.

CHARLES: Oh, yes. Last year they tried to promote me into more admin. and less teaching, but I wasn't having it. Those that can't aren't going to have *that* taken away from them. (*Smiles*.) By the way, did I mention to you, I've taken over the Junior Colts, soccer *and* cricket.

PETER: Really?

CHARLES: I thought that would surprise you.

PETER: For the exercise?

CHARLES: Partly. Of course I have to take further exercise to keep up with them. A run every morning before breakfast.

PETER: Christ!

CHARLES: I'm up to four miles.

PETER: Christ!

CHARLES: I really feel quite marvellous for it. (*Little pause*.) Well, how about you?

PETER: Oh, I'm not fit enough to take exercise.

CHARLES: But you're all right?

PETER: Yes. Oh yes thanks. Well, you know – (*Grunts vaguely*.)

CHARLES: And publishing? Anything changed? Last time you sounded a bit depressed –

PETER: Then nothing can have changed. I'm still editing the waste-products of immigrant intellectuals. We've just started a new paperback series. Mind-formers of our time. Monographs on people like Marcuse, generally by people on whom we can do monographs in a few years time.

CHARLES: But you *were* very excited over a novel you'd received – a quite unexpected first novel, I think it was.

PETER: Was I? Oh yes – that got a few nice reviews. Nothing special happened – I suppose one or two people might have bought it.

CHARLES: But you're still doing novels, aren't you?

PETER: Now and then. We have to keep up a list, for appearances sakes. But of course with rising costs and declining literacy – (*Gestures.*)

CHARLES: Still, it's good that you are, for whatever reason. (*Pause.*) What about your own – you had one on the way, didn't you?

PETER: No. Rather yes, but no. Not any longer.

CHARLES: Don't say you've given it up?

PETER: I've already done my bit as publisher to add to the world's stock of unread books. I have no right to add to it as an author. (*Pause.*) Besides, it wasn't any good.

CHARLES: How do you know?

PETER: I assessed it in my second capacity, I decided it was probably worth more than a straight rejection, but that I wouldn't have recommended it for publication. In fact, I'd probably have taken the author out to lunch and gently discouraged him. Which is precisely what I did do. A bloody good lunch, too – oysters, Guinness and strawberries. Thus proving that I may be a poor novelist, but I'm a decent enough editor.

CHARLES: Still, it must have been, well, painful for you.

PETER: It was a relief, actually. I haven't the stamina to drink, smoke *and* write, in the evenings.

CHARLES: Well, perhaps it would be worth giving up, for something really important.

PETER: That's what I did.

CHARLES: Under the circumstances – (*Hesitates.*)

PETER: What?

CHARLES: Oh just something rather ironic. But it can wait. (*Pause.*) Well, the thing is – (*Stops, looks towards the door.*) (PETER *also looks towards the door, which is opening. Cut to:*)

INT. MUSIC ROOM

MASTER, *in a gown, standing at the door.* BOY *and* BOWLER, *on their feet as Mozart comes to an end on the gramophone.*

MASTER: Mysteriously Mozart from the other side of the door.
While from the other side of the window something
fashionably atonal. Berg?

BOY: Sir.

MASTER: When it shouldn't really be either, as you're both down
to fag for seniors at Refec. Didn't you hear the Refec bells
between the Berg and the Mozart?

BOY: Sir, we were just going, sir.

MASTER: (*Looks at them thoughtfully*) Good. By the way, isn't
there some pettifogging regulation about the Music Room. *Is*
one allowed to use it before six o'clock prep?
(BOY *and* BOWLER *look at each other, seen from* MASTER'S
point of view.)

BOY: We thought on Sunday, sir . . .
(BOY *looks towards him, and as if we're going to see* MASTER
from his point of view. Cut to:)

INT. CHARLES'S STUDY

ALISON, *the pregnant lady from the garden, at the door.*

ALISON: What are you two chaps up to? Lunch is ready, at least
the children have all washed their hands, and Hilary's
arranging them around the table,
(PETER *is getting up*)
on which I'm just about to plonk the casserole, so if you're
going to get up some of our brew, darling, you'd better nip
about it sharpish.

CHARLES: Do you like home-made beer? I've been following that
chap in *The Guardian*, sometimes it turns out all right.

ALISON: It's actually jolly delicious.
(ALISON *holds the door open as first* PETER *then* CHARLES *pass,
see them from her point of view, and then her eye going to the
ashtray containing* PETER'S *stubs, and his glass and the Scotch,
as over:*)

PETER: As a matter of fact, I did bring along a small
contribution –

(ALISON *makes a sardonic expression, closes the door, and cut to:*)

INT.

Sound of voices. School refectory. Come in on knives and forks plying between plates and mouths, then cut to: BOY's *face, standing behind larger boys, who are eating. Then see him from the perspective of the* BOWLER, *also standing behind older boys, at a different table. There are other younger boys (clearly acting as fags) behind different tables.* BOY *smiles to* BOWLER, *then in response to an order from one of the older boys, moves to fetch a jug of water.* BOWLER *receives an order at the same time, comes back with bread, puts it down on the table, and cut to:*

INT. CHARLES'S KITCHEN

An enormous table, around which the four boys from the garden are seated. CHARLES, *behind the table, is on his feet and plonking bread down on the children's plates;* PETER *is moving around the other side, pouring out orange squash.* ALISON *is at the head of the table, serving casserole into bowls. Beside her, in a high-chair, is* NINDY, *the little girl.* HILARY *is seated, serving vegetables into the bowls. On the table several bottles of home-made beer, and two bottles of white wine. All this taken in fleetingly, then cut to* PETER's *face, sardonic, and then to* CHARLES, *intently the father.* CHARLES, *suddenly looks towards* PETER, *who smiles more intimately than in the study.* CHARLES *smiles back, while over:*)

ALISON: Does Jeremy eat aubergines?

HILARY: He's worth trying, doesn't Nindy manage her fork well.

EXT. SCHOOL YARD

Lots of boys milling about, talking, then come in on BOY's *face, as he and* BOWLER *slightly cut off from the others by a notice board.*

BOY: 'Gratters.

BOWLER: Oh, shut up!

BOY: I was only saying 'gratters, isn't that what chaps say to chaps when chaps get selected for the Junior Dolts.

BOWLER: Anyway, I'm only down because Duff is infirm.

BOY: Duff is infirm? But only mentally surely, not physically.

BOWLER: I mean, *in* infirm, you know jolly well. I didn't select myself, you know, I was selected, you know. Surely you can understand that.

BOY: What?

BOWLER: That it's not my fault.

BOY: What's not your fault?

BOWLER: If I happen to get selected because I was bowling off-spins in the nets, I didn't know I could bowl off-spin even, so it's not my fault, is it?

BOY: But it's your fault when you smirk about it.

BOWLER: I'm not smirking! (*Turning around on him.*)

BOY: No, it's quite true, you're not. Coming for a walk?

BOWLER: No.

BOY: Why not?

BOWLER: Because I can't.

BOY: Why can't you?

BOWLER: Because I'm meant to be playing, that's why.

BOY: But your match isn't until Thursday, it said on Notice.

BOWLER: It's squash, this afternoon.

BOY: Oh, squash!

BOWLER: It's the House Shield semi-finals.

BOY: 'Gratters!

(*Cut to:*)

EXT. CHARLES'S GARDEN

CHARLES *and the four boys are playing soccer on the lawn. See them from* PETER'*s point of view. Then take in* PETER *watching them. He is sitting in a deckchair at the end of the garden with a bottle of wine at his side, a cigarette in one hand, a glass in the other. He looks up suddenly, and to his right, at the approach of* HILARY, *not yet seen, and cut to:*

INT. SPECTATORS' BALCONY, SQUASH COURTS

Come in on MASTER's *face, looking down, as off, in the court,* BOWLER's *voice:*

BOWLER: (*Off*) Oh, jolly good serve.

> (*Sound of rallies punctuates the conversation.*)

MASTER: Some verse?

> (*Cut to* BOY *with an exercise-book open on his knees, a pencil in his hand.*)

BOY: Sir.

MASTER: Why here?

BOY: Well, supporting House too, sir. It's the House Shield semi-finals.

MASTER: Ah, well that's very keen of you. Let's hear a mite of applause then.

BOY: He hasn't done anything to applaud yet, sir, he's behind love – four.

BOWLER: (*Off*) Jolly good serve.

BOY: Five love.

MASTER: Then you must applaud his opponent. That's the done thing, isn't it?

BOY: Sir.

MASTER: Then kindly do it.

BOWLER: (*Off*) Jolly good serve!

> (BOY *applauds, and on him clapping and looking first down, into the court, then up again, as if at* MASTER, *see, as if from his point of view but cutting to:*)

EXT. GARDEN

HILARY's *face, from* PETER's *point of view, their voices carefully lowered, as over the sound of* CHARLES, *shouting encouragement.*

HILARY: You might show willing.

PETER: But I'm not.

HILARY: It's a little embarrassing for Jeremy, though, *his* father not playing.

PETER: It would be more embarrassing for him if I did. He hates football too.

HILARY: But at least he's joining in.

CHARLES: (*Off*) Oh, hard cheese, Jeremy.

PETER: Poor little sod had no option.

HILARY: Well, I must say, you present a very pretty spectacle –

ALISON: (*Off, advancing*) I say, would you mind looking?

PETER: What?

HILARY: (*Looking down*) O well done, Nindy.

    (PETER *looks down, on his face a sudden grimace.*)

    (*Under her breath*) Say something! (*Aloud.*) Marvellous darling!

PETER: Yes, brilliant.

    (*Cut to the* LITTLE GIRL, *holding chamber-pot for inspection.*)

ALISON: (*Behind*) Isn't she a clever girl! (*Claps.*)

    (HILARY *also claps.* PETER *also claps.*)

ALISON: Daddy, Daddy, Nindy's done a lovely little jobs for Pete, right into her pottie!

CHARLES: (*Bounds up, sweat running down his face, breathing deeply.*) What a clever girlie. (*Claps, and sinks exhausted to the porch.*)

PETER: (*Sotto voce, to* HILARY) What do they do when she does a lovely big jobs?

    (HILARY *lets out a laugh, suppresses it, turns, moves off after* ALISON *who is leading* NINDY, *carrying the pot, away. From the garden, noises of game continue.* CHARLES *sits recuperating, seen from* PETER'S *point of view then cut to:*)

You seem a bit done in for a chap who's up to four miles and the Junior Colts.

CHARLES: (*Over*) It's the heat. (*Panting.*)

    (*Cut as if back to* CHARLES, *and instead, to:*)

TWO SUNDAYS

INT. SCHOOL SHOWERS

BOWLER *is sitting beneath the clothes peg on a bench opposite the showers. He is stripped down to his shorts, and is taking off his socks. He sniffs at them in fascinated disgust, drops them to the floor, looks up, as voice over:*

BOY: (*Off*) Hard luck.

(*Cut to him as he enters, stands uncertainly.*)

BOWLER: I pong.

(BOY *comes over, sits down on the bench beside him.*)

BOWLER: I don't know how you can sit there.

BOY: Why not?

BOWLER: Because I pong.

BOY: That's because you've been running about, losing.

BOWLER: (*Gets up, takes off his shorts, goes to the shower.*) I wouldn't have, if you hadn't been there.

BOY: Run about?

BOWLER: Lost! You put me off.

BOY: But it doesn't matter, you losing. Master told me so.

(BOWLER *looks at him, goes under the shower and cut to:*)

INT. CHARLES'S BATHROOM

CHARLES *drying his face. He finishes, stares ahead, makes a face as if reaching a decision. Puts the towel back, and cut to:*

INT. CHARLES'S STUDY

PETER *is staring blankly ahead, hand around a glass; cigarette in his other hand. Suddenly sighs, as if with boredom. Coughs slightly.*

INT. SHOWERS

BOY *is still sitting, staring down. Cut to* BOWLER *sitting opposite him, towel around his waist, putting on socks. As he does so, glances furtively at* BOY. *Glances away. Draw the camera back, to take in the two of them. Then cut to:*

INT. CHARLES'S STUDY

CHARLES, *full face. He is closing the door, looks at* PETER. *Take in the two of them,* PETER *making a small effort at a greeting.* CHARLES *turns away. Camera on him. His face, for a second, desperate. Turns around, looks at* PETER.

CHARLES: Sorry.

PETER: What? What for?

CHARLES: All this. Family casseroles, soccer on the lawn, home-made beer. You must hate it.

PETER: Of course, I don't.

CHARLES: (*Smiles*) It's the only way Alison knows of doing things.

PETER: It's a splendid way. Besides, don't forget I didn't drink the beer or play soccer and the casserole was delicious. And so was the home-made bread.

CHARLES: The beer's really not at all bad.

PETER: Look, why don't we meet in town for lunch sometime.

CHARLES: We always decide to do that.

PETER: Nothing could be easier to arrange.

CHARLES: Fine.

(*There is a pause.*)

PETER: I'll give you a ring early in the week, just as soon as I've checked on my office diary –

CHARLES: Right. (*Little pause.*) One gets such odd fragments of information, doesn't one? From each other. But usually not the sequels.

PETER: Yes. It's very – tantalizing.

CHARLES: I mean. I take it everything's all right, to do with that girl –

PETER: Girl?

CHARLES: The one you were having an affair with.

PETER: Oh. Oh yes. (*Little pause.*) Which one was that?

CHARLES: The Australian.

PETER: Ah, yes. Long gone. All the way back to Australia, thank God! That was a long time ago.

CHARLES: You were worried that Hilary might find out, you thought she'd make trouble.

PETER: Hilary?

CHARLES: No, the Australian.

PETER: That's right. Yes, yes, she did go through a period of
Antipodean bluster. I think she just wanted to liven me up a
bit. She found me boring, when it came to it. She had some
idea that adultery should be, well, more spectacular,
especially in the literary world. At least a few *éclaircissements*.

CHARLES: Anyway, Hilary never did find out?

PETER: Christ no. She wouldn't really have done anything
underhand – she was all right. She was quite nice actually.
Her book's done quite well, too, considering it came at the
tail end of all that business. Have you read it?
(CHARLES *shakes his head.*)
In the Afterword, which she had stuck in afterwards, so to
speak, there's an account of an affair she had with a married
chap who used to bring a spare pair of knickers to her flat in
his briefcase. That was me. Hilary thought it was funny.

CHARLES: That it was you?

PETER: No, no – just the description. She read it out to me, bits
of it, of course she hadn't the least idea –

CHARLES: Good God, what did you do?

PETER: I laughed too. It struck me as really quite exceptional, to
lie in bed listening to one's wife innocently reading out an
account of one's adultery . . .

CHARLES: Yes, I can see . . . (*Laughs.*) Anyway, that's all over.

PETER: Mmmmm. Yes.
(*There is a pause.*)

CHARLES: I remember your saying that if you got out of *that* one
intact you'd make sure there'd never be another.

PETER: Did I say that?

CHARLES: Don't you remember?

PETER: Well, there have been so many since . . .

CHARLES: You mean now?

PETER: Not really, no. Well, one of the editor's secretaries . . .
she's worse than me. She keeps a supply of VD pills in her
bag, makes me take them . . . Extremely organized. Oddly
enough, I hear she's not a very good secretary.

CHARLES: Where do you do it?

PETER: Mmmm? (*Slightly shocked.*)

CHARLES: No, I was just curious. Sorry.

PETER: No, it's all right. In my office, at lunch-time, or after
hours – when she's not going on somewhere more interesting
and I don't have to get home for anything.

CHARLES: But isn't that risky?

PETER: Not really. I lock the door and leave the key in –

CHARLES: Surely people suspect.

PETER: I imagine there are the usual jokes. But as long as they
don't reach Hilary – (*Pause.*) The most depressing thing, you
know, *the* most depressing thing, is that I used to feel a
certain amount of post-coital tristesse. Well, guilt. But these
days I can scarcely be bothered to feel shifty when I get
home. Extra-marital sex is as over-rated as pre-marital sex.
And marital sex, come to think of it.

CHARLES: Then why do you have it?

PETER: (*Sighs*) I don't know. Well, the first time is still quite fun,
it's having to go on and on.

CHARLES: Why do you?

PETER: From politeness. I mean, one can't just have it off, tip
one's hat . . .

CHARLES: But you still love Hilary, don't you?

PETER: What?

CHARLES: Hilary.

PETER: What?

CHARLES: (*After a long pause*) Love Hilary.

PETER: Christ! (*Pause.*) Of course I do. (*Pause.*) There's not a
day at the office, when the telephone rings, not a day when at
least once (*Pause.*) I don't have a spasm of terror, and think:
'Not this time, please let nothing have happened to her this
time. Or Jeremy.' You know. I'm frightened for them. I
want to die before they do so at least I shan't spend my last
years – first me, and then Hilary, and then after a long
intermission – Jeremy. That seems only fair except that I
know that life doesn't work on fair principles, which are
anyway formulated by types like me in Greenwich . . . Who

knows? Who knows what . . . I'm frightened for them.
(*Pause.*) I know she is for me. (*Pause.*) Christ, that's a
marriage, isn't it? (*Pause.*) Bloody Hell, of course I love . . .
(*There is a pause.*) What do you mean?
(CHARLES *gets up, walks restlessly around the room.* PETER
watches him, then loses interest, concentrates on his drink.)

CHARLES: There's something . . . (*Stops.*)

PETER: (*Not paying attention*) Mmmm?

CHARLES: The irony is . . . (*Looks at* PETER, *then turns, opens the
drawer of his desk, takes out a bulky, and large, brown
envelope.*) Look.
(CHARLES *hesitates, then, making up his mind, carries it over to*
PETER, *hands it to him. Cut as if to* PETER's *face, but instead
to:*)

INT. SHOWERS

In on BOWLER's *face. He is now dressed and holding a sheet of paper.*
BOY *is standing, turned away from him.*

BOWLER: About me?

BOY: That's right. Didn't you recognize yourself, I thought you
would as it's so complimentary.

BOWLER: Well, I can't . . . I've only read it once. (*Little pause,
looks down, tries to read it again.*) It's difficult, with you
sitting there – well, you, I mean you just stick it in my hand –

BOY: I'm putting you off again, am I? You can't win at games
when I'm watching, you can't read when I'm watching –

BOWLER: Why don't you stop watching then?

BOY: You like being watched.

BOWLER: Rubbish, what bloody rubbish! It's a lousy poem, it's
just bloody rubbish!

BOY: (*Trying to control a shaking voice*) I'm glad I showed it to you.
I was sure I'd get an intelligent assessment.

BOWLER: They're right about you, what they say, you're just a
pseudo, really, loping about listening to music and scribbling
poems and not doing anything at all.

BOY: (*His voice now shaking*) The irony is that I thought you might have a touch of intelligence. The irony is that you're an extremely stupid sort of little person. The irony is I've been wasting my time on you.

BOWLER: (*Shouting*) Then why don't you leave me alone?

BOY: (*Shouting*) Yes, why don't I?

(*They stare at each other. Over the end of this scene:*)

CHARLES: (*Shouting*) That's enough, boys. Either play sportingly, or don't play at all. Don't forget, it's only a game.

(*Cut to:*)

INT. CHARLES'S STUDY

In on PETER *looking down at the envelope in his lap. He picks it up surreptitiously, as if weighing it, also tests its bulk with his thumbs. A general sense of his being aghast. Then looks towards* CHARLES, *and from his point of view.*

CHARLES: (*Leaning out of the window*) Ali darling, do you want me to come down . . .?

(ALISON, *off, in the garden, voice not audible.*)

Jolly good, thanks, darling. (*Straightens from the window, closes it, pauses staring out, then turns. Looks towards* PETER.) I was going through one of those passages that one goes through, you know, feeling a bit desperate, not sure I could go on – (*gestures*) then one day, just after I'd got back from my run I just – sat myself down and began it. I didn't intend it to come out as a full-length novel, I had no idea.

PETER: Well, these things happen.

CHARLES: Even now I can scarcely believe I've finished it. Or whether what I've finished is something *there*, you know, created. Or therapy. (*Little pause.*) I expect you'll be able to tell me, no punches pulled. (*Smiles.*)

(PETER *smiles.*)

What I do know is that it in a sense saved my life.

PETER: Well, that's certainly to its credit. Has anyone else read it?

CHARLES: No.

PETER: What does Alison feel about it?

CHARLES: Actually, she hasn't read it either. In fact, I'd better
warn you – mm, she doesn't even know I've written it. Oh,
she knows I've been working on something, of course, but
I've rather let her go on thinking that it's the Molière
translations, you know, the ones I started just after we came
down. (*Pause.*) Actually, I'd rather she didn't know, well, at
least just yet. You'll be able to help me there, too. You see,
it's about us?

PETER: Us?

CHARLES: Well, our marriage. (*Stares at him.*) It's *not*, of course,
but there are certain – well, I wouldn't want Alison to think
it *was* about us, is perhaps, the best way of putting it. There
are inevitable similarities – especially between myself and the
central chap. There's a chap who's a little like you in it too,
only superficially. For one thing, he commits suicide.

PETER: Well, there at least he's a little unlike me. If only
superficially.

CHARLES: No, no. I meant the other chap.

PETER: Oh, the chap a little like you?

CHARLES: Mmmm.

PETER: Can you tell me why, or would that ruin the suspense?

CHARLES: No, no. As he commits suicide on the first page. And
the last.

PETER: He does it twice?

CHARLES: No, it's the same suicide. The structure is complex.
Circular. But I hope organic. (*Pause.*) He commits suicide
because he's unhappy really, that's what it comes to. In his
work and his well, marriage. That's the part of it that Alison
might not understand – the difference between
autobiography and fiction.

PETER: It's frequently muddling.

CHARLES: Well, not for you – you'll know at once – his attitude to
the children, for example, his wife's pregnancies – and
various things that he does or feels at work –

PETER: What work does he do?

CHARLES: He's a teacher. A public school teacher. Not very
   imaginative that, I know, but in his real self he's so different
   from myself –
PETER: Anyway, *your* real self.
CHARLES: Exactly. Yes. Look – there is *one* thing – one section
   that I would like to clarify – where something's said,
   explicitly said, about his feeling for one of the boys. His
   sense of torture, and the way in which the word desire is used
   – (*painful pause*) well, that *is* – (*Hesitates.*) You'll understand.
   You'll understand. And also about friendship – there's a
   passage, a meditation – he thinks about his most important
   relationship and the tone of the passage is – well, intended to
   be – acerbic.
PETER: (*After a pause*) Don't worry, I'll read it as a novel.
CHARLES: I know. But I can't help feeling a little treacherous. In
   the sense that you meant years ago, when you first started
   being, mm, unfaithful – you said that for you the real
   treachery wasn't what you did with another woman, it was
   what you said to her about your wife.
PETER: Did I say that?
CHARLES: Anyway that's the sense in which I feel treacherous.
   Towards Alison. As if I had betrayed a deep confidence –
PETER: On that analogy, you haven't, yet. Not until I've read it –
   or somebody else has. Perhaps you ought to reconsider
   letting me see it.
CHARLES: No, no. You must read it.
PETER: But only if you're sure –
CHARLES: The treachery is finding it out. I can't go back on that.
   The truth is that it's all there. It's no good my fooling myself
   or trying to fool you, of all people. You'll know. It's all there.
PETER: (*After a pause*) Yes, well it usually is. (*Smiles.*)
CHARLES: How do you mean?
PETER: In a first novel.
CHARLES: If it hadn't been for you, I wouldn't have written it.
   You're the one –
   (*Bring them both in camera, drawing back slightly, looking
   towards each other.*)

To whom I've always privately addressed my most private feelings. Some friendships endure as what they were even though they *are*. No longer. What they were. Isn't that true? Isn't it the same for you?

(*Hold on the two of them, sitting in silence, for as long as possible. Then one beat longer than that, as fade into:*)

INT. SHOWERS

BOY *is sitting staring straight ahead.* BOWLER *is sitting opposite, staring down. He looks at* BOY.

BOWLER: Are you all right?

(BOY *remains immobile, staring blankly.* BOWLER *gets up, goes over to him slowly, apprehensively, hesitates, sits down beside him, clears his throat.*)

Are you?

(*They sit in misery. Fade to:*)

INT. CHARLES'S STUDY

As before.

PETER: (*Suddenly coughs, clears his throat*) I'm sorry.

CHARLES: Why?

PETER: Well, I hadn't realized you were un – well, unhappy.

PETER: Oh, I'm sure I'm not. Any more than anybody else, anyway. I'd be far more unhappy if Alison found out – well, aren't *you* unhappy?

PETER: Mmm, well – (*Coughs slightly and fade to:*)

INT. SHOWERS

The boys as before.

BOWLER: (*After a pause*) Well, liking me so much. (*In a mutter.*)

BOY: Because you've stopped liking me? (*Very low.*)

334

BOWLER: (*In a mutter*) No, well – it's not that, it's – (*Shrugs.*)

BOY: You don't like me any more.

BOWLER: Yes, I do. (*Embarrassed.*)

BOY: How do you know I like you?

BOWLER: Well, if you don't – I mean –

BOY: Why don't you go?

BOWLER: What will you do?

BOY: Stay here.

BOWLER: What for?

    (BOY *doesn't answer.*)

    Well, for how long?

BOY: Until I get up.

BOWLER: The Refec bell's gone. (*Pause.*) We're still on Fag.
(*Pause.*) Come on! (*Pause.*) We better go.

    (BOY *continues to sit.*)

BOWLER: Well – Well, I'm jolly well – (*Gets up, stands
indecisively.*)

BOY: You're very stupid.

    (BOWLER *still indecisive, takes* BOY'*s arm, tries to pull* BOY *up.*
BOY *resists passively, until he's hauled up, then begins to resist
violently, pushing* BOWLER *away, in a sudden, unexpected burst
of violence. They stand staring at each other. Sounds off, of a
door opening and closing. They swing their heads in alarm, left
and cut to:*)

INT. CHARLES'S STUDY

ALISON *is standing at the door,* NINDY *in her arms.*

PETER: Ah, is she? I'll be right down. (*Getting up.*)

ALISON: I'll dig Jeremy out of the cellar.

CHARLES: Aren't you staying for tea?

ALISON: (*Who has turned away, turns back, briefly*) It's rather a
long drive, Hilary feels.

CHARLES: Oh. (*Getting up.*)

    (ALISON *goes off.*)

    (As PETER *drains off the rest of his drink, stubs out his cigarette*)

We were just beginning to talk. Naturally.

PETER: It is a long drive and Jeremy gets tired – (*Moves towards the door.*)

(CHARLES *picks up the envelope, hands it to* PETER, *who has left it on the floor.*)

Ah!

(PETER *takes it, slips it under his arm,* CHARLES *holds the door open for him and as he passes, suddenly puts his hand on* PETER'*s arm.* PETER *turns, looks at him.* CHARLES *smiles.* PETER *smiles back, slightly awkwardly. They go out, leaving the door open, and fade the open door into:*)

INT. MASTER'S STUDY

A light, airy, and civilized place. Fading in on the open door, seen from MASTER'*s point of view from his desk. He is not yet seen, nor his room, just the open door, through which* BOWLER *and* BOY *enter, self-consciously. They stand in the room,* MASTER *comes into camera, but his face out of camera, passes the two boys, closes the door, turns, passes back. Sits down. His face coming into camera as he does so. Cut as if to the two boys, come in on:*

INT. CHARLES'S HALL

Front door open. PETER *and* CHARLES *standing at it. From behind, up the stairs, the cries of children, sound of bath-water running,* ALISON'*s voice.*

ALISON: (*Off*) Don't turn on the tap! Leave the taps alone!

PETER: I'll give you a ring –

(*Off sound of car honking.*)

Ah, there they are – Well, I'll give you a ring.

CHARLES: At the school. (*Low.*)

PETER: Right.

(ALISON *comes down, stands beside* CHARLES *as* PETER *moves outside.*)

ALISON: I was going to fix something up with Hilary, tell her I'll give her a ring.

PETER: Right, and thanks for a lovely – (*Gestures. He doesn't have the envelope in his hand.*)

ALISON: No, it was lovely –

CHARLES: Yes.

PETER: Well –

(*Stay on* CHARLES *and* ALISON *staring out from the hall, saluting as off. The sound of the car honking farewells. The door closes. Cut back into the hall.* ALISON *is going up the stairs,* CHARLES *is standing in the hall, looks down, sees in the pram the envelope. Come in on his face as he picks it up.*)

ALISON: He's certainly putting it on, isn't he?

CHARLES: What? Who?

ALISON: Surely you noticed? His face is quite –

(*A ring at the doorbell.* CHARLES *opens the door on* PETER.)

PETER: Christ, I nearly forgot, I thought I had it in my hand. I put it – (*Looks vaguely around.*)

(CHARLES *holds it out to him.*)

ALISON: (*Over*) Forgotten something?

PETER: No, got it thanks. Bye. Bye. (*The second to* CHARLES.)

(CHARLES *closes the door.*)

ALISON: (*Over*) What was it?

CHARLES: Oh just some cigarettes or something –

ALISON: (*Over*) Can you check in the bathroom, I'm doing Ophelia. They're meant to be washing their hands but they're mucking about with the bath-taps –

(CHARLES *during this, goes up the stairs, heavily, rather tired. Camera stays with him as he opens bathroom door, then cut to his face, as if from within the bathroom, from which splashes and shouts have been coming. Just for a second an expression of collapse, then a smile, and in pleasantly jocular tones:*)

CHARLES: What do you boys think you're doing? You're supposed to be washing your hands.

(*Cut instantly to:*)

INT. MASTER'S STUDY

In on his face, friendly and slightly satirical.

MASTER: . . . all over the school. Mr Jameson finds you in the
Music Room when you should be fagging at Refec, M. Fouce
wonders why you always sit in the back of the class and
whisper passionately over Baudelaire, he thinks, when you
ought to be translating *Le Malade Imaginaire*, and Mr James
stumbles across you in Change, when you should be fagging
in Refec. Mmm?

BOWLER: ⎱
BOY: ⎰ (*After a pause*) Sir.

MASTER: How's your chest?

BOY: I've still got asthma a bit, sir.

MASTER: You're still chitted for all games then?

BOY: Sir.

MASTER: How did the Shield match go?

BOWLER: Oh – oh all right, sir.

MASTER: You won then?

BOWLER: No, sir.

MASTER: Really. What they call in sporting circles a bit of an
upset?

BOWLER: (*Stammeringly*) Not really, sir, I mean I didn't mind too
much . . .

MASTER: Mmmm. (*Looks at* BOWLER, *see* MASTER'*s face from*
BOWLER'*s point of view. Smiles.*) Well, I've really got nothing
more to say to you than this. If you're going to be caught in
the wrong places at the wrong times, could you contrive to
do so separately?

BOWLER: Sir.

BOY: Sir. But it's all right to be in the Music Room together at the
right time, and other places at the right time?

MASTER: (*After a short pause*) There is no school regulation to
prevent boys from being friends. As you're in the same
House and the same Form there isn't even convention to
hold you back. (*Pause.*) I'd like a word with each of you
privately, if I may. Why don't you run along to Matron and

338

get your next week's chit, and then come back . . .

BOY: Sir.

> (BOY *turns, goes out, as he closes the door, see from his point of view* MASTER *and* BOWLER, *then cut to* MASTER'*s face, as behind, sound of door closing.*)

MASTER: You *are* friends, are you?

BOWLER: (*After a pause*) Sir.

MASTER: What sort of friends are you?

> (*Cut to his face, looking towards* BOWLER, *solicitously, then cut as if to* BOWLER, *and come in on:*)

INT. THE CAR

HILARY *driving,* JEREMY *strapped in behind,* PETER *beside* HILARY, *leaning back, eyes closed, cigarette between lips. In on his face:*

PETER: I suppose so. But he's, let's face it, one of those friends –

> (*Lets the sentence trail away.*)

HILARY: I wish you'd finish that sentence.

PETER: Oh, just that one can't bear seeing.

HILARY: Then why do we go on seeing them?

PETER: We scarcely do any more. Besides, *you* accepted. (*Pause.*) I was prepared for a ghastly day –

HILARY: Very well prepared, with your bottles of wine and cigarettes in every pocket –

PETER: But not sufficiently prepared for this? (*Beats the envelope with his hand.*) Christ, a bloody novel!

HILARY: You might like it.

PETER: Yes. (*Gives a half-laugh.*) That'd be a blow.

HILARY: To whom?

PETER: To me, of course. He had his purple passage at school, he doesn't deserve another go now I've settled him down as a successful failure.

HILARY: What an appalling thing to say. (*Pause.*) Besides, you used to claim he was very talented – in those days when you wanted to make your friends sound glamorous and mysterious. At least to me.

PETER: That was a long time ago, and even then I was going a long way back. When it was assumed we'd both of us go a long way.

HILARY: (*After a pause*) Well then, let's hope it's terrible. You can still make appropriate noises.

PETER: What are the appropriate noises for not wanting to publish it?

HILARY: Oh. Is that what he's after? (*Looks at* PETER.) You poor old sod.

(*Cut to:*)

INT. MASTER'S STUDY

BOWLER *is now sitting in a chair.* MASTER *on the edge of the desk, talking in a low, confidential voice.*

MASTER: . . . after all be a reason for choosing him among so many. You see, your interests are very different, or so it seems to an uninvolved eye. Aren't they?

BOWLER: Sir.

MASTER: I mean no reflection on your academic standing, you work as hard as can be expected from someone with so many obligations, in the squash courts, the cricket fields – I gather you've developed an off-spin of some consequence. (*Smiles.*) So I'm fairly confident that your general all-roundedness will stand you in some stead when you come to think between Oxford and Cambridge. All I mean is that I shouldn't have thought it was in the general run of your pursuits to listen to Berg or even Mozart when you should be fagging in Refec.

BOWLER: No, sir.

MASTER: But I'm not suggesting you give him up or anything so extreme. Just that you should reflect that too much too intense friendship can lead to too many complications for a chap who wants an uncluttered life. (*Pause.*) What do you say to that?

(*Pause, hold on his face then cut to:*)

340

INT. NINDY'S BEDROOM

Straight in on ALISON'*s face.*

ALISON: That I've got a perfect right to be pregnant.

CHARLES: (*Who is scrabbling around in a drawer*) Of course you have.

ALISON: (*Puts* NINDY *down on the pot*) She patronizes me.

CHARLES: I don't think she means to.

ALISON: Because she can't help it? Or because I make it unavoidable?

CHARLES: I can't find any with special caps on.

ALISON: There's a blue tin. (*To* NINDY) How are you doing, darling? That boy of theirs is a sly little brute.

CHARLES: Really? In what way?

ALISON: He's a mixer. He likes to stir things up – quite unnatural sophistication – piggy little eyes –

CHARLES: Darling, he's only six.

ALISON: (*After a pause*) If he doesn't look out, he's going to have a heart attack.

CHARLES: At six?

ALISON: You know perfectly well. He boozed all through the day.
(NINDY *on pot, sound of her peeing.*)
Oh clever girl! Look, Daddy, a wee-wee for you. (*She claps.*)
(CHARLES *claps.* ALISON *lifts* NINDY *off the pot, holds out her hand for the tin with the blue top, which she receives from* CHARLES, *spreads* NINDY *on the bed.*)
Can you honestly say that you still have anything in common?
(*Cut as if to* CHARLES'*s face, but come in, instead, on:*)

INT. MASTER'S STUDY

On BOY'*s face. He is sitting, as* BOWLER *was.*

BOY: Sir.

MASTER: Unless, that is, you've undertaken to supplement his education with some courses of your own.

BOY: (*After a pause*) Sir?

MASTER: Those subjects, that is, in which you have a natural
advantage.

(BOY *says nothing.*)

Is that what you're doing? (*Smiling.*)

BOY: We like talking about the same things, that's all.

MASTER: Really? Cricket, squash, athletics – you have an
interest?

BOY: I like watching.

MASTER: But only when he's playing. No doubt. (*Smiles.*) He
listens to you on Baudelaire because it's you he's interested
in, not Baudelaire. What do you think this is all about?

BOY: I don't know, sir.

MASTER: Well, I'm asking you to be careful, that's all.

BOY: Sir. (*Little pause.*) What of, sir?

MASTER: Of yourself, and of your feelings. It's hard for you, I
know, in that your health excludes you from a great deal of
companionship, although I suspect you don't much regret
that. You're very highly thought of, you know, by most of us
– even if we find you a little frightening. I for one wouldn't
dream of dictating the proper lines for friendship, there
aren't any. But do remember, won't you, that your capacity
for affection (*hesitates*) deserves various, mm, expressions.
(*Pause.*) I'm not saying anything at all, it's sheer nonsense.
(*Pause.*) You must find your own way. Nobody wishes you
any harm. Please believe that. Do you?

(*See* MASTER *from* BOY's *point of view. Cut as if to* BOY, *and in
fact go to:*)

INT. PETER'S STUDY

*He is lighting a cigarette. A suggestion of desperation; props his hand
under his chin, sits smoking.*

INT. CHARLES'S STUDY

He is sitting, staring ahead. A suggestion of despair.

INT. SCHOOL CHAPEL

BOWLER'*s face, as over the service (prayer). And cut to* BOY'*s face, his eyes moving purposefully, as if looking for* BOWLER. *And cut to:*

INT. PETER'S STUDY

Come in on him coughing slightly, the cough goes on and on, gets out of control. He stubs out his cigarette fiercely, sits shaken.

PETER: Christ!

> (PETER *gets up, hands not visible but sound of his pouring from a bottle to a glass. He sits down, coughs once or twice to clear his throat, then sits staring ahead.*)

INT. MUSIC ROOM

Light on. BOY *is staring out of window.*

EXT. MUSIC-ROOM WINDOW

From BOWLER'*s point of view.* BOY'*s face visible but indistinct. Cut to* BOWLER'*s face, undecided, and cut to:*

INT.

Very brief. CHARLES *staring ahead.*

INT.

Very brief. PETER *staring ahead. This in fact from* HILARY's *point of view although not yet established.*

HILARY: (*Over*) Will you be long?

PETER: (*Turns*) No, I won't be long.

HILARY: Jeremy's sound asleep. He's exhausted, poor child. Not a peep out of him.

PETER: Well, I won't be long.

HILARY: Thank you. What's it like?

PETER: It's bloody hand-written, that's what it's like.

HILARY: (*Takes in the ashtray, which has a number of butts in it. Then the glass*) Another drink? (*Pause.*) You're smoking too much.

PETER: Ah, that explains it.

HILARY: What?

PETER: Why I've got two hundred and fifty pages of handwritten novel to get through.

HILARY: Well, not tonight, I hope.

PETER: Some of it tonight.

HILARY: Why, if you're tired?

(PETER *sighs.* HILARY *looks at him, turns, goes out.* PETER *stares at the empty door a moment, lights another cigarette.*)
(*Reappears at the door*) Look, I didn't ask to spend the day with your old school friend and his dull wife, and I didn't fill you full of wine all day to help you get through it, and I'm not pouring Scotch down your throat to help you get over it. I don't know what's the matter with you, but I've had enough of everything today, including you.

PETER: (*With insulting courtesy*) Have you?

(HILARY *glares at him, slams the door.* HILARY [*Off*] *calls out something.*)

PETER: (*Sits still for a moment, then bellows*) What?

HILARY: (*Re-opens the door, glares at him*) Would you kindly remember that Jeremy is asleep.

INT. CHARLES'S STUDY

In on his face, briefly. Move back, to take in ALISON, *in her night-gown, holding two mugs.*

ALISON: But you are, I can tell.

CHARLES: No, contemplative.

ALISON: Then what are you contemplating?

CHARLES: I'm not sure. I don't think I'd fixed on a subject.

ALISON: (*Looks at him, troubled*) I wasn't trying to get at him, you know? (*Pause.*) Yes, I was.

CHARLES: I've never minded your not liking him.

ALISON: You mustn't. As long as you go on liking him –

CHARLES: Oh, I don't know. Old friends are like old habits. There comes a point when it doesn't matter any more whether you like them, they're what you've got.

ALISON: Is the same true of families?

CHARLES: Well, I don't keep adding to my circle of friends. But with my family, on the other hand – (*Smiles.*)

ALISON: (*Over*) I love you.

    (*Stay on* CHARLES's *face, smiling and cut to:*)

INT. MUSIC ROOM

BOY *bent over the gramophone. Then withdraw to take in* BOWLER, *hands in pockets, turned away.*

BOWLER: I can only stay for a little bit. (*Formally.*)

BOY: I can't stay long either. (*Formally.*)

    (*Cut to:*)

INT. PETER'S BEDROOM

HILARY *lying asleep. On her face, then* PETER *bends into camera, kisses her on the forehead, his face withdraws.* HILARY's *eyes open slightly, slight smile.*

345

INT. CHARLES'S BEDROOM

On his face, then cut to ALISON, *head on pillow, looking troubled,* CHARLES *puts out his hand, touches a lock of her hair, then moves out of camera.* ALISON *smiles. It is an unhappy smile. Over, Mozart and fade into:*

INT. MUSIC ROOM

As Mozart continues from previous scene, BOY *and* BOWLER *sitting, listening. And over this: Credits.*